First World War
and Army of Occupation
War Diary
France, Belgium and Germany

48 DIVISION
Divisional Troops
Royal Army Medical Corps
1/2 South Midland Field Ambulance
23 March 1915 - 31 October 1917

WO95/2752/2

The Naval & Military Press Ltd
www.nmarchive.com
Published in association with The National Archives

Published by

The Naval & Military Press Ltd

Unit 10 Ridgewood Industrial Park,

Uckfield, East Sussex,

TN22 5QE England

Tel: +44 (0) 1825 749494

www.naval-military-press.com

www.nmarchive.com

This diary has been reprinted in facsimile from the original. Any imperfections are inevitably reproduced and the quality may fall short of modern type and cartographic standards.

© **Crown Copyright**
Images reproduced by permission of The National Archives, London, England, 2015.

Contents

Document type	Place/Title	Date From	Date To
Heading	WO95/2752/2 1/2 South Midland Field Ambulance		
Heading	48th Division 1-2nd Sth Mid'd Fld Amb. Mar 1915-1917 Oct To Italy		
Heading	48th Div 121/4919 March 1915 1/2nd S Midland Field Ambulance Vol I		
Heading	War Diary Of 1/2nd S. Mid Fd. Amb From 23-3-15 To 31-3-15 Volume I		
War Diary	Margaretting	23/03/1915	23/03/1915
War Diary	Havre	24/03/1915	27/03/1915
War Diary	St Jans Capelle	28/03/1915	31/03/1915
Heading	48th Div 121/5161 April 1915 1/2 S. Midland Field Ambulance Vol II		
Heading	War Diary Of 1/2 S. Mid Fd Amb Pages 9 Appendix I One Pages		
War Diary	St. Jans Cappelle	01/04/1915	01/04/1915
War Diary	Armentieres	02/04/1915	06/04/1915
War Diary	Bailleul	07/04/1915	30/04/1915
Miscellaneous	5 Mid Div Rest Station	01/05/1915	01/05/1915
Heading	May 1915 48th Division 2nd S.M. Field Ambulance Vol III		
Heading	War Diary Of 1/2nd Sth Mid Fd Amb From 1.5.15 To 31.5.15 Vol I		
War Diary	Bailleul	01/05/1915	31/05/1915
Miscellaneous	Appendix 2	01/06/1915	01/06/1915
Miscellaneous	Admission To 7th April Rest Station 19 Rue De Music		
Miscellaneous	Admission To Field		
Miscellaneous	Appendix 3	01/06/1915	01/06/1915
Miscellaneous	Medical Officer	02/06/1915	02/06/1915
Miscellaneous	Number Of Men Bathed During 28 Working Days Of Month		
Miscellaneous	Appendix 4	01/06/1915	01/06/1915
Heading	48th Division 2nd S.M. Field Ambulance Vol IV June 1915		
Heading	War Diary Of 2nd Fd Amb 48 (S.M) Div From 1-6-15 To 30-6-15 Vol I Appendices		
War Diary	Bailleul	01/06/1915	27/06/1915
War Diary	Vieux Berquin	28/06/1915	28/06/1915
War Diary	Robecq	29/06/1915	29/06/1915
War Diary	Raimbert	30/06/1915	30/06/1915
Miscellaneous	Appendix 5		
Miscellaneous	Appendix 6		
Miscellaneous	Admission Discharges 2nd Field Amb Divine Rest Stn 48 Div		
Miscellaneous	Appendix 7		
Heading	48th Division July 15 1/2nd S.M. Field Ambulance Vol V		
Heading	War Diary Of 2nd Fd Amb. 48 (S.M) Div From 1-7-15 To 31-7-15 Vol I Appendices (8)		
War Diary	Raimbert	01/07/1915	20/07/1915
War Diary	Levincourt	21/07/1915	31/07/1915

Miscellaneous	Appendix 8		
Heading	48th Division August 15 1/2nd S.M. Field Ambulance Vol VI From 1-31.8.15		
Heading	War Diary Of 2nd Fd Amb (48 Div) From 1-8-15 To 31-8-15 Vol I Appendix IX		
War Diary	Louvencourt	01/08/1915	31/08/1915
Miscellaneous	Appendix IX	02/09/1915	02/09/1915
Miscellaneous			
Heading	48th Division Sept 15 2nd S.M. Field Ambulance Vol VII		
Heading	War Diary Of 2nd Fd Amb 48 Div From 1-9-15 To 30-9-15 Vol I Appendix 10		
War Diary	Louvencourt	01/09/1915	30/09/1915
Miscellaneous	Appendix X	01/10/1915	01/10/1915
Miscellaneous	Admissions Disposals		
Heading	48th Division 2nd S.M. Field Ambulance Vol VIII Oct 15		
Heading	War Diary Of 2nd Fd Amb 48 Div B.E.F. From 1.X.15-31.X.15 Vol II Appendix I		
War Diary	Louvencourt	01/10/1915	31/10/1915
Miscellaneous	2nd 5th Mid Fd Amb. 48 Div	02/11/1915	02/11/1915
Miscellaneous	Admissions Disposals		
Heading	1/2nd S.M. Fd Amb 48th Div Nov 1915 Vol IX		
Heading	War Diary Of 1/2nd Sth Mid Fd Amb 48 Div B.E.F. From 1.11.15 To 30.11.15 Vol II Appendix 2		
War Diary	Louvencourt	01/11/1915	28/11/1915
Miscellaneous	2nd 5th Mid Fd Amb 48 Div		
War Diary	Louvencourt	29/11/1915	30/11/1915
Miscellaneous	Admissions Disposals		
Heading	1/2nd Fd Amb (48in Div) Dec Vol X		
Heading	War Diary Of 1/2nd S.M Fd Amb From 1 Dec 1915-31 Dec 1915 Vol 3		
War Diary	Louvencourt	01/12/1915	31/12/1915
Miscellaneous	1/2 S.M. Fd Ambulance 48 Div	01/01/1916	01/01/1916
Miscellaneous	Admissions Disposals		
Heading	2 S M F A (48th Division) 2 Fd Amb Jan Vol XI		
Heading	War Diary Of 1/2nd Sth Mid Fd Ambulance 48 Div B.E.F. From 1-1-16 To 31-1-16 Vol 4 Appendix I		
War Diary	Louvencourt	01/01/1916	31/01/1916
Miscellaneous	1/2nd 5th Midland Fd Amb 48 Div	03/02/1916	03/02/1916
Miscellaneous	Admissions Disposals		
Heading	48th Division 1/2 S Midland F. Ambulance Feb Nov 1916		
Heading	1/2 S M Fd Amb Vol XIII		
Heading	War Diary Of 1/2nd Sth Mid Field Amb 48th Division B.E.F. From 1-2-16 To 29-2-16 Vol 5 Appendix I		
War Diary	Louvencourt	01/02/1916	21/02/1916
War Diary	Sarton	22/02/1916	29/02/1916
Heading	War Diary Of 1/2nd Sth Mid Fd Amb Vol 5 Appendix I		
War Diary	Louvencourt	01/02/1916	21/02/1916
War Diary	Sarton	22/02/1916	29/02/1916
Heading	War Diary Of 1/2 Sth Mid Fd Amb 48 Div B.E.F. From 1.3.16 To 31.3.16 Vol 6 Appendix I		
War Diary	Sarton	01/03/1916	26/03/1916
War Diary	Authie	27/03/1916	31/03/1916
Heading	1/2nd 5th Mid Fd Amb 48 Div Vol 6		

Miscellaneous	Appendix I 48th Div. Rest Station		
Heading	1/2 5th Mid Fd Amb 48 Div B E F 1-4-16 To 30-4-16 Vol 7 Pages 6 Appendix I		
War Diary	Authie	01/04/1916	30/04/1916
Miscellaneous	Appendix 1 To Vol 7		
Heading	1/2 South Midland Field Amb 48 Div B.E.F. 1.5.16 To 31.5.16 Vol 8		
Miscellaneous	To D.A.G Ag Office Base		
War Diary	Authie	01/05/1916	31/05/1916
Heading	Appendix 1 To Vol 8		
Heading	1/2 South Midland Field Amb 48 Div. B.E.F. 1-6-16 To 30-6-16 Vol 9		
War Diary	Authie	01/06/1916	30/06/1916
Miscellaneous	Appendix I To Vol 9		
Heading	1/2 5th Mid Fd Amb 48 Div July 1st July 31st 1916 Vol 10		
War Diary	Authie	01/07/1916	17/07/1916
War Diary	Warloy	18/07/1916	31/07/1916
Miscellaneous	Appendix I To Vol 10		
Heading	1/2 South Midland Field Ambulance B.E.F. 1 Aug 1916-31 Aug 1916 Vol II		
War Diary	Warloy	01/08/1916	02/08/1916
War Diary	Talmas	03/08/1916	03/08/1916
War Diary	Rederie Farm	04/05/1916	08/08/1916
War Diary	Beauval	09/08/1916	09/08/1916
War Diary	Raincheval	10/08/1916	12/08/1916
War Diary	Varennes	13/08/1916	31/08/1916
Miscellaneous	Appendix I To Vol 11 (Aug 1916)		
Heading	48th Div 1/2 South Midland Field Ambulance B.E.F. 1 Sept 1916 30th Sept 1916 Vol 12		
War Diary	Vaucelles	01/09/1916	07/09/1916
War Diary	Bois De Wariemont	08/09/1916	09/09/1916
War Diary	Ref	10/09/1916	10/09/1916
War Diary	Beauval	12/09/1916	18/09/1916
War Diary	Frauvillers	19/09/1916	30/09/1916
Miscellaneous	Summary Of Admissions & Discharges		
Heading	48th Div 1916 1/2 F Midland F. Ambulance Oct 1916		
Miscellaneous	Officer Commanding	31/10/1916	31/10/1916
Heading	1/2 South Midland Fd Ambulance B E F 1 Oct 1916-31 Oct 1916 Vol 13		
War Diary	Vanchelles	01/10/1916	01/10/1916
War Diary	W. 26 Cent	02/10/1916	08/10/1916
War Diary	Gaudiempre	19/10/1916	22/10/1916
War Diary	Beauval	23/10/1916	23/10/1916
War Diary	Talmas	24/10/1916	24/10/1916
War Diary	Behencourt	25/10/1916	25/10/1916
War Diary	Frauvillers	26/10/1916	31/10/1916
Miscellaneous	Summary Of Admissions & Discharges		
Heading	1/2 South Midland Fd Ambulance B.E.F. 1 Nov 1916-30 Nov 1916 Vol 14		
War Diary	Frauvillers	01/11/1916	24/11/1916
War Diary	Warloy	25/11/1916	30/11/1916
Miscellaneous	Summary Of Admissions & Discharges		
Heading	48th Div 1/2nd Field Ambulance Dec 1916		
Heading	1/2 South Midland Fields Ambulance B E F Vol 15 1 Dec-31 Dec 1916		

War Diary	Warloy	01/12/1916	31/12/1916
Miscellaneous	Summary Of Admissions & Discharges		
Heading	48th Div. 1/2nd S.M. Field Ambulance		
Heading	1/2 South Midland Field Ambulance B E F Vol 16 1 Jan 1917-31 Jan 1917.		
Miscellaneous	Summary Admission discharges		
War Diary	Warloy	01/01/1917	13/01/1917
War Diary	Frucourt	15/01/1917	29/01/1917
War Diary	Hamel	30/01/1917	31/01/1917
Heading	48th Div 1/2nd S.M. Field Ambulance Feb 1917		
Miscellaneous	A.D.M.S 48th Division	28/02/1917	28/02/1917
Heading	1/2 South Midland Field Ambulance B.E.F. Vol 17 1 Feb 1917-28 Feb 1917		
War Diary	Hamel	01/02/1917	02/02/1917
War Diary	Eclusier	03/02/1917	08/02/1917
War Diary	Cappy	09/02/1917	28/02/1917
Miscellaneous	Summary Of Admissions Discharges February 1917		
Heading	48th Div Mar 1917 1/2nd S.M. Field Ambulance		
Heading	1/2 South Midland Field Ambulance B.E.F. Vol 18 1 March 1917-31 March 1917 Vol 18		
War Diary	Cappy	01/03/1917	31/03/1917
Miscellaneous	Appendix Summary Of Admission Discharges March 1917		
Heading	48th Div 1/2nd South Midland F.A. April 1917		
Heading	1/2 South Midland Field Ambulance B.E.F. Vol 19 1 Ap 1917-30 Ap 1917 Vol 19		
War Diary	Cappy	01/04/1917	18/04/1917
War Diary	Doignt	19/04/1917	30/04/1917
Heading	Appendix Summary Admission Discharges April 1917		
Heading	May 1917 48th Div 1/2nd South Midland F.A.		
Heading	1/2 South Midland Field Ambulance B.E.F. Vol 20 1 May 1917-31 May 1917 Vol 20		
War Diary	Doignt	01/05/1917	11/05/1917
War Diary	Le Transloy	12/05/1917	12/05/1917
War Diary	Lebucquiere	13/05/1917	31/05/1917
Miscellaneous	Appendix Summary Of Admissions And Discharges May 1917	31/05/1917	31/05/1917
Heading	June 1917 1/2nd South Mid.F.A.		
Heading	1/2 South Midland Field Ambulance B.E.F. Vol 21 1 June 1917-30 June 1917		
War Diary	Lebucquiere	01/06/1917	30/06/1917
Miscellaneous	Appendix Summary Of Admissions & Discharges		
Heading	July 1917 1/2nd South Midland F.A.		
Heading	1/2 South Midland Field Ambulance B E F Vol 22 1 July 1917-31st July 1917		
War Diary	Lebucquiere	01/07/1917	03/07/1917
War Diary	Bihucourt	04/07/1917	04/07/1917
War Diary	Bellacourt	05/07/1917	22/07/1917
War Diary	Marcourt Farm	23/07/1917	24/07/1917
War Diary	L'ebbe Farm	25/07/1917	31/07/1917
Miscellaneous	Appendix Summary Of Admissions & Discharges July 1917		
Heading	Aug 1917 1/2nd South Midland F.A.		
Heading	1/2 South Midland Field Ambulance 1 Aug 1917-31 Aug 1917 Volume 23		
War Diary	L'ebbe Farm	01/08/1917	04/08/1917

Type	Description	Start	End
War Diary	Gwent Farm A.28.a.2.4	05/08/1917	05/08/1917
War Diary	Gwent Farm	06/08/1917	29/08/1917
War Diary	L'ebbe Farm	30/08/1917	31/08/1917
Heading	Sep 1917 1/2nd South Midland F.A.		
Heading	1/2nd South Midland Field Ambulance. 1st September 1917 To 30th September 1917 Volume 24		
War Diary	L'ebbe Farm	01/09/1917	15/09/1917
War Diary	Licques	16/09/1917	26/09/1917
War Diary	Zutkerque	27/09/1917	27/09/1917
War Diary	Gwalia Farm A 28 A 2.3 Sheet 28	28/09/1917	28/09/1917
War Diary	Gwalia Farm	29/09/1917	30/09/1917
Miscellaneous	XIX Corps Rest Station.		
Miscellaneous	XVIII Corps Main Dressing Station	30/09/1917	30/09/1917
Heading	Oct 1917 1/2nd South Midland F.A.		
Heading	1/2nd South Midland Field Ambulance 1st October 1917 To 31st October 1917 Volume 25.Pages 14 Appendix I		
War Diary	Gwalia Farm	01/10/1917	10/10/1917
War Diary	Tunnellers Camp	11/10/1917	13/10/1917
War Diary	In The Train	14/10/1917	14/10/1917
War Diary	Les Quartre Vents	15/10/1917	16/10/1917
War Diary	Mont St Eloi	17/10/1917	29/10/1917
War Diary	Aux Rietz	30/10/1917	31/10/1917
Miscellaneous	Summary Of Admissions And Discharges During Month Ending 31st October 1917		

WO/05/2752/2

1/2 South Midland Field Ambulance

48TH DIVISION

1-2ND STH MID'D FLD AMB.

MAR 1915-~~DEC 1918~~

1917 OCT

TO ITALY

121/4919
March 1915

JU 48th Div

1/2nd S. Midland Field Ambulance

121/4919

48

Ans

CONFIDENTIAL

WAR DIARY of 1/2nd S. Mid Ft Amb

From 23-3-15 to 31-3-15

Volume I

Place & Date	Summary of Events	Remarks & Appendices
MARGARETTING 23/3/15	First party (A & B secs) left 3.15 AM arrived Chelmsford Stn at 4.33 AM entrained in 40 mins. left 5.30 AM. Second party left at 5 AM. arrived CHELMSFORD Stn at 6.20 AM, entrained. First train arrived S'HAMPTON DOCKS at 11 AM, second at 1.30 PM Detained on Quayside remained at docks till 7 PM. Sailed 7 PM in QUEEN EMPRESS. Transport men, horses and vehicles in SS Lapland which did not leave till following evening.	left at 7.30 AM SB
HAVRE 24/3/15	Arrived 4 AM after very uncomfortable journey from overcrowding Disembarked at 7 AM - marched to shed R, stopped till noon Reported to Base commandant at 12.30 PM, men marched to No 1	

Place & Date	Summary of Events	Remarks & appendices	2
	rest camp, taking 2¾ hours - Guide having lost his way		
HAVRE 25/3/15	At rest camp all day; Transport arrived 7 PM, Ambulance wagon tyres defective. Completed equipment of Unit from Ordnance	French Interpreter Joined. Sergt Leay sent to Base	83 83
HAVRE 26/3/15	Left camp 3 PM arrived Gare des Marchandises at 5 PM. Entrained with No 2 Coy ASC 51 ID & transport details of 1/6 R Warwicks		
27.3.15	Left 8.59 PM, one horse shot at HARDELOT for broken leg. Arrived HAZEBROUCH 6 PM, detrained marched to farm at CROIX ROUGE - billeted		83
Sᵗ JANS CAPELLE 28.3.15	Left 10.30 AM by route march of 10 KM for Sᵗ JANS CAPELLE, Billeted at Convents & in neighbouring farm house - opened temporary hospital for Bgde sick evacuating to No 8 Cas Clearing Stn at BAILLEUL		83

Place & Date	Summary of Events	Remarks & references	3.
ST JANS CAPELLE 29/3/15	Visited BAILLEUL - lecture to B9th officers by General Smith-Dorrien		SB
ST JANS CAPELLE 30/3/15	Visited No 13, 14, 15 F.A. of V Dn with ADMS to see dispositions, two of my officers went at night to visit & see ambulances at work.		SB
ST JANS CAPELLE 31/3/15	Two more officers went at night to help in evacuation of sick & wounded at LOCRE and DRANOUTRE.		SB
			SB

Seymour Barling
Lt. Col. RAMCT.
O.C.
1/2nd S mid Fd Amb

121/5161
April 1915

48th Div

121/5161

1/2 S. Midland Field Ambulance

Vol II

CONFIDENTIAL.

War Diary of
1/2nd S. M'Sex F. Amb.

Pages 9.
+ Appendix I one page.

Seymour Barling
Lt Col RAMC(T)
O/C

Place & Date	Summary of Events	Remarks & references
ST. JANS CAPPELLE 1-4-15	By route march to ARMENTIERES with Warwickshire Infy Bgde. Left at 11.30 AM arrived 3 PM. Billeted Rue de Flanders. Reported to Col's in charge No 17, 18 F. Amb.	Capt. McCready Chaplain; attached. Left one HD horse SB behind under care of ADVS II Corps
ARMENTIERES 2-4-15	Shown over No 17, No 18 F.A. & went to Advanced Dressing Station of No 17 F.A. & method of evacuation explained. Two officers went out with 2 squads of 6 men each at night to evacuate from Reg. Aid Posts. Moving men & remainder of 2nd sub-division to hospital morning & afternoon.	SB
ARMENTIERES 3-4-15	Taken to Dressing Stations of No 18 F.A. & dispositions explained. Other officers & men went out at night to evacuate sick & wounded.	SB

Place & Date	Summary of Events	Remarks & appendices	2
ARMENTIERES 4/4/15	Sunday. Men of Unit all bathed at No 17 F.A.		SB
ARMENTIERES 5/4/15	Visited Divisional Baths & organisation explained. 2 Officers & 54 horses went out at night to evacuate sick & wounded	Sergt. Pyatt sick left at No 17 F.A.	SB
ARMENTIERES 6-4-15	By route march with Warwick Infy Bgde to BAILLEUL left 2.10 P.M. arrived 4.50 P.M. Into billets at Rue de Musée. Left 2 HD horses unfit to travel at Armentiers i/c of ADVS VI Div		
BAILLEUL 7.4.15	Strength 233 Officers & men Horses R=13 HD=43 Vehicles 21 7 GS 7 LGS 3 Ambulances 3 W Carts 1 Forges Cart		SB

Place & Date	Summary of Events	Remarks & appendices	3
BAILLEUL 8-4-15	Route march — Reported to ADMS 1/.st S.MD at 3PM. Strength O.11 O.R. 222 deficiency Horses 13 R 48 HD 1.R 4 HD Vehicles up to War Establishment		SB
BAILLEUL 9-4-15	Route March — Mens billets very overcrowded & insanitary Strength as on 8.4.15		SB
BAILLEUL 10-4-15	Men to Divisional Baths — very badly organised Strength as on 8.4.15		SB
BAILLEUL 11-4-15	Church Parade. Strength as on 8.4.15		SB
BAILLEUL 12-4-15	Route march 3 hrs. Strength as on 8.4.15 except Chaplain left & attached 6. Warwicks, Sergt Butler to office of ADMS.		SB

Place & Date	Summary of Events	Remarks & references to appendices
BAILLEUL 13/4/15	To collect sick from 5th Inf Bgde. Strength O 10 O R 222 Horses R 13 H D 43 Vehicles up to strength.	8B
BAILLEUL 14/4/15	Chaplain from 10th FA arrived with horse & batman Strength O 11 O R 223. Horses R 14 H D 44. 1 H D received today from Rouen. Men Detatched 2 ASC Sergt Pyott returned, to Div A.C. Vehicles up to strength	8B
BAILLEUL 15/4/15	Route march. Strength O 11 O R 223. Horses R 14 H D 44 7 M/cycle 1 M Cycle & 1 M men arrived 1 Horse Vehicles to strength.	8B

Place & Date	Summary of Events	Remarks Appendices
BAILLEUL 16.4.15	Fresh interpreter arrived, old interpreter reported St Omer; Two wagons (A) returned to HQrs ADMS - remain on our fighting strength. opened 19 Rue de Musée as F.A. Hosp / Div. Convalescent Hospital L⁺ WILKINSON & 20 tent subdivision took over Infectious Hospital L⁺ Col Thomas & debown arrived & one horse. Offrs 12 OR 238 Detached 1 A.Col 1 A.C. 4 Motor drivers (ADMS) 1 Roman Horses R. 15 HD 44. 4 Vehicles to schedule M.T. 1 Bicycle 5 MA 2 detached	SB

5

Place Date	Summary of Events	Remarks & appendices
BAILLEUL 17.4.15	Took in first batch of patients. O=nil OR= admissions 23 One man went sick (Jennings Pte) One man (Sgt of HT. [Injured]) Strength O 12 O.R. 236 Detached as 16/4 sick 2 Vehicles with exception of two detached & 2 MG up to Estab. Horses R 15 MD 44.	SB
BAILLEUL 18/4/15	Church Parade. Admissions O = 1 OR = 11 Strength as 17/4/15.	SB
BAILLEUL 19/4/15	Route March Strength as on 17/4/15 admissions O = 1 OR = 16	SB

Place & date	Summary of Events	Remarks & appendices
BAILLEUL 20/4/15	Admissions O= nil OR=10 Strength O=12 OR 235 Detached 16/4 Sick 3.	SB
BAILLEUL 21-4-15	Admissions O= nil OR= 14 Sick 4. Lt Sheridan joined 2 PM ex Rouen. One H.D. shot	SB
BAILLEUL 22-4-15	Admissions O= nil OR= 16. Sick 3 Capt. Handfield Jones left for Rouen.	SB
BAILLEUL 23-4-15	Admissions O=1 OR= Sick 3. Strength O=12 OR=234 Detached 1 A.Col. Horses R=15 HD=43 2 ASC H. Transport To Strength 4 MT Divs M.T. 7 MA (2 detached) 1 Rouen ADMS 1 328 Coy ASC 1 M Cy. Lt. Col. Thomas between returned to 7 divs	SB SB

Date & Place	Summary of Events	Remarks & Appendices
BAILLEUL 24-4-15	Admissions O = 1 OR = 14 Sick of Unit = 2 Strength O = 12 OR = 235 Capt. Oakey, horse & batman returned to 10th F.A.	SB
BAILLEUL 25/4/15	Admissions O = 0 OR = 45 Sick of unit = 2 Strength O = 11 OR = 234 One Riding & HD Horse received. Strength of Horses R 15 HD 46	SB
BAILLEUL 26/4/15	Admissions O = Nil OR = 17 Sick of Unit 2. Strength as on 25/4/15.	SB
BAILLEUL 27.4.15	Admissions O = Nil OR = 34 Sick of Unit 2. Strength as on 25/4/15	SB

Date & Place	Summary of Events	Remarks & appendices
BAILLEUL. 28.4.15	Admissions O = 1 OR = 16 Unit Sick 1 Strength as on 25/4/15 L⁰ Pitt 2 NCO's 11 men detatched to PONT NIEPPE for Div Baths.	SB
BAILLEUL. 29.4.15	Admissions O = nil OR = 39 Strength as on 25/4/15 Sick nil	SB
BAILLEUL. 30/4/15	Admissions O = 1 OR = 50 Sick = 1 wastage = 3 Strength O = 11 OR = 232 Horses R - 15 HD. 46 Horse transport to strength. In Transport of MA 1 MC	See appendix I SB

Seymour Barling
Lt. Col. RAMCT
o/c 1/2 5 Mid Fd Amb

APPENDIX I

5. Mid Div. Rest Station.

Admissions & Discharges from April 17 to April 30

Admitted	Disposal			
	To duty	To C.C. Stn.	To F Amb	Remaining
211	93	20	1	97

Seymour Barling
Lt Col. RAMC T.
O.C. 1/2 5. Mid F. Amb.

1 May 1915

121/5554

48th Division

2nd S.M. Field Ambulance

Vol III

121/5554
May
June 1918

CONFIDENTIAL

War diary of 1/2³ʳᵈ 5th Mid. Ft. Amb.

From   1.5.15   to   31.5.15.

Vol I

Place & Date	Summary of Events	Remarks appendices
BAILLEUL. 1/5/15	Admissions O = 1 OR = 13 Sick of Unit = 2 wastage 3 Belgian Interpreter joined Strength O = 11 OR = 232 Horses R = 15 HD = 46 Horse Transport to schedule M.T = 7 M.Cy = 7 2 NCO + 8 men attached for duty at Divisional Baths.	8B
BAILLEUL 2/5/15	Admissions O = 1 OR = 12 Sick nil Wastage 3	8B
BAILLEUL 3/5/15	Admissions O = 0 OR = 38 Sick = 3 wastage 3 French Interpreter returned	8B
BAILLEUL 4/5/15	Admissions O = 0 OR = 25 Sick = 4 Wastage 3	8B

Place & Date	Summary of Events	Remarks Appendices
BAILLEUL 5/5/15	Admissions O = O OR = 32 Sick 3 (admitted to FA) Wastage = 3	8B
BAILLEUL 6/5/15	Admissions O = O OR = 22 Sick 1 In FA = R Wastage = 3 1 NCO 1 man sent to Div. Baths 1 Off. 26 O.R. now at Baths	8B
Bailleul 7/5/15	Admissions O = O OR = 46 Sick 1 2 in FA Wastage = 3 one HD horse died & 2 mules join	8B
BAILLEUL 8/5/15	Admissions O = O OR = 24 Sick = 3 2 in FA Wastage = 3	8B
BAILLEUL 9/5/15	Admissions O = 1 OR = 17 Sick = 0 1 in FA Wastage = 3 Strength O = 11 OR = 233 Horses R = 15 HD 45 Mules 2. Horse Transport to schedule. Motor Transport MA = 7 MC = 1	8B

Place & Date	Summary of Events	Remarks & appendices
BAILLEUL 10/5/15	Admissions O = nil OR = 19 Sick 2 in FA = 1 Wastage = 3	SB
BAILLEUL 11/5/15	Admissions O = nil OR = 18 Sick = 4 Wastage 4 (1 M.T. Driver Sent down as Mentally Deficient) Workshop Unit taken on our Strength. Consists of O = 1 OR = 19 Interpreter = 1 OR deficient = 2 1 Packard Workshop 1 30 cwt Lorry 1 Napier Touring Car 1 3 ton Store wagon	SB
BAILLEUL 12/5/15	Admissions O = nil OR = 47 Sick = 0 in FA = 2 Wastage = 5 chit 4 WS = 1	SB
BAILLEUL 13/5/15	Admissions O = 1 OR 23 Sick = 2 in FA = 3 wastage = 5 / 4 Men of Unit paid 10f.	SB

Date & Place	Summary of Events	Remarks & Appendices
BAILLEUL 14/5/15	Admissions O = Nil OR = 30 Sick 1 In F.A. = 3 Wastage = 4	BB
BAILLEUL 15/5/15	Admissions O = 2 OR = 19 Sick Nil In F.A = 4 Wastage = 4 L. Col. Thomas left to join HQrs G+W. Bgde.	BB
BAILLEUL 16/5/15	Admissions O = Nil OR = 19 Sick = 1 In F.A. 3 Wastage = 4 Strength F.A. O = 10 OR = 229 Horses R = 15 HD 45 Mules 2 Horse transport to strength Motor Transport to strength Workshop As on 1/5 except one man in F.A.	BB
BAILLEUL 7.5.15	Admissions O = Nil OR = 34 Sick 1 In F.A. 4 Wastage 4 One Douglas M.C. received, passed to 3rd FA 18/5/15 One Electrician, Fitter joined workshop 16/5	BB

Place & Date	Summary of Events	Remarks appendices
BAILLEUL 18/5/15	Admissions O = 1 OR = 32 Sick = 2 In F.A = 2. Wastage 4. Two more patients sent to detachment at Isolation Hospital.	SB
BAILLEUL 19.5.15	Admissions O = Nil OR = 15 Sick = 1 In F.A = 1 Wastage F.A = 3+ = 1	SB
BAILLEUL 20/5/15	Admissions O = 2 OR = 29 Sick = 0 In F.A = 1 Wastage F.A 4. Shortage F.A 3. (Asc. M.T.) (not joined)	SB
BAILLEUL 21.5.15	Admissions O = Nil. OR = 33 Sick = 1 In F.A = 0 Wastage F.A 4 Shortage F.A 3	SB
BAILLEUL 22.5.15	Admissions O = 1 OR = 36 Sick = Nil In F.A = 0 Wastage = 4 Shortage = 3 4 mules Received	SB

Place & Date	Summary of Events	Remarks & initials
BAILLEUL 23/5/15	Admissions O = nil oR = 51 Sick = 1 Wastage 4 (shortage 3) Strength FA O = 10 oR = 232 Horses R = 14 HD 45 Mules 6 Horse Transport To strength M Transport To strength except 2 M Cy. Workshop O = 1 oR = 22 Vehicles to schedule. Lt. Shrivder proceeded on 8 days leave	SB
BAILLEUL 24/5/15	Admissions O = 1 oR = 29 Sick = 0 to FA = 1 Wastage 4 (shortage 3) One HD died probably volvulus.	SB
BAILLEUL 25/5/15	Admissions O = nil oR = 19 Sick ⊕ - FA = 4 wastage 4 shortage 3.	SB

Place & Date	Summary of Events	Remarks & appendices
BAILLEUL 26.5.15	Admissions O = Nil OR = 59. Sick = 4 To F.A = 2 Wastage 4 2 6 Shortage 3	SB
BAILLEUL 27.5.15	Admissions O = 1 OR = 82 Sick 3 To F.A = 7 Wastage 4 Shortage 3 L/Cpl Hughes removed to Flêtre replaced by Pte Price B S. Sergt. Ingham returned to 1/4 Gen Hosp Pte Hamblen removed from Isolation Hosp	SB
BAILLEUL 28.5.15	Admissions O = Nil OR = 24 Sick = 1 To F.A = 8 Wastage 4 Shortage 3	SB
BAILLEUL 29.5.15	Admissions O = Nil OR = 23 Sick = 1 To F.A = 6 Wastage 4 Shortage 3 Opened 100 bed Tent hospital by O.C. "C" Sect One BSA Motor Cycle received from 3rd F.A. (defective). Pte Keen J.W. Transferred to Isolation Hosp ? Typhoid	SB SB

Place. Date	Summary of Events		
BAILLEUL 30/5/15	Admissions O = 1 OR = 33 Sick = 0 to F.A. 4 Wastage 5 Shortage = 3		SB
BAILLEUL 31/5/15	Admissions O = Nil OR = 90 Sick = 2 to F.A = 3 Wastage 7 Shortage 3 P⁺ Taylor sent to C C S "otitis" P⁺ Christy to No 17 FA Armentières for Water Analysis study		SB
		Seymour Barling Lt Col RAMCT. 2nd Fd Ambulance 48th (S M) Div	

[Stamp: 2ND SOUTH MIDLAND FIELD AMBULANCE R.A.M.C. S.M.D.T.F. Date 1/6/15]

Appendix 2.

Resumé of admissions
& Disposal of cases
passing through Field
Ambulance & Divisional
Rest Station. May 1 – May 31

Admissions to F'd Amb & Rest Station
19 Rue de Musée

May	Officers	O.ranks	Total
1	1	13	14
2	1	15	16
3	-	38	38
4	-	28	28
5	-	35	35
6	-	24	24
7	-	46	46
8	-	24	24
9	1	17	18
10	-	19	19
11	-	18	18
12	-	47	47
13	1	23	24
14	-	30	30
15	2	19	21
16	-	19	19
17	-	34	34
18	1	32	33
19	-	15	15
20	2	29	31
21	-	33	33
22	1	36	37
23	-	51	51
24	1	29	30
25	-	19	19
TOTALS FORWARD	11	693	704

Admissions to Field Amb. & Rest Station
19 Rue de Musée.

May	Officers	O Ranks	Total
Totals forward	11	693	704
26	–	59	59
27	1	32	33
28	–	24	24
29	–	23	23
30	1	33	34
31	–	30	30
Total for May	13	894	907

— ANALYSIS —

	F. ambulance		D Rest Stn	
Admissions	Officers	O.R.	Officers	O.R.
	3	70	10	824

DISPOSAL	Officers	O.R.	
	7	754	To Duty
	6	122	Evacuated
	4	166	Remaining

Raymond Barley
Lt. Col. R.A.M.C.T
2nd ⁂ med ⁂
amb.
48th Div.

Appendix 3

Summary of cases passing through British Isolation Hospital - Bailleul -
May 1 - May 31. 1915.
under charge of
Lt. Wilkinson RAMC(T)
2nd S.M. Fd. Amb.
48 (S.M.) Div.

From Medical Officer i/c   June 2/15
       Isolation Hosp¹

To   O.C.
      2nd S.M.F. Amb.

Return of Admissions & Discharges
   for Month of May.

Infection	Number Admitted	Number Evacuated	
Measles	103	103	
German Measles	210	206	
Scarlet Fever	14	13	
Mumps	11	10	
Typhoid	26	25	
Para Typhoid	8	8	
Contact C.S.M.	9	9	
C.S.M.	7	6	
Influenza	11	11	
Non-infectious	23	20	
Totals	422	411	

W.A. Dickinson
Lieut R.A.M.C.

Number of men bathed during 28
working days of month
26,886
average per day 960

Each man supplied with clean,
new or mended garments in
exchange for dirty ones

Washing for month

Shirts   25,527
Pants   21,072
Vests   12,309
Towels   22,002
Socks (Prs) 25,157

Clothing replaced by new articles
Shirts   896
Pants   1808
Vests   665
Socks (Prs) 2164

Respirators to the number of 45,000
of different patterns were made
for the Division
Seymour Borley

Appendix 4

Summary of work at
48th (SM) Divisional Baths
under Lt Pitt RAMC(T)
2nd/1st Field Ambulance
RAMC(T)

1/6/15.

151/6023

ams.

47 48th Battalion

2nd S.M. Field Ambulance

Vol IV

June 1915

CONFIDENTIAL.

War Diary of 2nd Fd Amb.
48 (S.M) Div.

From 1-6-15 to 30-6-15

Vol I

Appendices

Raymond Barling
Lt. Col
O.C. 2nd Fd Amb.
48 (SM) Div

Pages. 8
Appendices 5-6-7.

Place & Date	Summary of Events	Remarks & references
1915 BAILLEUL 1 June	Admissions O = nil OR = 50 Sick = 1 In F.A = 3 Wastage = 7 officers Shortage = 3 Strength F.A - 10 OR - 230 Workshop - 1 OR = 22 Horses R = 14 HD = 44 Mules - 6 H.T. to strength M.T. MA = 7 M Cy - 2	SB
BAILLEUL 2 June	Admissions O = 2 OR = 47 Sick = 2 In F.A = 3 Wastage 7 Shortage 3 One Driver RAMC 2 privates RAMC arrived	SB
BAILLEUL 3 June	Admissions O = nil OR 31 Wastage = 4 Sick = 2 In F.A - 4 Shortage 3	SB

Date Place	Summary of Events	Remarks & appendices
BAILLEUL. June 4	Admissions O = 2 OR = 27 Sick = 4 In F.A. 4 Wastage 4 Shortage - 3. Three Motor Cyclists & 1 motor driver arrived from here.	SB
BAILLEUL June 5.	Admissions O = 2 OR = 29 Sick = 0 In F.A = 6 Wastage 3. Respirator Drill, Iron Rations & F.D. examined	SB
BAILLEUL. June 6.	Admissions O = Nil OR = 23 Sick = 2 In F.A = 5 Wastage = 3	SB
BAILLEUL. June 7	Admissions O = Nil OR = 26 Sick = 4 In F.A. = 6 Wastage = 3 Lt Murray & Servant for temporary duty at Bucks Bn.	SB

BAILLEUL June 8	Admissions O = Nil OR = 36
	Sick = 2 In F.A = 6 Wastage 3.
	Pte Cummings WA arrived
	  Stevenson E (1/2 Highland FA)
	    sent from here.
		SB

Date & Place	Summary of Events	Appendices
BAILLEUL 9.6.15	Admissions O = Nil OR = 23 Sick = 2 In F.A = 1 Wastage 1 Both Interpreters temporarily detached.	SB
BAILLEUL 10.6.15	Admissions O = 2 OR = 34 Sick = 3 In F.A = 2 Wastage = 3 Pte Bacon & Pte Herrington off the strength ? SF ~ ? enteric	SB
BAILLEUL 11.6.15	Admissions O = 1 OR = 17 Sick = 0 In F.A = 2 Wastage = 3	SB
BAILLEUL 12-6-15	Admissions O = Nil OR = 18 Sick = 2 In FA = 2 Wastage 3. Paid men 10/co. Interpreters Sergts 20/co. 4 Drivers (MT) from ROUEN rejoined	SB
BAILLEUL 13-6-15	Admissions O = Nil OR = 23 Sick = 2 In FA = 1 Wastage = 3	SB

Date & Place	Summary of Events	Remarks & references
BAILLEUL. 14-6-15.	Admissions O = Nil OR = 37 Sick = 4 In F.A. = 1 Wastage = 3	SB
BAILLEUL 15-6-15	Admissions O = 1 OR = 46 Sick = Nil In F.A. = 1 Wastage 1 P.e Bacon taken on strength from Isolation Hosp. P.e Rose received as reinforcement	SB
BAILLEUL 16-6-15	Admissions O = 1 OR = 43 Sick = 2 In F.A. = 2 Wastage 1	SB
BAILLEUL. 17-6-15	Admissions O = Nil OR = 31 Sick = 1 In F.A. = 3 Wastage 1 1 Riding Horse Cook. Officers OR = 2 on 6 days leave	SB
BAILLEUL. 18-6-15	Admissions O = 3 OR = 31 Sick = 2 In F.A. = 4 Wastage = 1 4 Drivers (MT) Returned to ROUEN as surplus to strength	SB

Place & Date	Summary of Events	Remarks & Appendices
BAILLEUL 19-6-15	Admissions O = 1 OR = 24 Sick = 2 in F.A. = 4 Wastage = 1	
BAILLEUL 20-6-15	Admissions O = 2 OR = 40 Sick = 0 in FA = 4 Wastage = 1	
BAILLEUL 21-6-15	Admissions O = 1 OR = 25 Sick = 2 in FA = 4 Wastage = 1	
BAILLEUL 22-6-15	Admissions O = 4 OR = 26 Sick = 5 in FA = 6 Wastage = 1 P⁄c Stonehouse arrived to replace wastage.	
BAILLEUL 23-6-15	Admissions O = Nil OR = 36 Sick = Nil in FA = 5 Wastage = 0 Major Halliday + 2 OR returned from leave 1 Riding Horse Shot.	
BAILLEUL 24.6.15	Admissions O = 1 OR = 2 Sick = 2 FA = 2 Wastage = 0 Handed over Baths at P⁄c de niffe	

Date Place	Summary of Events	Remarks & appendices
BAILLEUL 25-6-15	admissions = 1 Sick = nil W=tge = nil In F.A. = nil. Hospital closed. Fever Hospital Handed over	SB
BAILLEUL 26-6-15	admissions = 1 Sick = nil. in FA. nil W=tge	SB
BAILLEUL 27-6-15	Patients = nil Sick = 0 In FA = 0 W=tge = 0 Left by Route march for VIEUX BERQUIN at 9 PM. arrived 12.15 AM.	SB
VIEUX BERQUIN 28-6-15	Patients = 16 Sick = 2 In FA W=tge = 1 Left by Route march 7.30 PM arrived ROBECQ at 10.30 PM BILLETED at Farm 1 mile NE of Town	SB

Date & Place	Summary of Events	Remarks & appendices
ROBECQ 29-6-15	Patients = 9 Sick = 10 m FA 2 Wastage = 2 Left ROBECQ at 6 PM by route march to RAIMBERT arrived 9 PM billeted in houses on main street	SB
RAIMBERT 30-6-15	Patients admitted F.A = 7 Sick = 2 m FA = 2 Wastage = 3 Opened F.A. Hosp. Men into Tents.	APPENDICES 5 & 6 SB

Seymour Barling
Lt Col
OC 2⁻ 4ᵗʰ Amb.
48 Div.

30-6-15

Appendix 5

Cases admitted British Isolation Hospital II Army under Lt R.D. Dickinson RAMC. 2nd Fd. Amb. 48 Div.

Suspected Enterics	51
" Diphtheria	12
Scarlet Fever	6
Measles	22
German Measles	75
Cases proving Non infectious	34
Mumps	5
Cerebro Spinal Meningitis	8
Suspected Typhoid Carriers	18
Cerebro Spinal Contacts	12
	243

This is for the period June 1 – 25 when hospital was handed over to No 12 C. C. Stn.

Seymour Buley
Lt Col.
RAMC

OFFICER COMMANDING
2nd F.A. S.M.D., R.A.M.C.T.P.

Appendix 6.

Summary of Cases admitted
to 2nd Fd Ambulance
June 1 - 30th 1915

and to 48 Divl Rest
Station June 1 - 25th 1915.

Admissions & Discharges 2nd Field Amb & Divl Rest. Stn
48 Divn

Date	Fld Amb		Rest Stn		Total		To Duty		To C.C.S.		Total	
	OFF.	O.R.	OFF.	O.R.	OFF.	O.R.	OFF.	O.R.	OFF.	O.R.	OFF.	O.R.
June 1	.	4	.	46	.	50	.	20	.	.	.	20
2	1	5	1	42	2	47	1	28	.	1	1	29
3	.	11	.	20	.	31	1	27	.	.	1	27
4	.	6	2	21	2	27	.	23	.	3	.	26
5	.	1	2	28	2	29	2	29	1	.	3	28
6	.	4	.	19	.	23	2	23	.	.	2	23
7	.	11	.	15	.	26	.	36	.	1	.	37
8	.	9	.	27	.	36	.	30	.	2	.	32
9	.	10	.	13	.	23	.	23	.	1	.	24
10	.	6	2	28	2	34	.	20	1	5	1	25
11	.	3	1	14	1	17	1	28	.	1	1	29
12	.	1	.	14	.	15	.	23	.	1	.	24
13	.	2	.	21	.	23	.	23	.	.	.	23
14	.	15	.	22	.	37	.	13	.	2	.	15
15	.	16	1	30	1	46	1	30	.	.	1	30
16	.	20	1	23	1	43	1	35	.	1	1	36
17	.	10	.	21	.	31	.	30	.	4	.	34
18	.	3	3	28	3	31	.	26	1	1	1	27
19	.	.	1	24	1	24	1	25	.	2		
20	.	.	.	.	.	.	Died		.	1	1	28
20	.	8	2	32	2	40	.	32	.	.	.	32
21	.	4	1	21	1	25	.	22	1	2	1	24
22	.	8	4	18	4	26	.	21	3	2	3	23
23	.	2	.	34	.	36	2	30	.	2	2	32
24	1	2	.	.	1	2	1	64	7	103	8	167
25								44	.	1	.	45
	2	161	21	561	23	722	13	724	14	136	27	860

Date	Admitted F.A.		Discharges (OR)	
	Officers	OR	C.C.S.	Duty
June 25	–	1	1	–
26	–	1	1	–
27	–	–	–	–
28	–	16	12	–
29	–	9	5	1
30	–	7	–	7
	–	34	19	8

Total Admissions F.A. June 1 – 30
    Officers 2   OR 195

Total admissions Rest Station 48 Div
     June 1 – 20
    Officers   OR
     21   561

Disposal

Officers		Men	
Duty	C.C.S.	Duty	C.C.S.
13	14	732	154
			Died 1

Appendix 7.

Work at 48 Div. Baths
June 1st to June 24.

Under Lieut J.B. Pitt
R.A.M.C.T.

Twenty two working days
during which 23050
men were bathed & given
clean underclothing

Average per day. 1047.

Raymond Barling

LIEUT-COLONEL. R.A.M.C. (T.
OFFICER COMMANDING,
2nd F.A. S.M.D., R.A.M.C.T.F.

121/6344

48th Division/1

1/2nd S.M. Field Ambulance

Vol V

July '15

CONFIDENTIAL.

War diary of 2nd/1st Amb. 48(SM) Div
from 1-7-15 to 31-7-15.

VOL I
appendices (8)

Pages. 15
appendices (1)

Seymour Barling
Lt Col RAMCT.
O.C. 2nd/1st Amb.
48 Div.

Place / Date	Summary of Events	Remarks & references
RAIMBERT 1-7-15	Patients admitted F.A. O = 1 OR = 11 Disposal Duty 1 D.R.S. off 1 OR = 9 Remaining 9 Unit sick = 4 F.A. = 4 Wastage = 3	SB
RAIMBERT 2-7-15	Patients admitted FA ~~sick~~ ~~today~~ O = Nil OR = sick 7 Disposal Duty 5 DRS = 2 Remaining (9am) 5 } sick Evacuated 4 Unit Sick = 2. FA = 4 Wastage = 3	SB
RAIMBERT 3-7-15	Patients admitted FA O = Nil OR = sick 11 Wounded (acc'd) 1 Disposal Duty Nil Unit Wastage = 4 DRS = 7 Sick = 4 Remaining 10 58th Pyatt Evac. to L.of C. Evacuated nil	SB

Date. Place	Summary of Events	Remarks & Appendices

RAIMBERT
4-7-15
	Sick in FA = 13
	Disposal Duty —
	    Evacuᵈ 1 } sick
	    DRS 9
	Remaining = 13 sick
	Sick of Unit = 3 FA = 4 Dostage = 4
		SB

RAIMBERT
5-7-15
	Sick admitted FA. 16
	Disposal Duty 2
	    Evacuated —
	    DRS 11 } sick
	    Remaining 16
	Sick of Unit 2
	Dostage 4 Inspector of Transport In FA = 4
		SB

RAIMBERT 6-7-15	Sick admitted FA. sick 6 wd 2 Disposal Duty = 2 Evacuated = 3 Route march 6-9AM DRS = 6 Remaining.. 11 sick 2w Sick of Unit = 10 In FA = 4 Dostage = 4	SB

Date & Place	Summary of Events	Remarks & O/Defender
RAIMBERT 7.7.15	Kit Inspection. Sick admitted FA. O=10 off OR =10 　　Disposal　Duty 1 　　　　　　　DRS 4 　　　　　Evacuated 2 　　　　　Remaining 17. Unit In FA 4 Sick 10 Wastage = 4	SB
RAIMBERT 8/7/15	Sick admitted FA = 4 　　Disposal　DRS = 1 　　　　　　Duty = 2 　　　　　　CCS = 1 　　　　　Remaining = 17. Unit. In FA = 5 Sick 4 Wastage = 4.	SB
RAIMBERT 9/7/15	Route March. Sick admitted FA = 7 　　Disposal DRS. 6 　　　　　　Duty 5 　　　　　　CCS. 3 　　　　　Remaining 10 Unit In FA 3 Sick 8 Wastage = 4	SB

Date & Place	Summary of Events	Remarks & appendices
RAIMBERT. 10-7-15	Admitted to F.A. 11 Disposal Duty 1 Route March Evacuated 1 5 AM DRS 9 Remaining 10 Sick in Unit F.A. = 3 Sick = 8 Wastage = 4	SB
RAIMBERT 11-7-15	Church parade 9 AM. Admitted to FA 8 Disposal. Duty 6 DRS 3 Rem̄s. 9 Sick in Unit FA 4 Sick 12 W = 4 Two French Interpreters arrived	SB
RAIMBERT. 12-7-15	Route March 5.45 AM. Admitted to FA 19 Disposal Duty 16 DRS Evacuated 8 Rem̄g. 13 Sick = 8 F.A = 3 Wastage = 4 Lt Sheridan attached to Advres.	SB

Date & Place	Summary of Events	Remarks & reply
RAIMBERT 13-7-15	Admitted to F.A. = 1 Disposal Duty 4 　　　　　D.R.S. 5 　　　　　C.C.S. 1 　　　　　Remaining 4 Unit sick = 4　F.A. 4　Wastage = 6 　　　　　　　Pte Welford } to C.C.S. 　　　　　　　Pte at close Major Holly & Lt. Murray & Tents division of C to HESDINGUEUL to form advanced Dressing Stn. Took M.S. Cart, W. Cart & 2 M.A. Total personnel O = 2 O.R = 31	SB
RAIMBERT 14-7-15	Admitted to F.A. = 1 Disposal Duty = 2 　　　　　C.C.S. = 1 　　　　　D.R.S. = 0 　　　　　Remaining = 2 Unit sick = 6　F.A. = 4　Wastage = 6 Returned Tents C.S.6 36 to Ambulance 　also wagons L. & S. 3 to Divisional Train - three drivers & 6 H.D. Horses	SB

Date & Place	Summary of Events	Remarks & Appendices

RAIMBERT 15-7-15	Route March 15th at 5.45 AM
	Admitted to FA = 17
	Disposal Duty -
	          CCS = 2
	          Remaining 17
	Unit Wastage = 6 √ Sick = 3 FA = 2
	Strength RAMC T = 178 2 detached as wastage
	        Transport RAMC 32 2 over left
	        ASC (HT) = 2
	        ASC (MT) = 17 4 detached
	        Interpreter = 1
	        Chaplain Between = 1
	        Officers 11
	                               242
	Workshop OR = 22
	             off 1
	                      265
	MA = 5 MC = 2
	Horses HD = 35 mules 6 Riding = 13
	Wagons GS = 6 Water = 1
	        2 GS = 4 Ambulance 3
	        MC = 3
		1 Driver RAMC
		2 Ptes RAMC
		1 Chaplain
		  arrived

SPB

Date & Place	Summary of Events	Remarks & Appendices
RAIMBERT. 16-7-15	Admitted F A = 7 Disposal Duty 4. Evacuated = 2 Remaining 18 Unit Sick 2 FA = 3 Wastage = 3	SB
RAIMBERT 17-7-15	Admitted FA = 18 Disposal Duty = 8 Evacuated = 6 Remaining = 10 Unit sick = 5 Hosp = 5 Wastage = 3 Major Stobby + 2nd division R.C. returned midnight	SB
RAIMBERT. 18-7-15	Admitted to FA = 11 Disposal Duty = 1 Evacuated = 3 Remaining = 17 Unit sick = 0 Wastage = 3 FA = 5	SB
RAIMBERT. 19-7-15	Admitted to FA = 17 Disposal Duty = 7 Evacuated = 6 Remaining = 8 Unit sick = 2 Wastage = 3 In Hosp = 6. Major Kingston - Lt Murray - 2 NCO's 8 men to TERRAMESNIL	SB

Date Place	Summary of Events	Remarks & appendices
RAIMBERT 20-7-15	Admitted to F.A. =1 Disposal Duty =1 Evacuated =0 Remaining 8 Unit Sick = 0 F.A = 4 Wastage - 3 Transport & C sect left at 6.30 PM. Remainder at 8.30 PM – Entrained at LILLERS & left at 11 PM – arrived MODINCOURT at 5.30 AM detrained – left at 6.45 AM arrived at LEVINCOURT	3 8B
LEVINCOURT 21-7-15	Took over Chateau (B sect) & schools (A sect) Found 9 bad cases left by French Fd Amb. Unit Sick = nil Wastage = 3 Troops = 4 Admissions till 5.30 PM & including those taken in on previous day (A) = 83 Evacuated = nil	
LEVINCOURT 22-7-15	Unit Sick = 10 F.A = 4 Wastage 3. Field Amb. Admissions till noon 105 Capt. H R Burrows Disposal Duty = 5 Evacuated = 11 (Chaplain) arrived. DRS = 10	1W

Place & Date	Summary of Events	Remarks appendices

LOUVENCOURT 23/4/15	Admitted Officers in $ hd
	Men S = 38
	       W = nil
	Disposal Duty = 1
	          DRS = 20
	          Evacuated = 5
	          Remaining =
	Unit Ostge = 3 Hosp = 4 Sick 3	

LOUVENCOURT 24/4/15	Admitted Officers S = 1
	                    W = 2
	          Men S = 60
	                   W = 1
	Disposal Duty = 17
	          DRS = 26
	          Evacuated = 10 S off 1 wd
	          Remaining 0 sick 1 wd 1
	                           Men 72 " 2
	Men on Route march
	Unit Ostge = 3
	      DRS = 23
	      Hosp = 3
	      Sick = 4	

Date & Place	Summary of Events		Remarks & appendices
LOUVENCOURT 25-7-15	Admitted	Officers S=1, W=1 Men Sick=77, W=1	
	Disposal	Evacuated 0 = nil Men = 6 sick DRS 0 = nil Men = 39 (s), 1 (w) Duty 0 = nil Men = 3 (s)	
	Unit Wastage = 2 FA = 3 Sick = 3 Church Parade 8th Collins taken on strength.		SB
LOUVENCOURT 26-7-15	Admitted	Officers S=1, W=0 Men S=85, W=1	
	Disposal		Officers / Men C.C.S. S/W nil / S 15 W — DRS nil / 31 Duty nil / 9 Remained S 4 W 1 / S 127 W 3	SB

Date & Place	Summary of Events			Remarks & Appendices
	Unit. Wastage 2 Hosp 2 Sick 4			
LOUVENCOURT, 27-7-15	Admitted	Officers	Men	
		S = 2	60	
		W = —	8	
	Disposal			
	C.C.S.	S } nil W }	20 7	
	D.R.S.	S } nil W }	45 —	
	Duty	S = nil W = 1	13 —	
	Unit. Wastage 2 F.A. 5 Sick 3			
	Remaining in F.A.			
		S = 6	109	
		W = —	4	PB

Date & Place	Summary of Events.				Remarks & Appendices
LOUVENCOURT 28-7-15	Admitted		Officers	Men	
		S	nil	54	
		W		3	
	Disposal Duty	S	1	10	
		W	–	–	
	CCS	S	} nil	11	
		W		2	
	DRS	S	} nil	19	
		W		–	
	Remaining	S	5	123	
		W	–	5	
	Four Reinforcements arrived, 1 Dr. 3 Pte				SB
	Unit Surplus = 2 FA = 6 Sick = 4				

Date/Place	Summary of Events			Remarks & references
LOUVENCOURT 29-7-18	Admitted	Officers	Men	
	S	—	46	
	W	2	—	
	District. Duty S	1	14	
	W	—	—	
	C.C.S. S } nil		8	
	W		—	
	D.R.S S } nil		37	
	W		1	
	Remaining S	4	110	
	W	2	4	
	Unit Wastage Rifles of 3.			
	sick nil F.A. 6			
	Dr. Chilton arrived as reinforcement.			SB

Date, Place	Summary of Events				Remarks + Appendices
LOUTRE H:SQRT 30/7/15	Admitted	S. W.	1 -	29 1	
	Duxford CCS	S. W.	- -	11 1	
	DRS	S. W.	- -	19 -	
	Duty	S. W.	- -	19 -	
	Remng	S. W.	5 2	90 4	
	Unit Surplus + 3. Sick 2. FA. 6				SB
	Lnr Burrows OA joined 3rd FA temporarily.				

DATE & PLACE	Summary of Events				Remarks & references
LOUVENCOURT			Officers	Men	
31-7-15	Admissions	S	—	24	
		W	—	—	
	Disposals C.C.S.	S	—	9	
		W	—	—	
	Died.	S	1		
	Duty.	S	nil	11	
		W		2	
	Remaining	S	4	94	
		W	2	2	
	Unit Surplus + 3 Sick 2 Hosp = 3				SB

Appendix 8

Summary of sick & wounded admitted to 2nd F.? Amb 48 Divn during month of July 1915.

	Sick	Wounded
Officers	7	6
O. Ranks	762	27
	769	33

802

DISPOSAL

To Duty	162
To Divisional Rest Station	382
Evacuated	162
Died	1

Seymour Barling

121/6699

48th 15th Divi͞n

1/2nd L.M. Field Ambulance

Vol VI

From 1 - 31. 8. 15

August 15

CONFIDENTIAL.

War Diary of 2nd Ft. Amb. (48 Div)
From 1-8-15 to 31-8-15

Vol I

Appendices IX

Pages: 8
Appendices 1

Seymour Barling
Lt. Col. RAMC.
O.C. 2nd Ft. Amb
48 Div.

DATE / PLACE	Summary of Events	Remarks & appendices
LOUVENCOURT 1-8-15	Admitted sick 38 W.d 2 Disposal C.C.S. sick 2 Duty sick 5 DRS sick 22 To No 10 F.A. sick 20 Remaining Officers S=4 80 Lt Broderick Hope Hutton w=2 4 Unit Strength = 3 sick = 1 F.A.=2	
LOUVENCOURT 2-8-15	Officers men Admitted sick 2 38 W. — 3 Disposal CCS sick 1 4 DRS sick — 7 Duty sick 2 13 wounded — 1 Remaining sick 3 97 w. 2 6 Unit Strength = 3 sick=1 Men paid 10f.c. X. Amb=2	

DATE & PLACE	Summary of Events			Remarks & appendices
LOUVENCOURT 3-8-15	Admitted	officers S. 2 W. —	men 98 1	
	Disposal CCS	—	6	
	Duty	—	18	
	DRS	—	9	
	Remaining	S. 5 W. 2	102 7	SB
	Unit Surplus = 3 Sick = 7 F.A = 2.			
	Lt. Col. Thomas went on leave			
LOUVENCOURT 4-8-15 M.T. (ASC)	Nine men left for Rouen to join Ptes (A) Light T. Barton HJ (B) Light H. Johnston WF (A) (C) Ginders WH. White Cd. (C) (C) James DW. Bridges P. (B) (C) Morton HC.			(C)
	Wastage = 6. Sick = 4 FA = 1.	C Sect 5 A Sect 3 B Sect 1 B Sect — — 1 C " — — 5		SB Transport — +1

Date & Place	Summary of Events	Remarks & appendices
LOUVENCOURT 5/8/15	Two Ptes Allen & Goddard joined (C Coy) Pte James joined Transport. Pte Stonelowe transferred B to C. A — 1 B — 2 Unit Wastage 5 C — 2 Surplus 2 Transport (H) +2 Sick = nil. F.A. = 2	SB
LOUVENCOURT 6-8-15	Two Riding Horses taken on strength. HD = 34 R = 15 Mules 6 Shortage HD = 2. R = 2 Unit Sick = nil F.A. = 2 Wastage 5 Surplus = 2.	SB
LOUVENCOURT 7.8.15	Sick nil F.A. 2 Wastage 3 Sent for Chefferns lig. Surplus 2. to AMIENS.	SB

Date Place	Summary of Events	Remarks & references
LOUVENCOURT 8/8/15	Sick 3 Wastage 3 Hosp. 2 Church Parade noon. Pte Davis W. 165 F.P. No I Pte Davis J. 10 days F.P. No I Pte Welsh A. for Court Martial.	SB
LOUVENCOURT 9.8.15	Sick 1 Wastage 3 Hospl. 4 Chaplain Burrows to 20 Cas Clearing Stn at 5th Gmer. Pte Harper Returned. L/C Hughes returned from leave. Cpl Broderick " " " Cpl Sheridan + servant to 1/4" Glos.	SB
LOUVENCOURT 10.8.15	Sick 1 Hosp 3 Wastage 3	SB
LOUVENCOURT 11.8.15	Sick 1 Hosp 4 Wastage 3 Mr Morgan left for 5th met C.C. 8th. Mr Thomas Returned from leave. Two mules received for 1 HQ	SB

LOUVENCOURT 12/8/15	Unit Sick = 3	Hosp - 5	Wastage 3	
	1 Riding Hood cast to mobile Vet Sect.			SB
LOUVENCOURT 13/8/15	Unit Sick = 2	Hosp 7	Wastage - 3	
	Mr Fossling R.C. Chaplain arrived			SB
LOUVENCOURT 14/8/15	Unit Sick 4	Hosp 7	Wastage 3	
	Courtmartial Dr K Webb. 3 months I on P.D			SB
LOUVENCOURT 15/8/15	Unit Sick = 3	Hospital 7	Wastage 3	
	On leave to England Lt Col Bushing. Sgt Major Williams Lce Cpl Warburton Cpl Simpson A.S.C.			SB
LOUVENCOURT 16/8/15	Unit Sick = 1	Hospital 6	Wastage 3	SB
LOUVENCOURT 17/8/15	Unit Sick = 5	Hospital 6	Wastage 3	SB

LOUVENCOURT 18/8/15	Unit Sick = 4 Hospital = 5 Wastage = 3. Court Martial promulgated on Pte K Webb No 2147	Moir
LOUVENCOURT 19/8/15	Unit Sick = 2 Hospital = 2 Wastage = Nil Lt M. Connell proceeded to No 11 Field Ambulance Bertrancourt for temporary duty. 3 reinforcements arrived from Havre. Pt Ford, Pt Church, Pt Harrison J.	Moir
LOUVENCOURT 20/8/15	Unit Sick = 3 Hospital = 2 Wastage nil Rev Maude Roxby C.F. left for 3rd F Amb.	Moir
LOUVENCOURT 21st/8/15	Unit Sick = 4 Hospital = 2 Wastage nil Lt Murray & Servant (Pte Wilson) proceeded on detached duty to the 1/1st S.M.R.F Artillery.	Moir
LOUVENCOURT 22/8/15	Unit Sick = 1 Hospital = 2 Wastage nil Lt Trench ASC MT St Sergt Dancer LeCorp Hughes proceeded on leave to England.	Moir
LOUVENCOURT 23/8/15	Unit Sick = 9 Hospital = 2 Wastage nil Dr Newell AE detached as Lt McCarnett's batman in place of Pt Cartwright R returned. Sgt Major Williams & Pte Warburton returned from leave	Moir

Date & Place	Summary of Events	Remarks & Appendices
LOUVENCOURT 24/8/15	Unit Sick, Hosp = 0 Wastage = nil. Capt. McConnell and batman Returned to F.A. Horses 2 R short, 1 HD short I returned from leave. C/pl Simpson returned from leave.	SB
LOUVENCOURT 25/8/15	Unit sick = 2. Hosp = 1 Wastage nil Respirators inspected & cleaned. Horses (re cleanliness) HD 30 L.D. 4 Mules 8 Riding 14 Shortage H-D = 1 (one of these for chaplain) R = 3 not adjusted for before	SB
LOUVENCOURT 26/8/15	Unit sick 3 Hosp } nil. Wastage }	SB

Date & Place	Summary of Events	Remarks & references
LOUVENCOURT 27/8/15	Unit. Sick = 3 Hosp. 4 Wastage nil.	SB
LOUVENCOURT 28/8/15	Unit sick = 3 Hosp 6 Wastage nil	SB
LOUVENCOURT 29/8/15	Unit sick = 2 Hosp 5 Wastage (1) Pte Rainbow D.o.W. Church Parade 10 AM	SB
LOUVENCOURT 30/8/15	Unit sick = 2 Hosp = 6 Wastage 1. Horses. Chargers 6. L.D = 4 Riding 8. Mules = 8 H.D 30 Wastage R = 3 D = 1.	SB
LOUVENCOURT 31.8.15	Unit sick = 0 Hosp. 4 Wastage -1 Iron ration inspection.	SB Appendix 8

Appendix IX

Summary of Sick & Wounded treated by 2nd Fd. Amb. 48 Div. between 1-8-15 – 31-8-15

Seymour Barling
LIEUT. COL. R.A.M.C.T.
COMMANDING 2ND FD. AMB.
48 DIV.

DATE	ADMISSIONS				DISPOSAL						REMAINING	
	OFFICERS		O. RANKS.		DUTY.		DIV.REST.STN.		CAS.CLG.STN.			
	Sick	Wounded	Sick	Wounded	Officers	o.Ranks	Officers	o.Ranks	Officers	o.Ranks	Officers	o.Ranks
August 17	.	.	28	3	.	18	.	8	2	15	8	68
18	1	1	28	2	.	20	.	24	.	5	10	49
19	1	.	47	.	2	5	.	23	1	6	8	61
20	.	.	37	6	.	10	.	18	.	5	8	71
21	1	.	32	5	4	10	.	21	.	10	5	68
22	2	.	28	2	.	12	.	26	1	4	6	56
23	2	.	37	5	2	18	.	9	.	4	6	66
24	2	.	31	5	1	18	.	21	.	3	7	60
25	2	.	30	6	.	8	.	22	1	9	8	57
26	1	.	27	11	1	9	.	17	1	18	7	51
27	1	1	36	2	.	12	.	17	.	10	9	50
28	2	.	30	.	2	12	.	12	2	5	7	51
29	1	.	38	2	*	5	.	18	1	12	7	58
30	4	.	29	1	1	19	.	.	2	9	8	61
31	1	.	36	.	2	14	.	13	.	5	7	64
TOTALS.	50	3	1129	129	30	444	.	577	24	246	—	—
		53.	1258.									

DATE	ADMISSIONS				DISPOSAL						REMAINING	
1915	OFFICERS		O. RANKS.		DUTY.		DIV. REST. STN.		CAS. C.L.G. STN.			
	Sick	Wounded	Sick	Wounded	Officers	Ranks	Officers	Ranks	Officers	Ranks	Officers	Ranks
August 1	.	.	38	2	.	5	.	22	.	22		
2	2	.	38	3	2	14	.	7	1	4		
3	2	.	38	1	.	18	.	9	.	6		
4	.	.	41	.	.	18	.	18	.	12	7	102
5	.	.	41	6	1	18	.	19	.	10	6	102
6	1	.	45	4	.	23	.	29	.	1	7	98
7	1	.	30	.	.	13	.	24	.	1	8	91
8	3	.	41	4	1	17	.	.	1	2	9	117
9	6	1	44	10	3	11	.	30	5	11	8	120
10	4	.	55	3	4	19	.	40	1	10	9	107
11	2	.	49	30	.	8	.	43	1	16	10	91
12	1	.	35	2	.	13	.	7	.	3	11	110
13	-	.	31	2	.	20	.	16	1	6	10	101
14	1	.	58	4	1	22	.	38	.	11	10	93
15	2	.	34	4	2	14	.	8	2	8	8	101
16	4	.	17	4	1	21	.	18	1	3	10	79

121/6930

48th Highlanders

2nd S.M. Field Ambulance
Vol VII
Sept 15

Sept '15

CONFIDENTIAL.

War Diary of 2nd Fd. Amb.
48 Div
from 1-9-15 to 30-9-15

Vol I
Appendix 10

Pages. 7
Appendix 10

Seymour Barling
Lt. Col. RAMC T.
O.C. 2/S Fd. Amb.
48 Div.

Date & Place	Summary of Events	Remarks Appendices
LOUVENCOURT 1 Sept 1915	Unit Sick 4 / In FA 5 / Wastage 1	SB
LOUVENCOURT 2 Sept 1915	Unit Sick 1 / In FA 6 / Wastage 3. Cpl Grimley to CCS (sick) Pte Goodyear to CCS (Pleurisy)	SB
LOUVENCOURT 3/9/15	Unit Sick 2 / Hosp 4 / Wastage 3.	SB
LOUVENCOURT 4/9/15	Unit Sick = 4 / Hosp = 8 / Wastage = 6. Sgt Jones, Pte Hepburn, Pte Winter } to CCS.	SB
LOUVENCOURT 5/9/15	Unit Sick 3 / Hosp 10 / Wastage 3. Pte Winter at CCS & rejoined. Pte Grimley, Sgt Jones } rejoined from CCS. 10 Church Parade. Capt Sheridan & servant returned, Lt Broderick & servant to H/y at wick.	

Date & Place	Summary of Events	Remarks appendices
LOUVENCOURT 6/9/15	Sick 4 Hospital 10 Wastage 3 Capt Sheridan + Servant to 1/6 Warwicks Lt Pitt, St Sergt Ingham, D/O Stevenson from leave	SB
LOUVENCOURT 7.9.15	Sick 2 ~~Returned to Unit~~ D. Upton Hosp 6 Lt French + FAWV Wastage 1 taken on strength of 1/3 SMFA Pte Walford taken on strength	SB
LOUVENCOURT 8/9/15	Sick = 2 Hosp = 5 Pte Valentine to Wastage = 2 C.C.S. sick. Capt Sheridan gazetted to 2/7 Worcesters	SB
LOUVENCOURT 9/9/15	Sick = 2 Hosp = 1 H. 3 men Wastage = 2	SB

Date/Place	Summary of Events	Appendices/Remarks
LOUVENCOURT 10/9/15	Unit sick = 3 Wastage = 2 Hosp = 3	SB
LOUVENCOURT 11/9/15	Unit sick = 3 Wastage = 3 D. Brown to CCS Hosp = 1 off, 2 men Rheumatism P^{te} Bodman Returned to Unit Sergt Cross + P^{te} Goubl MT ASC on leave.	SB
LOUVENCOURT 12/9/15	Unit sick = 0 Wastage 3 Hosp 1 off, 1 men 10 AM Church Parade.	
LOUVENCOURT 13/9/15	Unit sick 3 Wastage 2 Hosp 1 off, 1 men P^{te} Valentine returned from CCS on 11/9/15.	

DATE & PLACE	Summary of Events	Remarks & Initials
LOUVENCOURT 14-9-15	Unit Hosp = 1 Off 2 men. Sick = 8 Wastge = 2. L. Broderick & Stewart returned to Unit	SB
LOUVENCOURT 15/9/15	Unit = 5 Hosp = 2 men, 1 officer. L. Allison-Jones unit. Wastge = 2 Pte Pooney Comfort to 1/7 RGA with one stretcher.	SB
LOUVENCOURT 16/9/15	Unit - sick 1 Hosp = off 1, men 0 Wastge = 2	SB
LOUVENCOURT 17/9/15	Unit sick = 7 Hosp = 1 off Wastge = 2.	SB

Place Date	Summary of Events	Remarks Appendices
LOUVENCOURT 18/9/15	Unit Hosp 2 1 off Sick 1 Wastage 2	SB
LOUVENCOURT 19/9/15	Unit Hosp 1 off, 1 OR Sick 2 Wastage 3. Cpl. Tundy to U.S Pte Stude Pte Jenkins — reinforcements Cpl Pemberton Pte Grubb ... from line	SB
LOUVENCOURT 20/9/15	Unit Hosp. 1 off 2 men Sick 3 Wastage 0 surplus ibid Cpl Wilkinson returned from leave Lt Mundy Cdt attached to unit Transport inspection.	SB
LOUVENCOURT 21/9/15	Unit Hosp 1 off 3 men Sick 3 Wastage - nil. L. Cpl + Pte Skell gone to Le Havre Henry Pte Bodum to HQ	SB

Date & Hour	Summary of Events	Remarks & initials
LOUVENCOURT 22/9/15	Unit sick 1 2 mules arrived Hosp. 4 Lt Murray discharged Hosp W.astge nil Lt Cox + 3 OR. returned from being detached	PB
LOUVENCOURT 23/9/15	Unit sick 5 Hosp 3 W.astge = nil.	PB
LOUVENCOURT 24/9/15	Unit sick 4 Hosp 3 W.astge nil	PB
LOUVENCOURT 25/9/15	Unit sick 4 Hosp 3 W.astge Nil	PB
LOUVENCOURT 26/9/15	Unit Hosp 1 off 8 OR sick 2 OR Pte Lyndon to W.astge 1/4 Ot Bucks L.I.	PB

Date & Place	Summary of Events	Remarks & Appendices
LOUVENCOURT 27/9/15	Sick 4 Hosp. Off. OR 4 Wastage 1 1 Riding Horse Cast.	SB
LOUVENCOURT 28/9/15	Sick 1 Hosp. Off. OR 4 Wastage 1 7 Men detatched temp to ASC MT 3 Riding Horses Received	SB
LOUVENCOURT 29/9/15	Sick 6 Hosp. Off. OR 3. Wastage = 1	SB
LOUVENCOURT 30/9/15	Sick 2 Hosp. Off. OR 2 Wastage = 2 Cpl. Perry to CCS	SB

Appendix X.

Summary of Sick & Wounded treated by 2nd Field Amb 48 Div between 1-9-15 and 30-9-15

Seymour Barling
LIEUT. COL. R.A.M.C.T.
COMMANDING 2ND FD. AMB.
48 DIV

1.X.15

	ADMISSIONS				DISPOSALS								REMAINING	
	OFFICERS		O.RANKS		DUTY		DIV.REST.STN		CAS.CLG.STN		DIED			
	S	W	S	W	Offrs.	O.R.	Offrs.	O.R.	Offrs.	O.R.	Offrs.	O.R.	Offrs.	O.Ranks
Sept. 1	.	.	27	3	1	10	.	18	2	12	.	.	4	54
2	1	.	40	1	1	6	.	11	.	8	.	.	4	70
3	3	.	34	9	.	5	.	21	2	10	.	.	5	77
4	1	.	26	1	1	16	.	9	1	10	.	.	4	69
5	.	.	54	4	1	10	.	17	.	12	.	.	3	90
6	.	.	20	.	.	11	.	8	.	11	.	.	3	80
7	2	.	44	1	.	17	.	13	2	22	.	.	3	73
8	.	.	30	.	1	11	.	12	.	11	.	.	2	69
9	4	.	39	4	.	9	.	7	.	17	.	1	6	80
10	1	.	45	2	.	9	.	21	1	15	.	.	6	82
11	4	.	25	6	.	13	.	14	2	10	.	.	8	76
12	1	.	52	2	.	21	.	10	.	8	.	.	9	91
13	1	.	34	1	1	11	.	14	1	9	.	.	8	92
14	.	.	35	5	1	18	.	25	.	19	.	.	7	70
15	3	.	25	7	.	24	.	2	1	7	.	.	9	49
16	1	.	25	8	.	2	.	10	1	14	.	.	9	56
17	2	.	66	3	1	9	.	35	4	11	.	.	6	70
	24	NIL	621	63	8	202	NIL	347	17	206	.	1	—	—

	ADMISSIONS				DISPOSALS								REMAINING	
	OFFICERS		O.RANKS		DUTY		DIV. REST STN		CAS.CLG.STN		DIED			
	S	W	S	W	Offrs	OR	Offrs	OR	Offrs	OR	Offrs	OR	Offrs.	oRanks
Forward	24	–	621	63	8	202	–	347	17	206	–	1	–	–
Sept. 18	1	.	40	4	1	7	.	18	1	18	.	.	5	71
19	2	1	38	3	.	10	.	16	1	25	.	.	7	61
20	1	.	37	4	1	18	.	16	.	13	.	.	7	55
21	2	.	37	1	1	9	.	22	1	11	.	1	7	50
22	2	1	29	7	1	30	.	18	.	12	.	.	9	26
23	.	1	27	3	4	15	.	.	1	17	.	.	4	24
24	.	.	17	2	.	9	.	.	.	11	.	.	4	23
25	2	2	22	7	.	6	.	.	.	5	.	1	8	40
26	2	.	2	1	2	12	.	.	2	3	.	.	6	27
27	2	.	1	1	1	2	.	.	2	4	.	.	5	24
28	.	.	.	3	.	.	.	.	2	3	.	1	3	23
29	.	.	.	.	.	3	.	.	.	1	.	.	3	20
30	2	.	3	.	.	.	.	.	.	2	.	.	4	21
	40	5	874	99	19	323	.	437	28	330	.	4	–	–

121/7429

1st Division

2nd J.M. Field Ambulance

Oct VIII

Oct 15

Oct-15

CONFIDENTIAL

War Diary of 2nd Fd Amb
48 Div.   B.E.F.
From 1.X.15 — 31.X.15
Vol. II
Appendix 1

Pages 9
Appendix 1

2nd SOUTH MIDLAND FIELD AMBULANCE
No ....
2 NOV 1915

Seymour Barling
LIEUT. COL. R.A.M.C.,
COMMANDING 2ND FD. AMB.
48 DIV.

Place Date	Summary of Events	Remarks appendices
LOUVENCOURT 1.x.15	Unit Sick = 3 Hosp. 1 off 2 OR Wastage 2 Capt Buckman attached. Horses HD 30 Riding 17 LD 4 Mules 10 A sect 2 men sick B sect 1 Transport one sick	SB
LOUVENCOURT 2.x.15	Unit Sick = 2 Hosp. 1 off 2 OR Wastage = 2	SB
LOUVENCOURT 3.x.15	Unit Sick = 4 Hosp. off - 1 OR = 2 Wastage = 2	SB
LOUVENCOURT 4/x/15	Unit Sick = 2 Hosp. OR 3 off 1 Wastage = 2 Pte Price R.B.S. returned from detached duty.	SB

Date & Place	Summary of Events	Remarks & references

LOUVENCOURT 5/7/15	Sick - 1
	Hosp - 4
	1 Dot. gr - 2
	
	Major Hobby Capt Dickson
	Capt Pitt Capt Gosling } to
	    4 or OR B sect
	    1 " OR C sect } Sailly
	    1 Motor Cyclist
	    2 Motor Ambulances & Drivers
	
	Capt Mummery 13 OR to Hebuterne
	    1 Motor Cyclist attached from 3rd F.A.
		R.B.

LOUVENCOURT 6/7/15	Sick 1
	Hospital 4 Pte. J. Mackay returned.
	1 Dot. gr. 2
	2 NCO's + 4 men to Hebuterne
	    2 men Sailly to Hebuterne.
	Sailly 4 Officers 54 men } includes
	Hebuterne 1 " 24 men } 5 Sailly cyclist
	Major Hobby admitted Hosp. } & 1 motor attached
	    1 Riding horse shot.	

Place & Date	Summary of Events	Remarks & appendices
LOUVENCOURT 7.x.15	Sick 2 Hosp. Off 1 OR 3 Wastage 2 Pte Phillips on leave. Sergt Henning returns from Sailly.	SB
LOUVENCOURT 8/x/15	Sick = 0 Hosp. = Off. 1 OR = 0 Wastage = 2	SB
LOUVENCOURT 9.x.15	Sick = 1 Hosp = 1 Off OR 3 Wastage = 2 Visited Helestone & Sailly one man returned from Sailly Pte Newman (Eyes)	SB
LOUVENCOURT 10/x/15	Sick = 1 Hosp = 1 Off 3 OR Sergt Saunders Wastage = 2. Pte Philpott on leave	SB

Date & Place	Summary of Events	Remarks & Appendices
LOUVENCOURT 11-X-15	Sick 1 Hosp. 1 off 3 OR. 11 on stge 2 Six privates returned from test for ASC MT 3 privates went to Pte Newman AE to SM OC 8th (Eyes)	SB
LOUVENCOURT 12-X-15	Sick 1 Hosp 1 off 3 OR. 11 on stge 2. Cpl Bee returned from Doullens	SB
LOUVENCOURT 13-X-15	Sick 2. Hosp. 1 off. 3. OR. 11 on stge 2. Pte Terry to CCS (Dental) Pte Griffin ex 1st F.A. arrived as reinforcement	SB
LOUVENCOURT 14-X-15	Sick: nil Hosp 1 off Hosp 3 Pte Rowe to CCS as wastage 11 on stge 2	SB

DATE & PLACE	Summary of Events	Remarks & References
15-10-15 LOUVENCOURT	Sick 1 Hosp OR 4. Wastage = 2 Major Hobbs to C.C.S.	SB
16-10-15 LOUVENCOURT	Sick nil Hosp OR 4 Wastage 2 Pte Phillips returned from leave.	SB
17.X.15 LOUVENCOURT	Sick nil Hosp OR 3 Wastage 2 Sgt Alloft, L/C Allen, Pte Hore, Pte Worrell FB on leave	SB
LOUVENCOURT 18/X/15	Sick nil Hosp = 4 Wastage = 1 Pte Jerry Returned from C.C.S.	SB

Date & Place	Summary of Events	Remarks & Attendances
Louvencourt 19.x.15	Sick = Nil Hosp. = 3 Pte Bacon discharged Hosp. 1 Wastage = 2 Sgt. Saunders Pte Philpott returned to duty	SB
Louvencourt 20/x/15	Sick Nil. Hosp. = 3 1 Wastage = 3 Pte Newman to Base (Eyes)	SB
Louvencourt 21.x.15	Sick = 3. Hosp = 3 Wastage 2. Pte Hanley 1st FA as Reinforcement.	SB
Louvencourt 22.x.15.	Sick = Nil Hosp = 2 1 Wastage = 3 Cpl. Langford ASC to CCS	SB

Place & Date	Summary of Events	Remarks & Initials
23/x/15 Louvencourt	Sick = 0 Hosp = 1 Wastage 3. 1 H.D. off strength Major Hobling to England 15/x/15 1 Officer 3 men on leave	SB
24/x/15 Louvencourt	Sick = 2 Hosp = 1 Wastage = 3. Cpl. Cole to England on leave	SB

29/x/15 Louvencourt	Sick = 2
	Hosp = 8
	Wastage = 10
	Sergt Jones
	Cpl Jones
	Pte Price
	Pte Lloyd } to Base
	Pte Symonds MT ASC
	  " Foster
	  " Butler
	Pte Pedley to Test at Supply Coy
		SB

Date Place	Summary of Events	Remarks appendices
26.x.15 Louvencourt	Sick = 2 Hosp = 1 1 Chaplain C.of.E Wastage 10. horse received	FB
Louvencourt 27.x.15	Sick nil Hosp = 0 Wastage 11 Sergt Saunders to Enlbt. 1 R Horse to D.A.D.R IV Army	FB
Louvencourt 28/x/15	Sick = nil Hosp = 2. Wastage = 12 Pte Pritchet to C.C.S. teeth.	FB
Louvencourt 29/x/15	Sick 1 Hosp 2 Wastage 12	FB

Louvencourt 30/x/15	Sick. — Hosp 2 Wastage 11	p⁰ Pritchett returned. Sergt McKinnon ⎫ p/c Hitchcock ⎬ leave to S/c Rowe ⎭ England Lt Whittaker	SB
	Posted sick — Helmhurst		
Louvencourt 31/x/15	Sick = 2 Hosp = 1 Wastage 11	p/c Chambers to hosp. Sergt Henning ⎫ p/c Brown NW ⎬ attached S/c Thornton ⎭ from Div.	SB

2nd 5th Midl Fd Amb.
48 Div

Appendix No 1. to war diary for the month of October 1915 showing admissions and discharges of cases treated in the Ambulance.

Raymond Barling

LIEUT. COL. R.A.M.C.T.
COMMANDING 2ND FD. AMB.
48 DIV.

Date	ADMISSIONS				DISPOSALS								REMAINING	
	OFFICERS		O.RANKS		Cas.Clg.Stn		Div. Rest Stn		Duty		Died		OFFICER	O.RANKS
	S	W	S	W	Offrs	O.R.	Offrs	O.R.	Offrs	O.R.	Offrs	O.R.		
Oct 16	–	–	25	4	–	7	–	12	–	12	–	–	1	79
17	3	–	39	3	3	10	–	11	–	9	–	–	1	79
18	–	1	5	18	–	29	–	8	–	7	–	1	2	70
19	3	–	2	7	–	7	–	10	–	19	–	1	5	48
20	2	–	27	5	–	11	–	10	–	17	–	1	7	41
21	1	–	29	3	2	4	–	5	1	12	–	–	5	52
22	4	–	46	5	2	14	–	10	1	9	–	–	6	70
23	–	–	40	3	1	19	–	10	–	6	–	–	5	78
24	1	–	42	1	1	14	–	12	–	5	–	–	5	90
25	–	–	21	–	–	15	–	5	1	11	–	–	4	80
26	1	–	30	2	–	10	–	13	1	9	–	–	4	80
27	–	–	32	1	–	10	–	12	1	11	–	–	3	80
28	1	–	20	3	1	11	–	15	–	21	–	–	3	56
29	2	–	30	–	–	5	–	11	–	14	–	–	5	56
30	1	–	57	4	–	15	–	14	1	6	–	–	5	82
31	2	1 acc.	21	3	4	12	–	9	1	12	–	–	3	73
Forward	15	1	400	56	9	173	–	142	10	81	–	–	67	607
	36	3	866	118	23	360	–	309	17	261	–	3	131	1,733

	ADMISSIONS				DISPOSALS								REMAINING	
	OFFICERS		O.RANKS		Cas.Clg.Stn.		Div.Rest Stn.		Duty		Died		OFFICERS	O.RANKS
	S	W	S	W	Offrs	O.R.	Offrs	O.R.	Offrs	O.R.	Offrs	O.R.		
Oct 1	-	-	3	3	1	3	-	-	-	3	-	-	3	21
2	1	-	-	-	1	-	-	-	-	5	-	-	3	16
3	1	-	-	-	-	-	-	-	2	3	-	-	2	13
4	1	-	1	1	-	2	-	-	1	3	-	-	2	10
5	4	-	3	1	-	5	-	-	-	1	-	-	6	8
6	1	-	34	4	-	15	-	8	1	4	-	-	6	19
7	2	1	40	18	2	24	-	13	-	5	-	-	7	35
8	-	-	37	5	-	14	-	7	1	5	-	-	6	51
9	-	-	41	6	-	19	-	16	-	2	-	-	6	61
10	3	-	35	3	2	16	-	14	-	14	-	-	7	55
11	-	-	40	1	-	23	-	22	2	10	-	-	5	41
12	-	-	35	3	-	4	-	13	1	6	-	-	4	56
13	1	-	47	9	-	16	-	19	1	4	-	-	4	73
14	1	-	34	2	-	14	-	21	-	7	-	-	5	67
15	-	-	50	-	3	18	-	9	1	9	-	-	1	81
	15	1	400	56	9	173	-	142	10	81	-	-	67	607

Nov 1915

13/11/31

[St. 2 Ame. 40 à 54]

Nov 1915

Vol IX

CONFIDENTIAL

War diary of 1/2nd 5th Mid
7th Amb 48 Div B.E.F
from 1·11·15 to 30·11·15
Vol II
Appendix 2

Pages.
Appendix 1

1 DEC 1915

Raymond Barling
LIEUT. COL. R.A.M.C.T.
COMMANDING 2ND FD. AMB.
48 DIV.

Date & Place	Summary of Events		Remarks & appendices
LOUVENCOURT Nov 1st 1915	Sick = 2 Hosp = 1 Wastge = 11		SB
LOUVENCOURT Nov 2 1915	Sick — Hosp one Wastge 12	Pte Brown to base on completion of service.	SB
LOUVENCOURT Nov 3.1915	Sick 5 Hosp 5 Wastge 12	(scabies) Dr. Glendon O.V. as reinforcement	SB
Louvencourt Nov 4.1915	Sick = nil Hosp = 5 Wastge = 11		SB
Louvencourt Nov 5th 1915	Sick 3 Hosp 4 Wastge = 11		SB

Place & Date	Summary of Events		Remarks & appendices
Louvencourt 6/xi/15	Sick = nil Hosp = 2 Duty = 11	Capt McConnell + 19 men to Halowtwe - Capt Murray + 19 men returned from H	SB
Louvencourt 7.xi.15	Sick 2 Hosp 1 Duty 11	Cpl. Twitchett to Water Duty 1/5 Glos. L/Cpl Martin returned to unit to revert to rank. 2 men returned from leave	SB
Louvencourt 8/xi/15	Sick 1 Hosp 3 Duty 11	2 men returned leave. 2 HD to Mobile Vet Sect	SB
Louvencourt 9/xi/15	Sick = nil Hosp = 2 Duty = 11		SB

Date/Place	Summary of Events	Remarks & appendices
Louvencourt 10/xi/15	Sick = 2 Wastage = 12. Hosp. 2 — Sergt Major Williams to C.C.S. chronic Rheumatism	8B
Louvencourt 11.xi.15	Sick = 1 Wastage = 12 Hosp. = 3 — 2 Riding Horses received.	8B
Louvencourt 12.xi.15	Sick = 2 Wastage = 12 Hosp = 3	8B
Louvencourt 13.xi.15	Sick 4 Hosp. 2 Wastage 13 — Br. Hygoons to C.C. 8th 1 officer 6 men on leave	8B

Date & Place	Summary of events	Remarks Authenticators
Louvencourt 14/xi/15	Hospital = 2 Sick = 2 1 HD recovered D-tye = 13 5 sick NCO + men 2 HD from mobile Vet. Section to Base, from leave	SB
Louvencourt 15/xi/15	Hosp = 2 Sick = 1 S/C Bennett D-tye. 13 returned from leave	SB
Louvencourt 16/xi/15	Hosp = 3 Sick = 2 Pte Lemon from D-tye = 13 leave	SB
Louvencourt 17.xi.15	Hosp. 3 Sick. 2 D-tye. 13	SB
Louvencourt 18.xi.15	Hosp nil Sick nil D-tye. 13	SB

Date Place	Summary of Events	Remarks appendices
Louvencourt 19.XI.15	Hosp. = 0 Sick = 5 Dutys = 13.	8B
Louvencourt 20/XI/15	Hosp = 0 Sick = 0 Dutys = 14	L/c. Stevenson to England.	8B
Louvencourt 21.XI.15	Hosp = 0 Sick = 0 Dutys 14	1 ok on leave.	8B
Louvencourt 22.XI.15	Hosp = 0 Sick = 0 Dutys = 14	Lt. Harrison returned from 28 days leave.	8B
Louvencourt 23/XI/15	Hosp = 0 Sick = 1 Dutys = 14.		8B

Date & Place	Summary of Events		Remarks & references
Louvencourt 24.11.15	Sick = 3 Hosp = 0 W. tge = 14	Capt Buchan & 2 OR to Sailly. Pte Slade, months leave	SB
Louvencourt 25/xi/15	Sick = 3 Hosp = 0 10n tge = 4	Capt Murray & Servant to Hebuterne	SB
Louvencourt 26/xi/15	sick = 0 Hosp = 1 10 - tge = 14	14 O.R to SAILLY 3 OR to HEBUTERNE	SB
Louvencourt 27/xi/15	Sick 2 Hosp = 2 10 n tge = 14	B sect to Ham C sect to SAILLY	SB
Louvencourt 28/xi/15	Sick 1 Hosp 3 10 n tge 14	8 men on leave	SB

2nd 5th Mid Fd Amb.
48 Div

Appendix to 2 to war diary for the month of November 1915 showing admissions and disposals of cases treated in the Ambulance

Raymond Bering
LIEUT. COL. R.A.M.C.T.
COMMANDING 2ND FD. AMB.
48 DIV.

Date & Place	Summary of Events	Remarks Attendances
Lunencourt 29.xi.15	Sick = 2. Hosp = 8 W.stge = 14	1 HD of strength
Lunencourt 30/xi/15	Sick = 2 Hosp 3 W.stge 14	7 OR returned from leave

November 1915	Admissions				Disposals								Remaining	
	Officers		O. Ranks		Cas. Clg. Stn.		Div. Rest Stn		Duty		Died		Officers	O. Ranks
	S	W	S	W	Offrs	O.R.	Offrs	O.R.	Offrs	O.R.	Offrs	O.R.		
Nov 1	–	–	16	–	–	11	–	2	–	9	–	–	3	67
2	3	–	35	–	3	12	–	7	1	9	–	1	2	73
3	2	–	29	–	1	9	–	7	–	19	–	–	3	69
4	1	–	54	4	1	12	–	10	1	22	–	–	2	83
5	1	1	36	5	–	13	–	26	–	11	–	–	4	74
6	–	–	54	2	1	15	–	12	1	7	–	–	2	96
7	2	–	24	5	1	10	–	15	–	16	–	–	3	84
8	2	1	43	7	3	18	–	28	–	15	–	–	3	73
9	2	–	48	2	1	11	–	16	–	12	–	–	4	84
10	3	–	48	–	2	9	–	22	–	18	–	–	5	83
11	–	–	28	4	–	13	–	9	–	10	–	–	5	83
12	–	–	36	3	2	11	–	25	–	15	–	–	3	71
13	–	–	52	1	–	5	–	14	–	13	–	–	3	92
14	–	–	37	2	–	8	–	24	–	16	–	–	3	83
15	1	–	25	2	1	23	–	14	1	15	–	–	2	58
Forward	17	2	565	37	16	180	–	231	4	207	–	1		

NOVEMBER 1915.	ADMISSIONS				DISPOSALS								REMAINING	
	OFFICERS		O.RANKS.		CAS.CLG.STN.		DIV. REST STN		DUTY		DIED		OFFICERS	O.RANKS
	S.	W.	S.	W.	Offrs	O.R.	Offrs	OR	Offrs	O.R.	Offrs	OR		
Nov. 16	1	–	46	–	–	9	–	12	1	7	–	–	2	76
17	2	–	49	2	2	13	–	10	–	10	–	–	2	94
18	–	–	48	2	–	20	–	23	–	11	–	–	2	90
19	1	–	37	2	1	12	–	21	–	18	–	–	2	78
20	–	–	47	–	–	11	–	7	1	14	–	–	1	93
21	–	–	46	–	–	12	–	19	–	12	–	–	1	96
22	2	–	35	1	1	19	–	15	–	22	–	–	2	76
23	–	–	43	2	–	11	–	15	–	23	–	1	2	71
24	1	–	30	9	1	20	–	10	–	7	–	–	2	73
25	3	–	37	2	2	14	–	12	–	9	–	–	3	77
26	1	3	36	15	2	18	–	8	1	10	1	–	3	92
27	1	–	53	9	–	23	–	16	–	11	–	1	4	91
28	2	–	40	1	1	16	–	29	1	12	–	–	4	85
29	–	–	35	2	–	23	–	25	–	21	–	–	4	53
30	2	–	40	4	–	9	–	21	–	16	–	–	6	51
Forward	16	3	622	51	10	230	–	243	4	203	1	2		
	17	2	565	37	16	180	–	231	4	207	–	1		
TOTAL	33	5	1,187	88	26	410	–	474	8	410	1	3		

1/2nd S. Mid
of Anne (48th Sr.)

Dee
Vol X.

121/7930

Dec 1915

CONFIDENTIAL

War diary of 1/2nd S.M. Fd Amb
from 7 Dec 1915 - 31 Dec 1915
Vol. 3
Appendix 1

Pages 7
Appendix 1

-1 JAN 1916

Seymour Barling
LIEUT. COL. R.A.M.C.T.
COMMANDING 1/2ND FD. AMB.
48 DIV.

Date & Place		Summary of Events		Remarks attendances
Louvencourt Dec. 1		Sick = 0 Hosp = 3 Wastge = 14		SB
Louvencourt Dec. 2		Sick = 2 Hosp = 2 Wastge = 14		SB
Louvencourt Dec. 3		Sick = 2 Hosp. 3 Wastge - 14	Two O.R. on leave to England	SB
Louvencourt Dec. 4		Sick 3. Hosp 5. Wastge 14	~~Officers~~ 1 H.D. struck off	SB
Louvencourt Dec. 5.		Sick = 1 Hosp = 4 Wastge = 14	1 Officer 6 OR on leave 2 H.D. received	SB

Date & Place	Summary of Events	Remarks & references to appendices
Louvencourt 6. Dec 15.	Sick = 1 Hosp. = 4 Wastage = 14	SB
Louvencourt 7. Dec.	Sick 3. Hosp = 3. Wastage = 14	P.d. sent to C.C.S. with 3/12/15 SB
Louvencourt 8/x/15	Sick 1 Hosp = 3. Wastage = 14	SB
Louvencourt 9.x11.15	Sick = 2 Hosp = 2 Wastage 14	2 OR returned 1 months leave 1 OR from C.C.S. SB
Louvencourt 10.x11.15	Sick = 2 Hosp = 3. Wastage 14	Lt. Col. Thomas Betoun Gig + 2 horses to 48 Div H.Q.	SB

Date & Place	Summary of Events			Remarks & Appendices
Louvencourt 11.12.15	Sick = 1 Hosp = 2. Wastage = 14	1 admitted to Hosp 2 released of Hosp		SB
Louvencourt 12-12-15	Sick — Hosp. 2 Wastage 14			SB
Louvencourt 13.12.15	Sick 4 Hosp. 1 Wastage 14	1 Officer 4 O.R. Leave.		SB
Louvencourt 14.12.15	Sick = 3. Hosp = 1 Wastage = 14	2 NCO returned from Leave. 5 O.R. from leave. Capt. Cox from detached duty		SB
Louvencourt 15/12/15	Sick = 3. Hosp = 1. Wastage = 14	Capt. McConnell from leave.		SB

Louvencourt 16. XII. 15	Sick - 2 Hosp - 1 (Pte Brothy) Officer 1 Wastge - 14.		SB
Louvencourt 17. XII. 15	Sick 3. Hosp 1 1 Officer Wastge 14 1 HD to mobile Vet Sect.		SB
LOUVENCOURT 18 XII.15	Sick - 2 Hosp 1 1 Officer discharged Wastge 14. Cpl Pitt attached Regt		SB
Louvencourt 19. XII.15	Sick 3 Hosp = 2 one officer discharged Wastge = 14 Pte Butler to SHD OCS 2 HD Received		SB
Louvencourt 20/XII/15	Sick 1 Hosp = 2 Wastge 14		SB

Date & Place	Summary of Events	Remarks & appendices
Louvencourt 21.12.15	Sick 1. Hosp 2 & 1 Officer Capt McConnell Wastge 14. 1 H.D. to hostile b.c. sick	SB
Louvencourt 22.12.15	Sick = 0 Hosp = 2 ; Officer, OR. Wastge = 14.	SB
Louvencourt 23.12.15	Sick 2. Hosp = 2 Wastge = 14	SB
Louvencourt 24.12.15	Sick = 3. Hosp = 1 OR , 1 Off. Wastge = 14	SB
Louvencourt 25.XII.15	Sick = 0. Hosp = 1 OR , 1 Off. Wastge = 15 Pte Davis W to Hosp (CCS) Sergt. _____ rejoined deftn SB	SB

Date & Place	Summary of Events		Appending Remarks
Lavencourt 26-12-15	Sick 2 Hosp. off. OR. 1 O. otys = 14		SB
Lavencourt 27-12-15	Sick = 4 Hosp = 2 1 O. otys = 14 Major Hoyston 6 OR on leave	Cpl McConnell to unit Pte Bouche admitted 2 H/D to Base from mobile Vet Sect	SB
Lavencourt 28.12.15	Sick 4 Hosp 2 1 O. otys 14.	Cpl Pitt to Sully, Cpl Buckner to Tydworth Pte Cornforth returned from 19 Skvry battery Mallein test on 87 Horses	SB
Lavencourt 29.12.15	Sick 6 Hosp = 4 1 O. otys 14	Dte Chilton } admitted Dte Webb } hosp.	SB

Date & Place	Summary of Events	Remarks & Initials
Louvencourt 30/XII/15	Sick = 2 Hospl = 4 Wastage = 14	SB
Louvencourt 31/XII/15	Sick = 5 Hospl = 4 Wastage = 14 Dvr Webb A.X. discharged " Hepburn Admitted Capt. Broderick & servant tempy det^d to 1st S.M. Bde. R.F.A.	SB

Seymour Bely
LIEUT. COL. R.A.M.C.T.
COMMANDING 2ND FD. AMB.
48 DIV.

2nd SOUTH MIDLAND FIELD AMBULANCE — 1 JAN 1916

1/2 S.M. Ft Ambulance
48 Div.

Appendix 1 to Vol 3 of
War Diary for Month
of December 1915 shewing
admissions and disposals
of Cases treated in
Ambulance

Seymour Barling
LIEUT. COL. R.A.M.C.T.
COMMANDING 2ND FD. AMB.
48 DIV.

Dec 1915	ADMISSIONS				DISPOSALS								REMAINING	
	OFFICERS		O. RANKS		Cas Clg Stn		Div. Rest Stn.		Duty		Died		Offrs	O. Ranks
	S.	W	S.	W	Offrs	O.R.	Offrs	O.R.	Offrs	O.R.	Offr	O.R.		
Dec 1	1	-	38	1	1	17		6	1	5			5	62
2	-	-	44	4	2	9		27	3	6			-	64
3	2	-	37	-	-	19		14	-	5			2	63
4	2	-	43	-	-	17		15	-	4			4	70
5	3	-	45	3	1	13		22	-	8			6	75
6	2	-	60	2	1	18		21	1	8		1	6	89
7	2	-	60	3	1	10		42	-	11		1	7	88
8	-	-	27	2	1	7		40	-	17			6	53
9	1	2	48	12	2	30		12	1	14		1	6	56
10	1	-	35	4	-	6		18	-	7			7	64
11	-	-	49	-	-	15		19	1	7			6	72
12	1	-	33	4	-	12		26	2	10			5	60
13	3	-	39	3	4	16		20	-	9			4	57
14	3	-	27	2	-	11		20	1	10			6	45
15	1	1	32	-	2	7		16	1	7			5	47
16	1	-	20	3	-	5		13	1	9		1	5	42
	23	3	637	39	15	212	-	331	12	134		4		

Dec' 1915	ADMISSIONS				DISPOSALS								REMAINING	
	OFFICERS		O.RANKS		Cas Clg Stn		Av. Rest Stn		DUTY		DIED		Offr	O.Rank
	S	W	S	W	Offr	O.R.	Offr	O.R.	Offr	O.R.	Offr	O.R.		
Dec (fwd)	23	3	637	39	15	212	—	331	12	137	4			
" 17	4	—	39	3	3	16		11	1	3			5	54
18	2	—	26	—	1	11		8	1	11			5	50
19	2	—	28	5	2	15		25	1	3	[1]		4	39
20	—	—	27	3	—	16		14	1	4			3	35
21	1	—	23	2	—	12		13	—	4			4	31
22	1	—	30	1	—	15		7	2	3			3	37
23	2	1	22	4	1	13		13	+	6			5	31
24	—	—	21	5	—	11		10	1	7	[1]	[1]	3	28
25	1	—	23	1	1	6		25	—	4			3	17
26	—	—	23	14	—	11		—	—	1		[2]	3	38
27	2	—	67	5	1	16		19	1	5			3	70
28	2	—	31	2	1	10		32	—	14		[1]	4	46
29	—	—	37	—	—	8		22	1	1			3	52
30	1	—	45	4	1	19		30	—	3		[1]	3	48
31	—	—	34	2	—	16		26	—	3			3	39
	41	4	1,113	90	26	407	—	586	21	209	1	10		

48

2 Fd Amb - 46(SM)XI
Jan
Vol XI

2 S.M. FA (4th Division)

F/213/1

Jan 1916

CONFIDENTIAL

War Diary of 1/2nd 5th Mid
Fd Ambulance 48 Div B.E.F
From 1-1-16 to 31-1-16
Vol 4 appendix 1

Pages 8
appendix 1

Seymour Barling
LIEUT. COL. R.A.M.C.T.
COMMANDING 2ND FD. AMB.
48 DIV.

Date & Place	Summary of Events	Remarks/ Appointments
Louvencourt 1.1.16	Sick = 1 Hosp - 4 Pte Chowley admitted (sales) Pte Boucher discharged D-tye = 14.	SB
Louvencourt 2.1.16	Sick = 2. Hosp - 4 D-tye - 14.	SB
Louvencourt 3.1.16	Sick 3 C Sect Returned Hosp = 4 from Sailly D-tye - 14 Capt Cox to 1/8 Warwick Regt	SB
Louvencourt 4.1.16	Sick = 0 - Hosp = 3 - Pte Brophy returned D-tye = 14 Capt Broderick to No 30 CCS 6 OR on leave	SB
Louvencourt 5.1.16	Sick = 2 Hosp = 3. 1 HD Charlie D-tye = 14 V/C Sect. 2 OR on leave	SB

Date & Place	Summary of Events	Remarks Initials
Louvencourt 6.1.16	Sick = 0 Hosp = 5 Wastge = 14. Dr Webb } admitted Pte Whitworth } 1 Officer 6 OR from leave	SB
Louvencourt 7.1.16	Sick = 2 Hosp = 5 Wastge = 14 Rtd Hingley Leave to England	SB
Louvencourt 8.1.16	Sick = 1 Hosp = 5 Wastge = 14 Capt Buchner Returned from 14 days 1 NCO 6 OR detached to MC.	SB
Louvencourt 9.1.16.	Sick. Hosp. 7 Wastge 15 1 extr wastge to complete War Estab.	SB

Date & Place	Summary of Events		Remarks & signature
Lowercourt 10.1.16.	Sick 2 Hosp. 6 1 Dr tge 15	Dr. 1 Welsh discharged	SB
Lowercourt 11.1.16	Sick: 2 Hosp: 5 1 Dr tge: 15	Pte Chambers discharged 4 OR on leave	SB
Lowercourt 12/1/16	Sick: 3 Hosp: 0 1 Dr tge = 15	4 OR on leave.	SB
Lowercourt 13/1/16	Sick = 0 Hosp 4 1 Dr tge 15	Pte Whitework Pte Jellyman } ex Hosp Capt Cox Returned	SB
Lowercourt 14/1/16.	Sick = 6 Hosp = 3 1 Dr tge 16 1 HD to H.V.S.	D/b OR Returned leave D/b: Chicton ex. Hospl. (Sgt Alsop to Home work) Capt Pitt & devl t/s to Glos.	SB

Date & Place	Summary of Events		Remarks & references
15-1-16 Amiens	Sick 4 Hospt 3 Wastge 16	1 H.D. to base. 1 R.H. to N.A.S. Capt Buchan + servant to 3rd S.M. Bgde.	SB
Louvencourt 16.1.16	Sick 3 Hospt 4 Wastge 16	Pte Roberts } admitted Dr Jillyman D. Whittaker discharged Pte Squires O.O. joined.	SB
Louvencourt 17.1.16	Sick 2 Hospl. 5 Wastage 15	Pte Edmonds admitted Lt. Col. Garling Leave.	alft.
Louvencourt 18.1.16	Sick 7 Hospl. 5 Wastage 15	Pte Elliott W admitted " Gibson. T. discharged 4. o.Ranks leave. Capt Murray's servant returned	alft.

Louvencourt 19.1.16	Sick 9 Hospital 6 Wastage 15	Pte Gibson } admitted " Butler J. } Hospital " Edmonds discharged	aof1
Louvencourt 20.1.16	Sick 5 Hospital 7 Wastage 15	Pte Betts C.Q. to 1st Fld Amb. (Dental) 3 o.ranks returned from leave Capt Broderick + servant returned from No 30 C.C.S. No 1854 Pte Baswell F, joined	aof1
Louvencourt 21.1.16	Sick 3 Hospital 10 Wastage 15	Pte Beech LCpl Bodman } admitted Pte Foster } Hospital " Harrison J to 1/5 Glos. for Water duty. Four other ranks returned from leave.	aof1

Louvencourt 22.1.16	Sick 2 Hospl 11 Wastage 15	Pte Elliott discharged Hospl " Wood W.E admitted " " Brophy " " 2 HD Horses to Mobile Vet	adjt.
Louvencourt 23.1.16	Sick 1 Hospital 8 Wastage 16	Pte Betts } discharged " Rowlands } Hospl. " Buck " Rose P. to Base Time expired	adjt.
Louvencourt 24.1.16	Sick 5 Hospital 10 Wastage 18	Drs. Buck & Newell admitted. Ptes Cottrell & Allen to 144 Bde M.G. Section for Water Duty	adjt.
Louvencourt 25.1.16	Sick 3 Hospital 9 Wastage 18	Pte Hudson E. } To Base for " Hopkins A } Munsterus Test " Gibson " Stanford } discharged	

Louvencourt 26.1.16	Sick 4 Hosp 9 Wastage 18	6 o.Ranks on leave. Capt Buchanan + servant Capt Pitt + servt rett. returned. L.t Col. Borley returned leave	SB
Louvencourt 27.1-16	Sick 1 Hosp. 10 Wastage 18	14 Reinforcements arrived A sect 5 P.te Jephcott B " 4 returned from C " 4 duty in trenches Water Duty 4	SB

Louvencourt 28-1-16	Sick 2
	Hosp. 8
	Wastage 6
		P.te Stonehouse
		  " Evans 4 Water Duty
		                 1 Books R.
		          4 o.R. from leave
		Master Cook reported for duty.
			SB

Louvencourt 29.1.16	Sick — Hosp 8 Wastage 6		SB

Place & Date	Summary of Events		Remarks & Appendices
Louvencourt 30-1-16	Sick = 1 Hosp = 5 Wastage = 7 1 R.H. to M.V.S.	Pte Hellgarth to bed Capt Buchanan - sewe to /4 Oxe Bucks Pte Butler } dis'c Buffey } Hosp L/c Robinson	SB
Louvencourt 31-1-16	Sick = 2 Hosp = 5 Wastage = 7	Capt Murray - struck to /6 Glos. Capt McConnell struck to /4 Glos. Capt Gosling from leave.	SB

Seymour Barling
Lt Col

LIEUT. COL. R.A.M.C.T.
COMMANDING 2ND FD. AMB.
48 DIV.

[Stamp: 2nd SOUTH MIDLAND FIELD AMBULANCE, 31 JAN 1916]

1/2nd 5th Midland Fd Amb.
48 Div.

Appendix 1 to Vol IV 1 Wer Diary.

Shewing admissions & disposals
of cases coming to Field Ambulance
for month of January 1916

Seymour Barling
LIEUT. COL. F A.M.C.T.
COMMANDING 2ND FD. AMB.
48 DIV.

3 FEB 1916

Jan 1916	ADMISSIONS					DISPOSALS								REMAINING	
	OFFICERS		O RANKS		Cas Clg Stn		Div Rest Stn		Duty		Died			
	S	W	S	W	Offrs	O.R.	Offrs	O.R.	Offrs	O.R.	Offrs	O.R.	OFFRS	O RANKS
Jan 1	2	-	28	4	-	8	24	-	2				5	33
2	1	-	19	9	-	12	10	-	-			1	6	38
3	2	-	34	2	2	14	17	-	-				6	43
4	2	-	30	8	1	6	19	1	6				6	50
5	3	-	36	-	3	7	14	1	2				5	63
6	2	-	39	4	-	15	19	-	1				7	71
7	1	-	23	4	1	6	25	1	3				6	64
8	2	-	34	10	2	11	25	1	3				5	69
9	1	-	35	3	2	10	22	-	8				4	67
10	-	-	24	4	-	8	17	-	5				4	65
11	2	-	35	1	-	7	19	-	6				6	69
12	1	-	29	3	1	3	23	-	9				6	66
13	1	-	25	7	-	10	20	2	5				5	63
14	2	-	25	1	-	11	24	1	6				6	48
15	2	3	31	1	3	9	14	-	5				8	52
	24	3	447	61	15	137	292	7	61		-	1		

Jan 1916	ADMISSIONS				DISPOSALS								REMAINING	
	OFFICERS		O. RANKS		Cas. Cl. Stn		Div Rest Stn		DUTY		DIED		OFFRS	O. RANKS
	S	W	S	W	Offrs	O.R.	Offrs	O.R.	Offrs	O.R.	Offrs	O.R.		
Jan 16	3	-	31	-	1	8	-	19	2	8	-	-	8	48
17	1	-	36	4	-	14	-	16	1	8	-	-	8	50
18	1	-	35	4	-	7	-	25	1	5	-	-	8	53
19	1	-	43	2	-	8	-	21	-	4	-	-	9	65
20	1	-	34	1	-	13	-	22	3	3	-	-	7	62
21	1	1	29	2	1	9	-	23	2	1	-	-	6	60
22	1	-	28	5	-	8	-	13	1	6	-	-	6	66
23	-	-	27	2	-	7	-	12	-	6	-	-	6	70
24	-	-	33	3	2	14	-	17	2	7	-	-	2	68
25	1	-	29	5	-	10	-	30	-	10	1	-	3	51
26	3	-	15	6	1	9	-	14	-	7	-	-	5	42
27	-	-	23	4	-	18	-	12	1	4	-	-	4	35
28	3	-	33	3	1	8	-	16	1	4	-	-	5	43
29	2	-	21	9	1	10	-	22	1	-	-	-	5	41
30	1	-	28	4	-	13	-	6	-	2	-	-	6	52
31	2	-	35	2	1	21	-	16	-	1	-	-	7	51
Fwd.	24	3	447	61	15	137	-	292	7	61	-	1		
TOTAL	45	4	929	117	23	314	-	576	22	137	-	2		

48th Division

1/2 S Midland F. Ambulance

Feb } 1916
Mar }

48

½ S M 7ª Amb

Vol XIII

Army Form C. 2118.

WAR DIARY
or
INTELLIGENCE SUMMARY
(Erase heading not required.)

CONFIDENTIAL.

War Diary of 1/2nd S.M. Md. Field Amb.
49th Division. B.E.F.
From 1-2-16 to 29-2-16
Vol. 5. appendix 1.

Pages 8
appendix 1.

Seymour Barling
LIEUT. COL. R.A.M.C.T.
COMMANDING 2ND FD. AMB.
48 F...

Army Form C. 2118.

WAR DIARY
or
INTELLIGENCE SUMMARY
(Erase heading not required.)

Place	Date	Hour	Summary of Events and Information	Remarks and references to Appendices
LOUVENCOURT	1/2/16	noon	Sick = 5 Hospital = 5 Wastage = 4	2 HD 2 Rating } received	SD3
LOUVENCOURT	2/2/16	noon	Sick = 0 Hospital = 4 Wastage = 4	Pioneer Hand admitted Hospl Pioneer Brown } discharged " Stephens 36 O.R. to HEBUTERNE for duty in trenches. 3 O.R. to England on months leave.	SD3
LOUVENCOURT	3/2/16	noon	Sick = 1 Hospl. = 4 Wastage = 10	Sgt James admitted Hospl Cpl Birch discharged Bapt PITT leave to England	SD3
LOUVENCOURT	4/2/16	noon	Sick = 4 Hospital = 5 Wastage = 10	L. Cpl Cartwright admitted Hospl.	SD3

Army Form C. 2118.

WAR DIARY
or
INTELLIGENCE SUMMARY
(Erase heading not required.)

Instructions regarding War Diaries and Intelligence Summaries are contained in F. S. Regs., Part II. and the Staff Manual respectively. Title Pages will be prepared in manuscript.

Place	Date	Hour	Summary of Events and Information	Remarks and references to Appendices
LOUVENCOURT	5/2/16	noon	Sgt Farmer ex Hospital Dvr Wanton do 6 O.R. from leave Sick = 3 Hospl = 3 Noolage = 10	SPS
LOUVENCOURT	6/2/16	noon	Driver Newell T.B. to Cav. Rep. Station Sick = 4 Hospl = 2 Noolage = 11	SPS
LOUVENCOURT	7/2/16	noon	Driver Stowe ex Hospl. 36 O.R. returned from HEBUTERNE. Sick = 4 Hospl = 1 Noolage = 11	SPS
LOUVENCOURT	8/2/16	noon	Driver Wheeler to Hospl. Sick = 1 Hospl = 2 Noolage = 11	SPS
LOUVENCOURT	9/2/16	noon	1 Officer 3 Ranks on leave 1 O.R. to Expended for Commission. Sick = 2 Hospl = 2 Noolage = 12	SPS

Army Form C. 2118.

WAR DIARY
or
INTELLIGENCE SUMMARY

(Erase heading not required.)

Instructions regarding War Diaries and Intelligence Summaries are contained in F. S. Regs., Part II. and the Staff Manual respectively. Title Pages will be prepared in manuscript.

Place	Date	Hour	Summary of Events and Information	Remarks and references to Appendices
LOUVENCOURT	10/2/16	noon	Sick = 1 Hospital = 2 Nondays = 11	Pte Cartwright ex Hospl. Pte Hepburn to Hospl. 3 o.R. on leave Sgt Allcott returned from one months leave	SB
LOUVENCOURT	11/2/16	noon	Sick = 2 Hospital = 1 Nondays = 12	Pte Wheeler ex Hospl. L/Cpl Mannie to Base on discharge 5 o.R. from leave 4 o.R. reinforcements arrived from...	SB
LOUVENCOURT	12/2/16	noon	Sick = 2 Hospital = 3 Nondays = 8	Pte Drew " Chambers } to Hospl Fire in Village. 1 Riding Horse burnt 3 sets Saddlery destroyed.	SB
LOUVENCOURT	13/2/16	noon	Sick = 2 Hospital = 4 Nondays = 8	Pte Pritchett admitted Capt McConnell returned returned L/Cpl Howcutt A.S.C. returned from leave	SB

Army Form C. 2118.

WAR DIARY
—or—
INTELLIGENCE SUMMARY
(Erase heading not required.)

Instructions regarding War Diaries and Intelligence Summaries are contained in F. S. Regs., Part II. and the Staff Manual respectively. Title Pages will be prepared in manuscript.

Place	Date	Hour	Summary of Events and Information	Remarks and references to Appendices
LOUVENCOURT	14/2/16	noon	Sick = 1 Hope = 7 Wastage 8	Pte Jones & Cpl R. } admitted Hope Norrace # B 1 Riding Horse received	SB
LOUVENCOURT	15/2/16	noon	Sick = 1 Hope 4 Wastage 5	1 Farrier arrived.	SB
LOUVENCOURT	16/2/16	noon	Sick = 1 Hope = 5 Wastage 7	L/Cpl Jones Pte Shepherd } ex Hospital L/Cpl Huxley admitted 1 Riding Horse shot following burns.	SB
LOUVENCOURT	17/2/16	noon	Sick = 5 Hope = 5 Wastage 7	L/Cpl Ernsley Pte Christopher Pte Chambers ex do. 5 Remts on leave	SB
LOUVENCOURT	18/2/16	noon	Sick = 2 Hope = 6 Wastage 9	Pte Baker admitted Pte Hudson Hopkins } to Base Munition Works Capt Munday Cox from leave	SB

2449. Wt. W14957/M90 750,000 1/16 J.B.C. & A. Forms/C.2118/12.

Army Form C. 2118.

WAR DIARY
or
INTELLIGENCE SUMMARY
(Erase heading not required.)

Instructions regarding War Diaries and Intelligence Summaries are contained in F. S. Regs., Part II. and the Staff Manual respectively. Title Pages will be prepared in manuscript.

Place	Date	Hour	Summary of Events and Information	Remarks and references to Appendices
LOUVENCOURT	19/2/16	noon	Sick = 0 Hosp = 3 Lcpl Morbey } ex hosp. Wastage = 9 Pte Morrall 2/5 }	SB
LOUVENCOURT	20/2/16	noon	Sick = 0 Hosp = 1 oR 1 officer Major Hugglton Wastage = 9 4 Lcpl Emsley } discharged Pte Pidcock } discharged 2/Lt Cross from leave one month 3 Ptes from leave 4 Reinforcements arrived "C" SECTION to SARTON.	SB
LOUVENCOURT	21/2/16	noon	Sick = 1 Hospital = 2 oR Sgt Allcroft to hosp. Wastage = 4 officers "B" Section to SARTON.	SB

2449 Wt. W14957/M90 750,000 1/16 J.B.C. & A. Forms/C.2118/12.

Army Form C. 2118.

WAR DIARY
—or—
INTELLIGENCE SUMMARY
(Erase heading not required.)

Instructions regarding War Diaries and Intelligence Summaries are contained in F. S. Regs., Part II and the Staff Manual respectively. Title Pages will be prepared in manuscript.

Place	Date	Hour	Summary of Events and Information	Remarks and references to Appendices
SARTON	22/2/16	noon	Sick 1 Hosp. 1 off 10 OR Nostopo 4	Capt Mitchman rtd to 3rd A/B Fld Amb. Sgt Alcott to Hosp. "A" Section and remaining details move to SARTON	SPB
SARTON	23/2/16	noon	Sick = 1 Hosp = 1 off. 2 OR Nostopo 4	2/Lt Preston admitted Hosp. H sR leave to England	SPB
SARTON	24/2/16	noon	Sick = 0 Hosp. = 2 1 off. Nostopo = 4	Capt Kingsley servant to Fd. Field Amb	SPB
SARTON	25/2/16	noon	Sick = 2 Hosp. = 5 Nostopo = 4	The Matto " Capt K. A.J. } to Hospital " Lloyd H Major Hungston Discharged Hosp.	SPB
SARTON	26/2/16	noon	Sick = 0 Hosp = 5 Nostopo = 4	Capt Ewing servant to 1/3rd A/Mo Field Amb	SPB

Army Form C. 2118.

WAR DIARY
or
INTELLIGENCE SUMMARY
(Erase heading not required.)

Instructions regarding War Diaries and Intelligence Summaries are contained in F. S. Regs., Part II. and the Staff Manual respectively. Title Pages will be prepared in manuscript.

Place	Date	Hour	Summary of Events and Information	Remarks and references to Appendices
SARTON	27/9/16	noon	Pte Morrell J.E. } admitted Hosp. "Mannington" Capt Prosser's demand to 7th Oxon & Bucks Pte Ford for Mater duty to 7th Oxon & Bucks. Capt M Connell's demand returned. Sick = 3 Hosp = 7 Wastage = 5	85
SARTON	28/9/16	noon	Pte Yardley arrived as reinforcement. Pte Speirs for Mater duty to 1/1st Bucks Bn. Lieut Butler reported for duty. Sick = 0 Hosp = 1 Wastage = 5	86
SARTON	29/9/16	noon	Pvt. Webb A.H. admitted Hosp. Sick = 3 Hosp = 8 Wastage = 5	85 / 83

2449 Wt. W14957/M90 750,000 1/16 J.B.C. & A. Forms/C.2118/12.

Army Form C. 2118.

WAR DIARY
or
INTELLIGENCE SUMMARY

(Erase heading not required.)

Place	Date	Hour	Summary of Events and Information	Remarks and references to Appendices
			War Diary of 1/2nd S.M. Field Ambulance Vol 5 Appendix 1. Summary of admissions and evacuations during the month of February 1916. [signature] Lieut. Col. R.A.M.C. Commanding 2nd S.M. Fd. Amb. 48 Div	

Instructions regarding War Diaries and Intelligence Summaries are contained in F. S. Regs., Part II. and the Staff Manual respectively. Title Pages will be prepared in manuscript.

Army Form C. 2118.

WAR DIARY
or
INTELLIGENCE SUMMARY

(Erase heading not required.)

Instructions regarding War Diaries and Intelligence Summaries are contained in F. S. Regs., Part II. and the Staff Manual respectively. Title Pages will be prepared in manuscript.

Summary of Events and Information

Place	Date	Hour	ADMISSIONS				DISPOSALS								REMAINING		Remarks and references to Appendices
			OFFICERS		O.RANKS.		Cas.Cg.Stn		In.Rest.Stn		Duty		Died		OFFRS	O.RANKS.	
			S.	W.	S.	W.	Offrs	O.R.	Offrs	O.R.	Offrs	O.R.	Offrs	O.R.			
LOUVENCOURT	Feb. 1	Noon	1	1	31	3	1	5	-	21	-	5	-	-	7	54	
do	2	do	-	1	26	7	-	7	-	18	-	8	-	1	7	54	
do	3	do	-	-	28	1	1	12	-	17	1	5	-	-	6	51	
do	4	do	3	1	26	1	1	7	-	19	-	4	-	1	7	46	
do	5	do	1	-	39	7	2	14	-	16	3	5	-	-	3	57	
do	6	do	1	-	37	1	-	13	1	21	-	4	-	1	4	57	
do	7	do	-	1	28	2	1	23	1	17	1	7	-	-	4	39	
do	8	do	2	-	29	2	1	5	1	16	1	4	-	1	5	45	
do	9	do	1	-	26	8	1	12	1	16	1	1	-	-	6	46	
do	10	do	1	1	21	8	2	14	1	20	2	6	-	1	6	35	
do	11	do	1	1	27	17	1	11	1	10	-	5	-	-	7	53	
do	12	do	2	1	46	6	3	9	1	22	1	2	-	-	7	72	
do	13	do	1	-	27	2	1	11	1	25	-	5	-	-	6	60	
do	14	do	1	1	34	5	3	13	1	19	-	9	-	1	7	58	
do	15	do	1	-	13	5	1	6	1	31	1	6	-	-	6	38	
do	16	do	1	1	17	1	-	3	-	13	1	4	-	-	5	34	
do	17	do	1	-	20	1	-	1	-	12	3	5	-	1	4	38	
do	18	do	-	1	13	1	-	5	-	14	1	5	-	-	1	29	
do	19	do	1	-	15	5	-	6	-	17	-	2	-	-	1	16	
do	20	do	1	2	60	1	5	4	-	16	-	-	-	1	2	19	
do	21	do	1	-	-	-	2	1	-	-	1	-	-	3	-	64	
Carried Fwd.			28	5	519	81	22	181	-	352	16	91	1	3			

Army Form C. 2118.

WAR DIARY
or
INTELLIGENCE SUMMARY
(Erase heading not required.)

Instructions regarding War Diaries and Intelligence Summaries are contained in F. S. Regs., Part II. and the Staff Manual respectively. Title Pages will be prepared in manuscript.

Summary of Events and Information

Place	Date	Hour	ADMISSIONS					DISPOSALS								REMAINING		Remarks and references to Appendices
			OFFICERS		O.RANKS		Cas.Cg.Stn		Div.Rest Stn		DUTY		DIED		OFFICERS	O.RANKS	
			S.W.	W.	S.W.	W.	Offrs	O.R	Offrs	O.R	Offrs	O.R	Offrs	O.R			
SARTON	22	Noon	–	1	–	–	1	4	–	–	–	–	–	–	1	60	
	23		–	–	2	–	–	–	–	–	–	–	–	–	1	68	
	24		1	1	23	3	1	1	–	–	–	19	–	–	1	73	
	25		2	–	26	1	1	–	–	–	1	12	–	1	1	88	
	26		2	1	17	–	–	3	–	–	–	2	–	–	3	99	
	27		–	1	23	–	1	9	–	–	–	16	–	1	2	97	
	28		3	–	24	1	4	19	–	–	–	4	1	1	1	98	
	29		1	–	23	–	–	6	–	–	–	12	–	1	2	104	
			28	5	159	81	22	181	–	–	–	352	16	91	1	3	
Brought Fwd.			37	6	702	88	30	223	–	–	–	352	17	156	1	3	

Army Form C. 2118.

WAR DIARY
or
INTELLIGENCE SUMMARY

(Erase heading not required.)

CONFIDENTIAL.

War diary of 1/2 5th West Lg. Amb.
48 Div. B.E.F.
From 1.3.16 to 31-3-16.
Vol. 6 Appendix 1.

Pages 6.
Appendix 1.

Seymour Barling
LIEUT. COL. R.A.M.C.T.
COMMANDING 2ND FD. AMB.
48 DIV.

[Stamp: 2nd SOUTH MIDLAND FIELD AMBULANCE — No. FA 78 — 4 APR 1916]

Army Form C. 2118.

WAR DIARY
~~INTELLIGENCE SUMMARY~~

(Erase heading not required.)

Instructions regarding War Diaries and Intelligence Summaries are contained in F. S. Regs., Part II. and the Staff Manual respectively. Title Pages will be prepared in manuscript.

Place	Date	Hour	Summary of Events and Information	Remarks and references to Appendices
SARTON	1/3/16	Noon	Sick = 4 Hospital = 5 Wastage = 5 Pte Hoyall " Morris S.E. } discharged Hospital " Watts E.E. Capt Buchanan on leave to England Capt Broderick & servant returned	SPS
SARTON	2/3/16	Noon	Sick = 4 Hospital = 3 Wastage = 5 Pte Cooke H } discharged Hospital Dvr Preston 1 H.D. off strength 29.2.16 Capt Murray and servant returned.	SPS
SARTON	3/3/16	Noon	Sick = 3 Hospital = 4 Wastage = 3 Dvr Hatfree admitted Hospital Pte Foster } reinforcements " Baker - from one month's leave	SPS
SARTON	4/3/16	Noon	Sick = 5 Hospital = 4 Wastage = 1 Pte Archer } reinforcements " Emmons	SPS

Army Form C. 2118.

WAR DIARY
or
INTELLIGENCE SUMMARY
(Erase heading not required.)

Instructions regarding War Diaries and Intelligence Summaries are contained in F. S. Regs., Part II. and the Staff Manual respectively. Title Pages will be prepared in manuscript.

Place	Date	Hour	Summary of Events and Information	Remarks and references to Appendices
SARTON	5/3/16	noon	Sick = 3 Hospital = 4 Wastage = 1	Lt Butler & on Leave Gun Taylor Jr. do.	SB
SARTON	6/3/16	noon	Sick = 3 Hospital = 4 Wastage = 0	Lt Hadley & returned from one months leave Pte Watt discharged Hospital " Boucher J.A. admitted do.	SB
SARTON	7/3/16	noon	Sick = 4 Hospital = 5 Wastage = 0	Gun Davies J admitted Hospl.	SB
SARTON	8/3/16	noon	Sick = 2 Hospital = 5 Wastage = 0	1 H.J. to Mobile Vet. Section	SB
SARTON	9/3/16	noon	Sick = 1/6 Hospital = 1 Wastage = 0	Capt McCance & 20 men to COUIN. Pte Matthews Admitted	SB

Army Form C. 2118.

WAR DIARY
or
INTELLIGENCE SUMMARY
(Erase heading not required.)

Instructions regarding War Diaries and Intelligence Summaries are contained in F. S. Regs, Part II. and the Staff Manual respectively. Title Pages will be prepared in manuscript.

Place	Date	Hour	Summary of Events and Information	Remarks and references to Appendices
SARTON	10/3/16	noon	Pte Matthews E.b. discharged Hosp. Sick = 8 Hosp = 5 Wastage = 0	
SARTON	11/3/16	noon	Dvr Brown J & discharged Hospital Pte Coy R admitted to Pte Foley admitted to Rouxhur Discharged Hosp. Sick = 6 Hospital = 3 Wastage = 0	
SARTON	12/3/16	noon	Sick = 9 Hosp = 3 Wastage = 0	
SARTON	13/3/16	noon	Pte Pritchett Matthews } to Hospital Lieut Bulbro kept Sick and for duty. Sick = 6 Hosp = 5 Wastage = 0	
SARTON	14/3/16	noon	Sick = 4 Hosp = 5 Wastage = 0	

Army Form C. 2118.

WAR DIARY
or
INTELLIGENCE SUMMARY
(Erase heading not required.)

Instructions regarding War Diaries and Intelligence Summaries are contained in F.S. Regs., Part II and the Staff Manual respectively. Title Pages will be prepared in manuscript.

Place	Date	Hour	Summary of Events and Information	Remarks and references to Appendices
SARTON	15/3/16	noon	Sick = 1 Hospl = 2 Wastage = 1	The Madonnas ex Hospl " do " Mitchett NCO to C.C.S. + off strength	SB
SARTON	16/3/16	noon	Sick = 3 Hospl = 84 Dutys = 1	Cpl Rogers admitted Hospl 9.16. Drv Taylor admitted.	SB
SARTON	17/3/16	noon	Sick = 5 Hospl = 84 Dutys = 1	Cpl Murry + Smart to 2 S/17 R.F.A. (Rent) G.E. Long Dri Pte Shothree out	SB
SARTON	18/3/16	noon	Sick = 3 Hospl = 86 Wastage = 1	Lt Geary P. to Ft Freed Amb. Pte Taylor to Hospl. Cpl McConnell + party returned Cpl Buchman returned from leave.	SB
SARTON	19/3/16	noon	Sick = 4 Hospl = 9 Dutys = 1	Pte Tye Pte Stim. At. } to Hospital Dr 15 nect.	SB

2449 Wt. W14957/M90 750,000 1/16 J.B.C. & A. Forms/C.2118/12.

Army Form C. 2118.

WAR DIARY
or
INTELLIGENCE SUMMARY
(Erase heading not required.)

Instructions regarding War Diaries and Intelligence Summaries are contained in F. S. Regs., Part II. and the Staff Manual respectively. Title Pages will be prepared in manuscript.

Place	Date	Hour	Summary of Events and Information	Remarks and references to Appendices
SARTON	21/3/16	pm	Sick=1 Shot=8 Wastage=1 Cpl Bird & Pte Ogilvie transferred to hospital. Pte Taylor discharged hospital do. 4 HD Howrs + 2 OS LP gun from HQ 1 Bren, 1 RH to Beauval 1 Alpha + horse + batman attached	SB
SARTON	22/3/16	pm	Sick=0 Shot=8 Wastage=0 Cpl George (W) att 1/4 O+B L.I.) returned to unit + went to AUTHIE P.a. Sgt Smith sent as advance party to AUTHIE to prepare huts for reception	SB
SARTON	23/3/16	noon	Sick=2 Shot=6 Wastage=0 Pte Abbott Cpl Rogers to hospital. Cpl Wotherston + 6 men returned from Armee Bau signallers + sharers attached to Authie Portion of equipment	SB
SARTON	24/3/16	am	Sick=1 Shot=5 Wastage=0 Pte Long nc to hospital Move to Authie ambulance	SB
SARTON	25/3/16	noon	Sick=3 Hospital=4 Wastage=0 Surplus=1 Pte Tay discharged hospital Pte Evans off sick from Maker duty + taken on strength Lubbock re went on leave	SB

Army Form C. 2118.

WAR DIARY
or
INTELLIGENCE SUMMARY
(Erase heading not required.)

Instructions regarding War Diaries and Intelligence Summaries are contained in F. S. Regs., Part II. and the Staff Manual respectively. Title Pages will be prepared in manuscript.

Place	Date	Hour	Summary of Events and Information	Remarks and references to Appendices
SPARTON	26/3/16	a.m.	S.O.K. = 2 Shot = 2 N.D. Cge = 1 Cpl Army + Scrivens returned to Unit. Pte Colley to Hosp. GC. Cpl Reed Ot ex hospital	SB
RUTHIE	27/3/16	p.m.	S.O.K. = 0 Shot = 2 N.D. Cge = 1 Capt Brunning Pte Crocs SJ to Shot Pte Hall at Shot Pte Shine, it took Capt Brodrick's Serving Unit moved to Hosh a.c. Ambl. Reminder of Serving Unit Instruction Cpl Cole returned from Hosh SCRUTON to BASE time deferred	Pte Barr 16 CCS Pte Baird to CCS SB
RUTHIE	28/3/16	a.m.	S.O.K. = 0 Shot = 2 N.D. Cge = 2	Capt + 9 N.C.O's + 3 men on leave Capt Butler + 20 O.R. remain a.c. SPARTON to run O. Rec. Stn.	SB
Aukie	29/3/16	a.m.	S.O.K. = 3 Shot = 2 N.D. Cge = 4	Pte Elloff Pte Price JS J to water duty Serg C. Jones to BASE - temporary demobilised.	1/4 Ox + Bucks L.I. SB
Aukie	29/3/16	a.m.	S.O.K. = 1 Shot = 2 N.D. Cge = 4	Pte Weel at Hosp C.E Buncher JHJ to Hosp t.C. Pte Lines ASC 717 Ptes Sowell + Slain all to 48 Div Dn Pte Allan returned from Hosp	SB

2449 Wt. W14957/M90 750,000 1/16 J.B.C. & A. Forms/C.2118/12.

Army Form C. 2118.

WAR DIARY
or
INTELLIGENCE SUMMARY
(Erase heading not required.)

Place	Date	Hour	Summary of Events and Information	Remarks and references to Appendices
AUTHIE	21/3/16	from	Strck = 3 Shot = # Body = 4	Attestation sheets Capt. Durrang & servant to 1st Bucks Bn. A/sergt Rutherford ASC to be Sergt. Brought F. ASC to be O/C mechanical tpt.	JB

Army Form C. 2118.

WAR DIARY
or
INTELLIGENCE SUMMARY

(Erase heading not required.)

1/2 5th Mid. Fd. Amb.
48 Div.

Vol. 6
Appendix 1.

Summary of admissions & discharges
Divisional R.S.C. Station 48 Div.

Edward Barley
LIEUT. COL. R.A.M.C.T.
COMMANDING 2ND FD. AMB.
48 DIV.

2nd SOUTH MIDLAND FIELD AMBULANCE — No. FA.93 — 4th APR 1916

Place	Date	Hour	Summary of Events and Information	Remarks and references to Appendices

WAR DIARY or INTELLIGENCE SUMMARY

Army Form C. 2118.

(Erase heading not required.)

Instructions regarding War Diaries and Intelligence Summaries are contained in F. S. Regs., Part II. and the Staff Manual respectively. Title Pages will be prepared in manuscript.

Place	Date	Hour	Summary of Events and Information	Remarks and references to Appendices
			Appendix 1. 48th Div. Rest Station March 1916	

	Admissions		Discharges		
	Sick	Wded.	C.C.S.	Duty	
OFFICERS	57	7	45	14	
O.RANKS	631	6	127	533	

Remaining 29.6 / 2 / 3   Officers 2   O.R. 106
21.6 / 7   88

Seymour Darby
LIEUT. COL. R.A.M.C.T.
COMMANDING 2ND FD. AMB.
48 DIV.

2nd SOUTH MIDLAND FIELD AMBULANCE
No. FA 78
Date APR 1916

WAR DIARY
INTELLIGENCE SUMMARY

Army Form C. 2118.

CONFIDENTIAL

April 1916. 1/2 5th Midd. F¹ Amb

4⁵ Div BEF

1-4-16 to 30-4-16

Vol XIV

Vol 1 - Pages 6.
Appendix 1.

Seymour Barling
Lt Col
RAMCT

COMMITTEE FOR THE
MEDICAL HISTORY OF THE WAR
Date 9-JUN 1916

Army Form C. 2118.

WAR DIARY
or
INTELLIGENCE SUMMARY

(Erase heading not required.)

Instructions regarding War Diaries and Intelligence Summaries are contained in F. S. Regs., Part II. and the Staff Manual respectively. Title Pages will be prepared in manuscript.

Place	Date	Hour	Summary of Events and Information	Remarks and references to Appendices
Authie	1/4/16	from	Sick = 3. / Hosp. = 2 / 1 Dis. to Br. = 4	St Gros at Hosp. / 2 H.D. from 1/3 SM FA in exchange for 3LD	SB
Authie	2/4/16	from	Sick = 2 / Hosp = 2 / 1 D. to Br. = 5	— in Hosp. / Br. Sprague into Hosp — evacuated to CCS from Bresle	SB
AUTHIE	3/4/16	from	Sick = 2 / Hosp = 3 / 1 D. to Br. = 5	Lt.Col. Hughes to Hosp. / Br. Naughton to SM D CCS / Brit. / 11.30 A.M. Conference by CDC. / 2 P.M. " ADMS / 2 P.M. Pvts. 3 drivers 2 orderlies to ADMS. 2 y Div	Dr. Lewis / 1s Bercher at Hosp.	SB
AUTHIE	4/4/16	from	Sick = 3 / Hosp = 3 / 1 D. to Br. = 5	OC Wyldon from C.C.S. / 2Lt Set R. to base / Cpl. McDonald & 31 OR from Colincamps / OR 18 of FAMC attached to H.B. Supply Col. / Officers = 1	SB
Authie	5/4/16	from	Sick = 3 / Hosp = 1 / 1 D. to Br. = 6	Archie Bathe started. / 30 OR inoculated	SB

2449 Wt. W14957/M90 750,000 1/16 J.B.C. & A. Forms/C.2118/12.

Army Form C. 2118.

WAR DIARY
or
INTELLIGENCE SUMMARY
(Erase heading not required.)

Instructions regarding War Diaries and Intelligence Summaries are contained in F. S. Regs., Part II. and the Staff Manual respectively. Title Pages will be prepared in manuscript.

Place	Date	Hour	Summary of Events and Information	Remarks and references to Appendices
AUTHIE	6/4/16		Sick = 2 Shot = 1 Dosage = 6	SS
Authie	7/4/16		Sick = 3 Shot = 4 Dosage = 6	Pte Hunter } to Hosp Pte Horace Scott Arthur } 3 Brown belongs to Gen. 21/14 Column to FANY	SS
Authie	8/4/16		Sick = 2 Shot = 5 Dosage = 6	Pte Winter to 1st FA for dental treatment Hosp Hosp Infl ex Hosp C/C me Cornwall & Savage to H/Q Bn 14L C/C Col 3 Franks leave Htq. 8 days. 3 Franks leave Htq. months. or. Scrutated.	SS
AUTHIE	9/4/16		Sick = 3 Hospital = 4 Package = 9	Pte Brown MM to Hosp " Monters } ex Hosp " Bowyer } 1 H.D off Strength to Authie Ret. 1 HD died 2 L.D. horses received	SS

2449 Wt. W14957/M90 750,000 1/16 J.B.C. & A. Forms/C.2118/12.

WAR DIARY
or
INTELLIGENCE SUMMARY

(Erase heading not required.)

Army Form C. 2118.

Instructions regarding War Diaries and Intelligence Summaries are contained in F. S. Regs., Part II. and the Staff Manual respectively. Title Pages will be prepared in manuscript.

Place	Date	Hour	Summary of Events and Information	Remarks and references to Appendices
AUTHIE	10/4/16	Noon	Sick – 3 Hosp. – 3 + O.Coy – 9	Pte Goodard to hosp GC. RE Authie fatigue with R.E. Authie. 1 NCO + 9 men for strily fatigue work on Nave line 1 NCO 5 men took over Nave line	PS 1
Authie	11/4/16	Noon	Sick – 1 Hosp – 4 + O.Coy – 10	Pte Whitnick to hospital Cpls L Cornell to Highbury OCS Seniors went to Cpls Tenney + Service from regimental duty. Conference at D.HQ by A.O.C.	PS
Authie	12/4/16	am	Sick – 5 Hosp – 8 O.Coy – 11	P/o Thornton to Hosp. Pte Walker to watering duty 1/4 Berks Rgt Cpls + 2 McGowan 2 orderlies returned from 29 Div. 1 HD Review. Lt R Booth (RAMC)	PS
Authie	13/4/16	Noon	Sick – 2 Hosp – 8 + O.Coy – 11	Browne TNT at hosp.	PS
Authie	14/4/16	Noon	Sick – 1 Hosp – 2 + O.Coy – 11		PS
Authie	15/4/16	am	Sick – 1 Hosp – 2 + O.Coy – 10	Pte Whitnick to hosp CH Bue returned from Nrc E hosp Pte Moore to hosp 1/2 A.S.C. stable fire mystery to 10 villagers	PS

Army Form C. 2118.

WAR DIARY
or
INTELLIGENCE SUMMARY

(Erase heading not required.)

Instructions regarding War Diaries and Intelligence Summaries are contained in F. S. Regs., Part II. and the Staff Manual respectively. Title Pages will be prepared in manuscript.

Place	Date	Hour	Summary of Events and Information	Remarks and references to Appendices
RUTHIE	16/4/16	Noon	Sick = 6 Hosp = 1 D-ty = 10	P.G. Mackie to Hosp.	JB
RUTHIE	17/4/16	Noon	Sick = 6 Hosp = 2 D-ty = 10	Pte. McClain into Hosp. 1 R.H. to mobile V.G. sec.	JB
Authie	18/4/16	am	Sick = 3 Hosp = 2 D-ty = 10	Cpl. Cox & Pte. C Kerr return from duty.	JB
Authie	19/4/16	Noon	Sick = 5 Hosp = 3 D-ty = 10	Pte. Hardy to Hosp.	JB
Authie	20/4/16	am	Sick = 3 Hosp = 4 D-ty = 10	Pte. Shaw to Hosp. 2 hubs Reserve 1 R.H.	JB
Authie	21/4/16	Noon	Sick = 2 Hosp = 4 D-ty = 10	Pte. Bennett to Hosp. P.O. 19 Chris H.	JB

Army Form C. 2118.

WAR DIARY
or
INTELLIGENCE SUMMARY

(Erase heading not required.)

Instructions regarding War Diaries and Intelligence Summaries are contained in F.S. Regs., Part II. and the Staff Manual respectively. Title Pages will be prepared in manuscript.

Place	Date	Hour	Summary of Events and Information	Remarks and references to Appendices
Authie	22/4/16	noon	Sick - 5 Shot - 4 10 Btge - 6	Pte Bellinger " Tucker } as reinforcements " James 21/4/16 " Raveron CpL Washington to Hospl	SB3
			Increase of one in PSC TF under New Est. Part VII Wastage = 1	
Authie	23/4/16	noon	Sick - 4 Shot - 4 10 Btge - 7	1 R.H. sick	SB3
Authie	24/4/16	am	Sick - 5 Shot - 4 10 Btge - 7	Pte Sumner to Hosp. Pte Lawes sick / went to hosp. Cas on L 19/2/16 1 R.H. to home / never to hosp Cas on L 19/2/16	SB
Authie	25/4/16	noon	Sick - 5 Shot - 5 10 Btge - 7	Pte Thomas to Hospl Lt Col Baring leave to England	ACyl

Army Form C. 2118.

WAR DIARY
or
INTELLIGENCE SUMMARY
(Erase heading not required.)

Place	Date	Hour	Summary of Events and Information	Remarks and references to Appendices
AUTHIE	26/4/16	noon	Sick 4 OR. 18 NH. Capt Mundy Ex to Hospital. Hosp. 5 OR. 18 NH. Lt. Butler + Party (19 OR) take over new adv. dressing station MAILLY. Wastage 7. Capt HINGLEY + servant } attached at A.D.S. " FRITH " servant Cpl. Mathewson + H OR. det. to MS N. Supply Col. - Leave Barn. Cpl. Mathewson to Hospl.	a.y.l.
AUTHIE	27/4/16	noon	Sick 4 Pte. Stevenson E. } to Hospital Hosp. Off. 1. OR. 16 " Harris J.F. } Wastage 7. Capt BUCHANAN - servant to Ht SM13 (How) RFA. Camp.	a.y.l.
AUTHIE	28/4/16	noon	Sick 5 L.M. Trafford + 3 OR leave to England. Hosp. Off. 1. OR. 6 Pte Hudson returned from det. duty. Wastage 7.	a.y.l.
AUTHIE	29/4/16	noon	Sick 1 Pte Brown. W.M. to Hospl. Hosp. Off. 1. OR. 7 Wastage 7.	a.y.l.
AUTHIE	30/4/16	noon	Sick 1 Pte Glenn Arth } ex Hospital. Hosp. Off. 1. OR. 5 " Harris J.F. } Wastage 7. 2 L.D. Horses received.	a.y.l.

2449 Wt. W14957/M90 750,000 1/16 J.B.C. & A. Forms/C.2118/12.

Army Form C. 2118.

WAR DIARY
or
INTELLIGENCE SUMMARY
(Erase heading not required.)

Instructions regarding War Diaries and Intelligence Summaries are contained in F. S. Regs., Part II. and the Staff Manual respectively. Title Pages will be prepared in manuscript.

Place	Date	Hour	Summary of Events and Information	Remarks and references to Appendices
			Appendix 1 to Vol 1. Summary of admissions & discharges 48 Div. Fd. Amb. — April 1 – 30 1916 [signature] LIEUT. COL. R.A.M.C.T. COMMANDING 2ND FD. AMB. 48 DIV.	

2449 Wt. W14957/M90 750,000 1/16 J.B.C. & A. Forms/C.2118/12.

WAR DIARY
or
INTELLIGENCE SUMMARY
(Erase heading not required.)

Army Form C. 2118.

Place	Date	Hour	Summary of Events and Information	Remarks and references to Appendices
	8 - MAY 1916			

	Admissions		Disposals	
	Sick	Wounded	C.C.S.	Duty
OFFICERS	40	5	36	12
O. RANKS	819	73	146	632

Remaining 38/16 Offrs. SR.
9   .   7   88
90/16 4 205

Raymond Ewing
LIEUT. COL. R.A.M.C.T.
COMMANDING 2ND FD. AMB.
48 DIV.

Army Form C. 2118.

WAR DIARY
or
INTELLIGENCE SUMMARY
(Erase heading not required.)

CONFIDENTIAL.

1/2 South Midland Field Amb.
48. D⁻⁰
B.E.F.
1-5-16 to 31-5-16

Lieut. Col. R.A.M.C.T.
Commanding 2nd Fd. Amb.
48 Div.

COMMITTEE FOR THE
MEDICAL HISTORY OF THE WAR
Date 26 JUN 19

Vol. 8
Page 6.
Appendix 1

To: D.A.G.   SECRET
A.G's Office
Base.

Herewith please
A.F's C2118 - War Diary
& Appendix, for this
Unit during the
month of May, 1916.

[signature]

LIEUT. COL. R.A.M.C.T.
COMMANDING 2ND FD. AMB.
48 DIV.

2nd SOUTH MIDLAND FIELD AMBULANCE — No. M.962 — Date 2 JUN 1916

WAR DIARY
or
INTELLIGENCE SUMMARY

(Erase heading not required.)

Army Form C. 2118.

Place	Date	Hour	Summary of Events and Information	Remarks and references to Appendices
AUTHIE	1/5/16	noon	Sick 3, Hosp. Offr. 1, OR. 5, Machine G. 7	The Revd. Jackson, R.C. attended at A.D.S. SAILLY.	ayl.
AUTHIE	2/5/16	noon	Sick 1, Hosp. Offr. 1, OR. 5, Machine G. 7	Pte Skiris adm'd to Bie Supply Col. Hutton Evacuated. Leave Gren.	ayl.
AUTHIE	3/5/16	noon	Sick 3, Hosp. OR 5, Machine G. 7	Capt Cox ex Hosp.	ayl.
AUTHIE	4/5/16	noon	Sick 4, Hosp. 5, Machine G. 7	Advanced Dressing Station moved from SAILLY to J.16.A.6.	ayl.
AUTHIE	5/5/16	noon	Sick —, Hosp. 3, Machine G. 7	Pte Henley to C.C.S + off Strength. " Lowrie to Hospital. Lt. Qr. Sc. WRIGHT + 2 OR leave to England	ayl.

Army Form C. 2118.

WAR DIARY
or
INTELLIGENCE SUMMARY
(Erase heading not required.)

Instructions regarding War Diaries and Intelligence Summaries are contained in F.S. Regs., Part II. and the Staff Manual respectively. Title Pages will be prepared in manuscript.

Place	Date	Hour	Summary of Events and Information	Remarks and references to Appendices
Authie	6/5/16	Noon	Sick = 0, Hosp = 0, Dutys = 2. Lt. Col. E Bertrey returned from leave. W.W. Bowman. Pte Sherman E. J Sn Hosptl. Pte Thomas C. 6 O.R. on reinforcements.	P3
Authie	7/5/16	Noon	Sick = 1, Hosp = 0, Dutys = 2+1. Two O.R. from Sibley Pk. Pte Chiffers, La Chance. Pte Robinson to base reinforced.	P3
Authie	8/5/16	Noon	Sick = 1, Hosp = 0, Dutys = 5+1. 1 NCO & 6 O.R. to Smilly for fatigue work. Pte Elliott transfered to 1st Army Artillery Grpd. COURCELLES. "winters" Sergt Major Jeffrey from leave.	P3
Authie	9/5/16	Noon	Sick = 0, Hosp = 6, Dutys = 6. Pte. 13 one P.E. to Hosp. 1 O.R. check to 2 SA.B.F.A on route Boly. 3 O.R. from leave. Capt Nicolson same Staff Sergt Allison from leave. Lieut on strength Division from sick.	P3
Authie	10/5/16	Noon	Sick = 2, Hosp = 1, Dutys = 4. P.G. Blewett on one month leave. Capt Mc Cannel from Base. One army recruit to 1/4 R Bork.	P3
Authie	11/5/16	Noon	Sick = 1, Hosp = 1, Dutys = 8+7.	P3

Army Form C. 2118.

WAR DIARY
or
INTELLIGENCE SUMMARY
(Erase heading not required.)

Instructions regarding War Diaries and Intelligence Summaries are contained in F. S. Regs., Part II. and the Staff Manual respectively. Title Pages will be prepared in manuscript.

Place	Date	Hour	Summary of Events and Information	Remarks and references to Appendices
Authie	12/5/16	pm	Strik = 2, Hosp = 1, N/dge = 7. 1 MD transfd. to E.A.M.C. 3 O.R. on leave	SP3
Authie	13/5/16	am	Sick = 0, Hosp = 1, N/dge = 7.	SP3
Authie	14/5/16	am	Sick = 0, Hosp = 1, Dutge = 7. At St Aubin as reinforcements. No. 4 Coy. 16 { SP & Sergt fellow temp. attahd. from line 2d. 18 nights. P & Funnell men returned	SP3
Authie	15/5/16	am	Sick = 0, Hosp = 1, N/dge = 6.	SP3
Authie	16/5/16	am	Sick = 0, Hosp = 1, Dutge = 6.	SP3
Authie	17/5/16	am	Sick = 1, Hosp = 1, N/dge = 6.	SP3
Authie	18/5/16	am	Stat = 1, Hosp = 2, N/dge = 6. Capt C Buckman + Brig. train to 4th Gen. train	SP3

WAR DIARY
or
INTELLIGENCE SUMMARY

Army Form C. 2118.

(Erase heading not required.)

Place	Date	Hour	Summary of Events and Information	Remarks and references to Appendices
Authie	19/5/16		Sick = 3 Hosp = 2 1 O.R. to Base + 3 O.R. on leave	OB
Authie	20/5/16	am	Sick = 0 Hosp = 3 1 O.R. to Base Pte Farrell to Hosp. S.S. Retnd returned from detached duty to 14 C.T. Coy.	OB
Authie	21/5/16	noon	Sick = 3 Hosp = 4 1 O.R. to Base Pte Ware att K Hosp. Cpl Whitley } to 14b Inf. Bde. Cpl Smith } Signallers Cpl Pritt L.C. Returned.	OB
Authie	22/5/16	noon	Sick = 0 Hosp = 3 1 O.R. to Base Pte Reynolds to Hosp. Posted to 14th Inf. Bde. O.C. 1 L/O strength from R.E.S. 1 L/O	OB
Authie	23/5/16	am	Sick = 0 Hosp = 4 1 O.R. to Base 3 O.R. from leave. Sergt Welsh to Hosp.	OB
Authie	24/5/16	am	Sick = 6 Hosp = 6 1 O.R. to Base Cpl Cole Cpl Taylor 1 Dog. to Hosp. 14 O.R. returned from leave.	OB

Army Form C. 2118.

WAR DIARY
or
INTELLIGENCE SUMMARY

(Erase heading not required.)

Instructions regarding War Diaries and Intelligence Summaries are contained in F. S. Regs., Part II. and the Staff Manual respectively. Title Pages will be prepared in manuscript.

Place	Date	Hour	Summary of Events and Information	Remarks and references to Appendices
Authie	25/5/16	from	Sick = 3 Cyst Coe to CCS. Shot = 4 (Cyst Stewart slightly wounded this morning by enemy aeroplane) 1 Dis Coys = 8	JBS
Authie	26/5/16	am	Sick = 4 Shot = 4 1 Dis Coy = 8	JBS 1 L.D. to mobile vet. sec. 4 O.R. reinforcements arrived
Authie	27/5/16	am	Sick = 4 Shot = 4 1 Dis Coy = 3 P.te Small	JBS 1 R.H. 1 L.D. 1 M.D. just been to 143 Inf. Bde. Horse lens - struck off strength 4 O.R. reinforcements arrived
Authie	28/5/16	am	Sick = 2 Shot = 4 1 Dis Coy = 3	JBS Cyst Buchan & Saying C returned from detached duty Pte Stewart to hos. L/C Capt. Murray on leave Cyst Cox & Sergeant to 4th Army Gas school
Authie	29/5/16	pm	Sick = 1 Shot = 5 L/Sgt = 3	JBS P.te Hancock to hos.
Authie	30/5/16	am	Sick = 1 Shot = 4 1 Dis Gr. = 2	JBS Lt. Col. Ole returned from C.O.S. Cyst Jas Gunner C from leave Cyst Wheatcroft & Samuels to 6th struck off strength 1 N.D. vacant Lt. Slough Lieut.

Army Form C. 2118.

WAR DIARY
or
INTELLIGENCE SUMMARY
(Erase heading not required.)

Instructions regarding War Diaries and Intelligence Summaries are contained in F. S. Regs., Part II. and the Staff Manual respectively. Title Pages will be prepared in manuscript.

Place	Date	Hour	Summary of Events and Information	Remarks and references to Appendices
Bulke	31/5/16	Noon	S Coll = 3. Hos = 4 Ds Gr = 2	SB

Seymour Barling
LIEUT. COL. R.A.M.C.T.
COMMANDING 2ND FD. AMB.
48 DIV.

[Stamp: 2nd SOUTH MIDLAND FIELD AMBULANCE — 2 JUN 1916]

WAR DIARY
or
INTELLIGENCE SUMMARY

Army Form C. 2118.

2 S.M. 3ª Amb.

Vol.

Appendix 1 to Vol. 8

Summary of admissions to 2/8 Fd. Amb. Rec. Stn.
May 1 to May 31, 1916

LIEUT. COL. R.A.M.C.T.
COMMANDING 2ND FD. AMB.
48 DIV.

Army Form C. 2118.

WAR DIARY
or
INTELLIGENCE SUMMARY
(Erase heading not required.)

Instructions regarding War Diaries and Intelligence Summaries are contained in F. S. Regs., Part II. and the Staff Manual respectively. Title Pages will be prepared in manuscript.

Place	Date	Hour	Summary of Events and Information	Remarks and references to Appendices

	Admissions		Discharges	
	Sick	Wound	C.C.S.	Unit.
Officers	42	5	20	25
O.R.	822	28	162	693 Buri 1.

Remained
30-4-16
31. 5.16

Officers 6
O.R. 205
   98

Seymour Barling
LIEUT. COL. R.A.M.C.T.
COMMANDING 2ND FD. AMB.
48 DIV.

WAR DIARY
or
INTELLIGENCE SUMMARY

Army Form C. 2118

1/2 SM Fd Amb
48
Vol 16

CONFIDENTIAL

1/2 South Midland Field Amb
48 Div
B.E.F.

1-6-16 to 30-6-16

Reymond Batey
LIEUT. COL. R.A.M.C.T.
COMMANDING 2ND FD. AMB.
48 DIV.

COMMITTEE FOR THE
MEDICAL HISTORY OF THE WAR
Date 31 AUG. 1915

Vol = 9
Pages = 6
Appendix = 1

WAR DIARY
or
INTELLIGENCE SUMMARY
(Erase heading not required.)

Army Form C. 2118.

Place	Date	Hour	Summary of Events and Information	Remarks and references to Appendices
Authie	1/6/16	pm	S.O.R. = 1 Hot = 4 1 Sgt. Cpl = 2		SDS
Authie	2/6/16	am	S.O.R. = 3 Hot = 4 1 Sgt. Cpl = 2	Dr. Billerjin to Hosp G.C. 2 R.W. received.	SDS
Authie	3/6/16	am	S.O.R. = 2 Hot = 5 1 Sgt. Cpl = 2	Col. O. & Serval returned from 4th Army Leave School.	SDS
Authie	4/6/16	am	S.O.R. = 2 Hot = 3 1 Sgt. Cpl = 2	Six O.R. on leave — 2 for 1 week — & for 4 days.	SDS
Authie	5/6/16	am	S.O.R. = 2 Hot = 4 1 Sgt. Cpl = 4	Dr. Billerjin in hosp. Offr. & 3 attendan returned from Gas Course. Gas Instructions kit in men and at 2 p.m.	SDS
Authie	6/6/16	am	S.O.R. = 3 Hot = 4 1 Sgt. Cpl = 4	Gas instruction 2 p.m.	SDS

Army Form C. 2118.

WAR DIARY
or
INTELLIGENCE SUMMARY
(Erase heading not required.)

Instructions regarding War Diaries and Intelligence Summaries are contained in F. S. Regs., Part II. and the Staff Manual respectively. Title Pages will be prepared in manuscript.

Place	Date	Hour	Summary of Events and Information	Remarks and references to Appendices
Authie	7/6/16	a.m.	Sick = 3 Hosp = 4 Dutys = 3	Sgt. maintain 2 PM Reduction of the Est. A.S.C.T. – Sergeant	JB
Authie	8/6/16	a.m.	Sick = 0 Hosp = 2 Dutys = 8	Pte Taylor 27 D. Hosp. Regt. Albit J Dr Wott P. to 46 mount pack on remounts of 10 – E.G. to 240 13th R.F.A. Capt Broderick	JB
Authie	9/6/16	a.m.	Sick = 2 Hosp = 3 Dutys = 2	To Bologne to Hosp. Pte fifted sick as reinforcement	JB
Authie	10/6/16	a.m.	Sick = 1 Hosp = 1 Dutys = 4	Pte a Sword R.E. (T.F.) to CCS to Bologne (not sick)	JB
Authie	11/6/16	a.m.	Sick = 1 Hosp = 1 Dutys = 4	NCO + 12 men to DDMS for days fatigue working party removing from field, 3 or on leave 7 days. 3 OR Dispatch Horse Overseer	JB

2449 Wt. W14957/M90 750,000 1/16 J.B.C. & A. Forms/C.2118/12.

WAR DIARY
or
INTELLIGENCE SUMMARY

(Erase heading not required.)

Army Form C. 2118.

Instructions regarding War Diaries and Intelligence Summaries are contained in F.S. Regs., Part II. and the Staff Manual respectively. Title Pages will be prepared in manuscript.

Place	Date	Hour	Summary of Events and Information	Remarks and references to Appendices
Authie	12/6/16	a.m.	Stk=0 Hrs=2 ·on ege 4·	Pte Mcintosh on trek Sergt Hampton] to Hosp. Pte Irons S]	SB
Authie	13/6/16	p.m.	Stk=1 Hsh=2 10 on cge=3	Sergt Allsopp to CCS. Duodenal ulcer.	SB
Authie	14/6/16	noon	Stk=4 Hsh=2 on cge=3	Capt McConnell & Ramsey returned from 24th Fd.A. R.F.A.	SB
Authie	15/6/16	a.m.	Stk=3 Hsh=2 on cge=5	Capt Hughes G.S. RAMC T(F) attached	SB
Authie	16/6/16	p.m.	Stk=1 Hsh=0 on cge=5	Pte Brown S. Sergt Hampton	SB
Authie	17/6/16	noon	Stk=1 Hsh=1 on cge=3	Pte Chatterton Pte Riley as reinforcements. Capt Ashby & Ramsey to 20 or to Hebuterne	SB

Army Form C. 2118.

WAR DIARY
or
INTELLIGENCE SUMMARY

(Erase heading not required.)

Instructions regarding War Diaries and Intelligence Summaries are contained in F. S. Regs., Part II. and the Staff Manual respectively. Title Pages will be prepared in manuscript.

Place	Date	Hour	Summary of Events and Information	Remarks and references to Appendices
Authie	17/6/16	am	SCK=3 Hosp.=1 ?D~Gge=3	Pte Panton from Hospital. 242 SAC and 6 B.o.R Bn for W.a. Duty. Cpl Broderick returned from 240 Bde Bde. Cpl McDonnell & Panton reported to Sitn arrived. hr. gun shypsh in hand.	SPB
Authie	18/6/16	noon	SCK=4 Hosp=2 ?D~Gge=3	Pte certificate to hosp. Cpl Att & position of A.D.C.S A.D.S. (5) Lieve Dinn Ruby returned 14 OR from Palestine	SPB
Authie	24/6/16	am	SCK=4 Hosp=2 ?D~Gge=5	Pte Ransom to duty with 241 Bde RFA. Pte Scott Cpl Dalton attached temporarily.	SPB
Authie	2/6/16	am	SCK=2 Hosp=1 ?D~Gge=5	Pte Whitworth to Hosp. Sgt Snyder to Colly on Hosp. 3 OR from leave	SPB
Authie	24/6/16	am	SCK=2 Hosp=1 ?D~Gge=5		SPB

Army Form C. 2118.

WAR DIARY
or
INTELLIGENCE SUMMARY
(Erase heading not required.)

Instructions regarding War Diaries and Intelligence Summaries are contained in F. S. Regs., Part II. and the Staff Manual respectively. Title Pages will be prepared in manuscript.

Place	Date	Hour	Summary of Events and Information	Remarks and references to Appendices
Authie	23/6/16	Noon	Sick = 4 Res. to bath unit Hosp = 2 Sgt. Smith on staff D. to G. = 4 Cpl. C. Derry T.B. on to 23 C.C.S. from duty Bgn. Hughes from base (colony) Cpl. Buchannan & recruit from leave	SPB.
Authie	24/6/16	Noon	Sick = 1 Pte. Silver to Hosp. Hosp = 4 Pte. Clutsel D. to G. = 4	SPB
Authie	25/6/16	Noon	Sick = 0 Dr. Drew to Hosp. Hosp = 5 D. to G. = 4	SPB
Authie	26/6/16	Noon	Sick = 1 at Brei M.B.) to 1.45 op meeting F.C. Hosp = 5 Pte. Shata) D. to G. = 7 P.T.O. attg C.D. to mens funeral (Nurses) 2050 2nd Lewell transfd to A.O.C. T HT. (auth. no.6 at 10/5676 A.4/5/16) I.O.R. leave to Eng.	SPB
Authie	27/6/16	Noon	Sick = — Pte. Mitchener to Hospital Hosp. 1 A.m. Bailey Nodays 7 Pte. Silver J. ex Hospital Am Prew to J. ex Hospital I.O.R. leave to Eng.	SPB

2449 Wt. W14957/M90 750,000 1/16 J.B.C. & A. Forms/C.2118/12.

WAR DIARY
or
INTELLIGENCE SUMMARY
(Erase heading not required.)

Army Form C. 2118.

Instructions regarding War Diaries and Intelligence Summaries are contained in F. S. Regs., Part II. and the Staff Manual respectively. Title Pages will be prepared in manuscript.

Place	Date	Hour	Summary of Events and Information	Remarks and references to Appendices
Authie	28/8/16	noon	Sick - 1 Hospital - 1 Wastage - 1	Revd Hughey } Pte Smith } attached. 1 Rainer	OP3
Authie	29/8/16	noon	Sick - 1 Hospital - 1 Wastage - 1	Revd Hughey to C.C.S. sick.	OP3
Authie	30/8/16	noon	Sick - 5 Hospital - Wastage - 1	Pte Cleveland ex Hospital. 27 O.R. returned from A.D.S. SAILLY	OP3

WAR DIARY or INTELLIGENCE SUMMARY

Army Form C. 2118.

Appendix I to vol 9

Summary of admissions to 1/2 Field Amb.
48 (S. Mid) Div.
June 1st to June 30th 1916

Seymour Riley
LIEUT. COL. R.A.M.C.T.
COMMANDING 2ND FD. AMB.
48 DIV.

WAR DIARY
or
INTELLIGENCE SUMMARY

Army Form C. 2118.

	Admissions		Discharges	
	Sick	Wnd.	C.C.S.	Unit
Officers	16	7	16	12
O.R.	638	52	184	598

Died Officers — O.R. 8

Remaining O.R. 97.

Seymour Barling
LIEUT. COL. R.A.M.C. T.
COMMANDING 2ND FD. AMB.
48 DIV

Army Form C. 2118.

WAR DIARY
or
INTELLIGENCE SUMMARY
(Erase heading not required.)

Vol 17

CONFIDENTIAL.

1/2 2nd South Midland Fd. Amb.
48 DIV.
July 1st – July 31st 1916.

Seymour Barling
LIEUT. COL. R.A.M.C.T.
COMMANDING 2ND FD. AMB.
48 DIV.

Vol. 17
Pages of
Appendix. 1

COMMITTEE FOR ...
MEDICAL HISTORY OF THE WAR
Date 13 SEP. 1916

2nd SOUTH MIDLAND
31 JUL 1916
FIELD AMBULANCE

WAR DIARY
or
INTELLIGENCE SUMMARY

(Erase heading not required.)

Instructions regarding War Diaries and Intelligence Summaries are contained in F. S. Regs., Part II. and the Staff Manual respectively. Title Pages will be prepared in manuscript.

Place	Date	Hour	Summary of Events and Information	Remarks and references to Appendices
AUTHIE	1/7/16	noon	Sick — Hospt — Wastage 7	"C" Section complete with transport to 144th Infantry Brigade at MAILLY-MAILLET. Rev Goring, Servant + Horse attacked.	SP3
AUTHIE	2/7/16	noon	Sick — Hospt 1 Wastage 7	Pte Whitewick to Hospital 16 o.Ranks to MAILLY MAILLET.	SP3
AUTHIE	3/7/16	noon	Sick — Hospt 1 Wastage 7	"E" Section returned to Headquarters = 3 Offrs + 97 O.R. Capt Michael, Ramc(TC) joined VIII Corps Operating Unit on Aveluy field. (4/7/16)	SP3
AUTHIE	4/7/16	noon	Sick 3 Hospt 2 Wastage 7	L. Cpl. Rowe, admitted Hospital.	SP3
AUTHIE	5/7/16		Sick 2 Hospt 2 Wastage 7	Nursingsister Parslow joined VIII C.O.U. 1 o.r. returned from leave	SP3

WAR DIARY
or
INTELLIGENCE SUMMARY
(Erase heading not required.)

Army Form C.

Instructions regarding War Diaries and Intelligence Summaries are contained in F.S. Regs., Part II. and the Staff Manual respectively. Title Pages will be prepared in manuscript.

Place	Date	Hour	Summary of Events and Information	Remarks and references to Appendices
AUTHIE	6/7/16	noon	Sick. 6 Hospl. 1 Wastage 7	Pte Whitworch acch. Hospl.	SB
AUTHIE	7/7/16	noon	Sick. 2 Hospl. 1 Wastage 5	Pte Hood M E } returned from 10 m/o leave Dvr Wheeler WN } on strength.	SB
AUTHIE	8/7/16	a.m.	S/Sgt = 2 Hosp = 1 Woolwich = 1	L/Cpl Pane re Hosp. - Pte Yonge G Hosp. 4 Reinforcements Received 1 NCO & see returned from SOMMET	SB
AUTHIE	9/7/16	noon	Sick = 1 Hospl = 1 Wastage = 1		
AUTHIE	10/7/16	noon	Sick Nil Hospl 1 Wastage 1	Pte Elliott M ret. from Water duty. On strength. " Percy H admitted off strength - with 17 HAG for Water duty. J Muller sent to 3 Echelon DAC off strength.	

2449 Wt. W14957/Mgo 750,000 1/16 J.B.C. & A. Forms/C.2118/12.

Army Form C. 2118.

WAR DIARY
or
INTELLIGENCE SUMMARY
(Erase heading not required.)

Instructions regarding War Diaries and Intelligence Summaries are contained in F. S. Regs., Part II. and the Staff Manual respectively. Title Pages will be prepared in manuscript.

Place	Date	Hour	Summary of Events and Information	Remarks and references to Appendices
AUTHIE	11/7/16	Noon	Sick = 2 Hospl. = 1 Furlough = 2	Pte Moffatt to C. to 144th Coy M.G.C. for Motor duty. Eff. Strength.	883
AUTHIE	12/7/16	Noon	Sick = 3 Hospl = 0 Furlough = 2	Pte George discharged Hospl. Revd Robins, servant, & Rolling Horse detached O.K.C Room to Bde Sick.	883
AUTHIE	13/7/16	Noon	Sick = 2 Hospl = 0 Furlough = 2	6 Reinforcements arrived. Cpl Buchan & servant returned to about 2 O. + 39 OR to Colincamps.	883
Authie	14/7/16	noon	Sick = 2 Hospl = 0 1 Duty = 0 Supple ,, ASC 3 Rgmt.		883
Authie	15/7/16	Noon	Sick = 0 Hospl = 0 1 Duty = 0 Supple = 4		883

2449 Wt. W14957/M90 750,000 1/16 J.B.C. & A. Forms/C.2118/12.

WAR DIARY
or
INTELLIGENCE SUMMARY
(Erase heading not required.)

Army Form C. 2118.

Place	Date	Hour	Summary of Events and Information	Remarks and references to Appendices
Authie	16/7/16	Morn.	Sick = 0 Hosp = 0 Employ = 4 Bn Hqrs & B Sec Left Authie & C Sec complete to WARLOY by route march	SBS
Authie	17/7/16	Morn.	Sick = 0 Hosp = 0 Sept = 4 Handed over camp & equipment etc CHATEAU AUTHIE to 131 F.A. Capt Ingles } at strength Capt Gibson } 8 Sisters Proceeded to F.A. to WARLOY by motor Lorry & took over Running advanced & Quietly hospital Orts quietly station & Quietly hospital 8 Sisters Lt Coulter Capt Ruttan Capt Turin Lt Jost 8 Officers, 12 men 3 RAMC orderlies 25 Stretcher bearers W. Raby F.A. } attached for duty 8+ orderly men }	SBS
WARLOY	18/7/16	Morn	Sick = 0 Hosp = 0 Employ = 4	SBS

Army Form C. 2118.

WAR DIARY
or
INTELLIGENCE SUMMARY
(Erase heading not required.)

Instructions regarding War Diaries and Intelligence Summaries are contained in F. S. Regs., Part II. and the Staff Manual respectively. Title Pages will be prepared in manuscript.

Place	Date	Hour	Summary of Events and Information	Remarks and references to Appendices
WARLOY	19/7/16	Noon	Sick = 0 Hosp = 3 Duty = "Tenby" "Clarke" to hospital. Surplus = 4 2 officers 21 OR 1/3 W.R. Z.S. had returned to duty 2 officers 21 OR 1/1 S. Mid. Regt. a.b. attached	SB
WARLOY	20/7/16	Noon	Sick = 0 Hosp = 3 Pte Chance to CCS Surplus = 3 Cpl Thornton to hospital. 1 NCO 36 Bearers to Amiens for Conv.	SB
WARLOY	21/7/16	Noon	Sick = 0 Hosp = 3 24 Bearers to BAPAUME POST. Surplus = 3 1 R.H. to M.V.Sec. one made or strong W. 1 R.H. missing to 3rd Infantry Bn.	SB
WARLOY	22/7/16	Noon	Sick = 0 Hosp = 3 Lt. Culpitt + 3 men to 3rd Infantry Bn. Surplus = 3	SB
WARLOY	23/7/16	Noon	Sick = 0 Hosp = 4 (gas) 4 O.R. gassed. Surplus = 0 3 OR wounded to CCS. Gas.ge = 0 L. Burke + servant to 1/4 Berks Regt.	SB

2449 Wt. W14957/Mg0 750,000 1/16 J.B.C. & A. Forms/C.2118/12.

Army Form C. 2118.

WAR DIARY
or
INTELLIGENCE SUMMARY
(Erase heading not required.)

Instructions regarding War Diaries and Intelligence Summaries are contained in F. S. Regs., Part II. and the Staff Manual respectively. Title Pages will be prepared in manuscript.

Place	Date	Hour	Summary of Events and Information	Remarks and references to Appendices
Warloy	24/7/16	Noon	Sick = 3 Shot = 4 Duty = 0 Surplus = 1	Sgt Kirkoff, ASC. T. on Strength.	SB
MARLOY	25/7/16	Noon	Sick = 0 Hospital = 5 Mishap = 0 Surplus = 1	Capt Cox and 23 OR returned from BAPAUME POST.	SB
Warloy	26/7/16	Noon	Sick = 1 Hospital = 5 Surplus = 1	Capt Murray + 31 OR from Arrivées X. Two Officers W.R. Gri + remainder rejoined unit.	SB
Warloy	27/7/16	Noon	Sick = 3 Shot = 8 Surplus = 1	A/Sgt Dancer Cpl Harrison A. } to hospital 26" Pte Barker A. do 26" " Cooper	SB
Warloy	28/7/16	Noon	Sick = 0 Hospital = 3 Surplus = 1	H.O.L. (Evans) ex hospl. Pte Cooper ex " Capt McRuby, devond thought 1 mule off Strength. to 3rd Field Amb.	

Army Form C. 2118.

WAR DIARY
or
INTELLIGENCE SUMMARY
(Erase heading not required.)

Instructions regarding War Diaries and Intelligence Summaries are contained in F. S. Regs., Part II. and the Staff Manual respectively. Title Pages will be prepared in manuscript.

Place	Date	Hour	Summary of Events and Information	Remarks and references to Appendices
Marley	29/4/16	noon	Officers Lieut Nelson McKewan Rej 6th Australian Field Amb. Sick = 6 Dropt = 8 Backape = 0 Surplus = 1	SB
Derly	30/4/16	noon	Sick = 5 Dropt = 3 Surplus 2 (ASC) Wastage 1 (RAMC)	FX3
Derly	31/4/16	noon	Sick = 9 Dropt = 3 Surplus = 2 (ASC) Wastage = 1 (RAMC)	SPS

Seymour Bishop
Lt. Col.
RAMC (T)

[Stamp: 2nd SOUTH MIDLAND FIELD AMBULANCE 1 JUL 1916]

2449 Wt. W14957/M90 750,000 1/16 J.B.C. & A. Forms/C.2118/12.

Army Form C. 2118.

4 8

WAR DIARY
or
INTELLIGENCE SUMMARY

(Erase heading not required.)

Appendix 1 to Vol. 10

1/2 South Midland Field Amb.

B.E.F.

WAR DIARY
or
INTELLIGENCE SUMMARY

Army Form C. 2118.

Summary of admissions & discharges
July 1 - 31 1916.

	ADMITTED			DISCHARGED		
	Sick	Wounded	C.C.S.	to duty	Died
Officers	35	105	89	24	13
O.R.	495	1456	1475	350	177
	530	1561	1564	374	190

LIEUT. COL. R.A.M.C. T.
COMMANDING 2ND FD. AMB.
48 DIV.

WAR DIARY
or
INTELLIGENCE SUMMARY

(Erase heading not required.)

Army Form C. 2118.

1/2 S.M. Fd Amb.

Vol II

Place	Date	Hour	Summary of Events and Information	Remarks and references to Appendices

Aug. 1916. Confidential

1/2 South Midland Field Ambulance.
B.E.F.

1 Aug. 1916 – 31 Aug. 1916.

Vol II

Seymour Barling
LIEUT. COL. R.A.M.C.T.
COMMANDING, 2ND F⁹. AMB
48 DIV.

1/2nd
SOUTH MIDLAND
FIELD AMBULANCE.
No.
Date 31 AUG 1916

Vol. II
pages 6
appendix 1

WAR DIARY
or
INTELLIGENCE SUMMARY
(Erase heading not required.)

Army Form C. 2118.

Place	Date	Hour	Summary of Events and Information	Remarks and references to Appendices
WARLOY	1/6/16	Noon	Sick = 5 Hosp = 4 Surplus = (2 ASC) 10-strength = (1 RAMC)	Detached 2/Lt S.M.R. C.C.S. took over special hosp/bll at Nuoy 3 Sergeants off strength	SP3
"Darby"	2/6/16	A.m.	Sick = 10 Hosp = 4 (2 ASC) Surplus = (1 RAMC) 10-strength	13 Ambulance truck took over R.tg + intoxic unit. 4 sec left Warloy complete, by route march at 6.30 pm - reached TALMAS at 10 pm. Bivouacked	SP3
TALMAS	3/6/16	Noon	Sick = 7 Hosp = 4 Surplus = (2 ASC) 10-strength = (1 RAMC)	A/p. route march to REDERIE FARM. left 5.30 pm arrived 10 pm. Bivouacked	SP3
REDERIE FARM	4/6/16	A.m.	Sick = 5 pts. Cont to Hosp Hosp = 4 Eye Nuron " Surplus = 2 ASC 5 RAMC	E Reinforcements arrived	SP3
	5/6/16	Noon	Staff = 9 Hosp = 9 (on char) Surplus (on char)	Kit inspection Divisional Rehearsal SRTC	SP3

Army Form C. 2118.

WAR DIARY
or
INTELLIGENCE SUMMARY
(Erase heading not required.)

Instructions regarding War Diaries and Intelligence Summaries are contained in F. S. Regs., Part II. and the Staff Manual respectively. Title Pages will be prepared in manuscript.

Place	Date	Hour	Summary of Events and Information	Remarks and references to Appendices
REDERIE FARM	6/8/16	Noon	Sick = 9 Hosp. = 0 Surplus = 2 ASC 5 RAMC	2 Nursing orderlies 4 RAMC Bearers to Special Hosp. & Duty	SB3
REDERIE FARM	7/8/16	Noon	Sick = 8 Surplus = 2 ASC 3 RAMC	Route march shows. 2 Water duty men to 1/4 Roy'l Rers Pte Hardly N P.E. F. HALL	SB3 SB1
REDERIE FARM	8/8/16	Noon	Sick 9 Surplus 5		SB1
BEAUVAL	9/8/16	Noon	Sick 6 Surplus 5	By route march from REDERIE FARM Left 6.30 a.m. arrived 12.30 p.m.	SB3
RAINCHEVAL	10/8/16	Noon	Sick 14 Surplus 5	By route march from BEAUVAL Left 5.30 a.m. arrived 9.15 a.m.	SB3

WAR DIARY
or
INTELLIGENCE SUMMARY

(Erase heading not required.)

Army Form C. 2118.

Place	Date	Hour	Summary of Events and Information	Remarks and references to Appendices
RAINCHEVAL	21/8/16	Noon	Sick = 9 Surplus = 5.	In Rest.	SPS
RAINCHEVAL	22/8/16	Noon	Sick = 10 Surplus = 6 Hospital = 5	6 OR RANC — to hospital at Wartoy for duty.	SPS
VARENNES	23/8/16	Noon	Sick = 6 Surplus = 5 Hospital = 4	By motor truck C. Sec. to CLAIRFAY FARM to take over II Corps Collecting station. 37 all ranks. A.C. Sec. to VARENNES took over from 86 F.A. hut at noon. Capt Arnold MC & Service to 1/4 Royal Berks area. Capt Lt Butler on leave Capt Lt Butler's arrival returned for duty.	SPS
Varennes	24/8/16	noon	Sick = 9 Surplus = 5 Hospital = 1	2 NCO's + 36 men of horse orderlies sent to ADS under 1/Lt SPS for Leave	SPS
Varennes	25/8/16	am	Sick = 6 Surplus = 5 Hosp = 1	Revd Jackson temporarily attached will service here & between	SPS

Army Form C. 2118.

WAR DIARY
or
INTELLIGENCE SUMMARY
(Erase heading not required.)

Place	Date	Hour	Summary of Events and Information	Remarks and references to Appendices
Varennes	26/5/16	Am	Sick = 6 Surplus = 7 Hosp = 1	2 Reinforcements RAMC arrived.	JS
Varennes	7/6/16	Non	Sick = 5 Surplus = 7 Hosp = 1	1 R.H. received 2 Others attached G/1 S.M.F.A. B 1/3 S.M.F.A	JS
Varennes	16/6/16	Am	Sick = 5 Surplus = 7 Hosp = 1		JS
Varennes	19/6/16	Non	Sick = 3 Surplus = 7 Hosp = 1	Rev. Graham & servant attached " McNally & servant attached 1 Rider attached. Pte Rowlands J to 1/4 Glam Yeo for water duty.	JS
Varennes	27/6/16	Am	Sick = 4 Surplus = 6 Hosp = 2	L/S Jolly sent L/C wounded C. Younger RAMC on Straff.	JS

2449 Wt. W14957/M90 750,000 1/16 J.B.C. & A. Forms/C.2118/12.

Army Form C. 2118.

WAR DIARY
or
INTELLIGENCE SUMMARY

(Erase heading not required.)

Instructions regarding War Diaries and Intelligence Summaries are contained in F. S. Regs., Part II. and the Staff Manual respectively. Title Pages will be prepared in manuscript.

Place	Date	Hour	Summary of Events and Information	Remarks and references to Appendices
Vorenne	21/8/16	noon	Sick = 3. Hosp = 2. Sniplus = 6.	SPB
Vorenne	22/8/16	noon	Sick = 4. Hosp = 2. Sniplus = 6.	Pte Tuck attached to 1/5 Glo. Regt. Pte Davis & L.S. Evers att 1/5 Worc. Regt. from Salinge. Cpl Johns Baker	SPB
Vorenne	23/8/16	noon	Sick = 2. Hosp = 2. Sniplus = 6.	A/Cpl Mc Nulty O.R. attached 33 TMB. Cyclist Jackson C.R. moved to duty with Divn. Sig. Comp.	SPB
Vorenne	24/8/16	noon	Sick = 6. Hosp = 3. Sniplus = 5.	Pte. T. Evans to England (release from army). L/c Youngson) temporarily attached men old sched. Cyc. N. Wrigley)	SPB
Vorenne	25/8/16	noon	Sick = 3. Hosp = 2. Sniplus = 4.	1 H.D. on strength. Pte. Phelan Co 2D attached 1/4 or 1/3-ck L.I. Capt Mc Connell & Sadleir returned to duty	SPB
Vorenne	26/8/16	a.m.	Sick = 4. Hosp = 2. Sniplus = 4.	3P Bevan returned from MDS.	SPB

Army Form C. 2118.

WAR DIARY
or
INTELLIGENCE SUMMARY
(Erase heading not required.)

Instructions regarding War Diaries and Intelligence Summaries are contained in F. S. Regs., Part II. and the Staff Manual respectively. Title Pages will be prepared in manuscript.

Place	Date	Hour	Summary of Events and Information	Remarks and references to Appendices
Vanannes	27/6/16	am	Sick = 4. Hosp = 2. I.D = O. Surplus = 4.	Pte Mackay to Hosp. No 77 F.A. took over R.6 Stn. at Clairfaye ; R.H. on Staff (Cpl Dickson) ; L.D off Staff.	JB
Vanannes	28/8/16	am	Hosp = 1. Sick = 4. Surplus = 4.	Pte Gadby to C. Rec Stn. Nervus Beavy Statn taken over by No 75. F.A. Cpl McConnell to Hospital (CCS) Ambulances by road to VAUCHELLES Bivouacked.	JB
Vauchelles	29/6/16	am	Sick = 4. Hosp = 1. Surplus = 4.	Pte Schuler to Hosp. 20 OR to duty No 29 CCS. Ambulances out on ...	JB
Vauchelles	30/6/16	am	Sick = 2. Hosp = 4. Surplus = 4.	Pte Schuler at Hosp. to Details ES. to Hosp. Pte Sircck Pte Rawlings	Route march 6.30 am. Ambulances out ...	JB
Vauchelles	31/6/16	am	Sick = 2. Hosp = 2. Surplus = 4.	Ambulances out ...	JB

Army Form C. 2118.

WAR DIARY
or
INTELLIGENCE SUMMARY
(Erase heading not required.)

Appendix 1 to vol. 11. (Aug 1916)

1/2 South Midland Field Amb.

B.E.F.

Seymour Barling

LIEUT. COL. R.A.M.C.T.
COMMANDING 2ND FD. AMB.
48 DIV

1/2nd
SOUTH MIDLAND
FIELD AMBULANCE.
31 AUG

Army Form C. 2118.

WAR DIARY
or
INTELLIGENCE SUMMARY
(Erase heading not required.)

Instructions regarding War Diaries and Intelligence Summaries are contained in F. S. Regs., Part II. and the Staff Manual respectively. Title Pages will be prepared in manuscript.

Place	Date	Hour	Summary of Events and Information	Remarks and references to Appendices
			Summary of admissions & discharges ½ S mid Fd. Amb. Aug. 1916.	

ADMITTED			DISCHARGED		
	Sick	Wnd.	C.C.S.	Duty	Died	Transferred
Officers	27	72	77	—	2	27
O.R.	138	2091	1682	315	21	249
Total	165	2163	1759	315	23	276

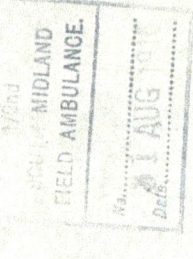
2/2nd MIDLAND
FIELD AMBULANCE.
No.........................
Date 3 AUG 1916

Seymour Barling
LIEUT. COL. R.A.M.C.T.
COMMANDING 2ND FD. AMB.
48 DIV

WAR DIARY
or
INTELLIGENCE SUMMARY

Army Form C.2118

48 Div

Confidential

1/2 South Midland Field Ambulance
B.E.F.

1 Sept 1916 – 30th Sept. 1916.

Col. 12.

[Signed] Major
R.A.M.C.T.
Commanding 2nd Fd. Amb.
48 Div

1/2nd SOUTH MIDLAND FIELD AMBULANCE
Date 0 SEP 1916

COMMITTEE FOR THE MEDICAL HISTORY OF THE WAR
Date 26 OCT. 1916

Col. 12
Page 5.
Appendix 1.

Sept. 19

WAR DIARY
or
INTELLIGENCE SUMMARY

(Erase heading not required.)

Army Form C.21?

Instructions regarding War Diaries and Intelligence Summaries are contained in F.S. Regs, Part II. and the Staff Manual respectively. Title Pages will be prepared in manuscript.

Place	Date	Hour	Summary of Events and Information	Remarks and references to Appendices
Vendelles	1/9/16	am	Sick 1 Hosp 6. MSC = 2 Ryfles RAMC = 1	Pte Jandly to CCS. Route march 6-30 AM. Pte Pully to duties	SBS
Vendelles	2/9/16	am	Sick = 8 Hosp = 6 Ryfles = 3	Lt Booth returned from leave & attached to Gen HQrs for duty until remounted. Capt Bretton & 3 remounts returned from ½ Royal Scots	SBS
Vendelles	3/9/16	pm	Sick = 1 Hosp = 6 Ryfles = 4	Pte Mandly returned from A.C.S. to duty, Pte RH & Return for Lt Busk also died.	SBS
Vendelles	4/9/16	am	Sick = 5 Hosp = 6 Ryfles = 4	Route march 6-30 AM.	SBS
Vendelles	5/9/16	pm	Sick = 2 Hosp = 3 {13 settled Ryfles = 4 {20 unsettled	Cpl Murray & Pte C Robertson CH Downs G Pridey to Pte Fully in Hosp.	SBS

2449 Wt. W14957/Mg0 750,000 1/16 J.B.C. & A. Forms/C.21:8/12.

WAR DIARY
or
INTELLIGENCE SUMMARY

Army Form C. 2118

(Erase heading not required.)

Instructions regarding War Diaries and Intelligence Summaries are contained in F.S. Regs., Part II. and the Staff Manual respectively. Title Pages will be prepared in manuscript.

Place	Date	Hour	Summary of Events and Information	Remarks and references to Appendices
Vandeleths	6/9/16	am	Sick = 1 Pte Sutton Hosp = 6 S. Price } — Hosp. Pte Brown Stragglers.—	SP3
Vandeleths	7/9/16	am	Sick = 1 Hosp = 6. Stragglers = 3.	Pte Buckhore taken sick. Remainder of unit by route march to Bois WARIEMONT at 2.30 PM 1 NCO. 10 men returned from No 29 CCS.	SP3
Bois de WARIEMONT	8/9/16	am	Sick = 4 Hosp = 6. Stragglers = 3.		SP3
Bois WARIEMONT	9/9/16	am	Sick = 2 Hosp = 6 Stragglers = 3	A/Cpl Walker F. L/Clayton W.T. } in Hosp. Cpl Cox returned from leave.	SP3
Ref.	10/9/16	am	Sick = 1 Hosp = 4 Stragglers = 3	Pte Sutton „ Dowell } to hosp „ Powell Sgt Price	SP3
Ref.	11/9/16	noon	Sick = 4 Hosp = 4 Stragglers = 3.	1 Sergt + 11 O.R. left at Bois de Warienont. Unit with 145 Fd Amb. to Beaume by Route march.	SP3

2449 Wt. W14957/M90 750,000 1/16 J.B.C. & A. Forms/C.2118/12.

Army Form C. 2118

WAR DIARY
or
INTELLIGENCE SUMMARY
(Erase heading not required.)

Instructions regarding War Diaries and Intelligence Summaries are contained in F. S. Regs., Part II. and the Staff Manual respectively. Title Pages will be prepared in manuscript.

Place	Date	Hour	Summary of Events and Information	Remarks and references to Appendices
BEAUVAL	12/9/16	a.m	Sick - 1 Hosp - 4 Duty - 3	Lt. Broderick on leave. Returned to ORS to AMIENS temporary duty.	APP 1
Beauval	13/9/16	a.m	Sick - 2 Hosp - 4 Duty - 3	Pte Clayton } on " Brown } poison " Parsons } in hosp.	APP 2
Beauval	14/9/16	a.m	Sick - 4 Hosp - 2 Duty - 3	Pte A.C.C. Pte Potter & J.Q. to hospital. Review by G.O.C. Divn.	APP 3
Beauval	15/9/16	a.m	Sick - 1 Hosp - 2 Duty - 3	C/S.M. Cox to 1st Back Rs. C/C. Mitcham to Divl. H.Qrs. details. 1 Light draught horse received	APP 4
Beauval	16/9/16	noon	Sick - 3 Duty - 2 Hosp - 2 Supply - 4	Pte Culliff returned from hospital. No strength. 4 Other ranks returned from Amiens (Baths). Lt Col Badcock to Staff for duty. Major A.A. Thompson took over command of Ambulance	App 1.

WAR DIARY
or
INTELLIGENCE SUMMARY

(Erase heading not required.)

Army Form C.2

Place	Date	Hour	Summary of Events and Information	Remarks and references to Appendices
Beauval	17/9/18	noon	Sick 4. Hospt 2. Surplus 4. Service by Capt Jackson.	AYP
Beauval	18/9/18	noon	Sick 2. Hosp 3. Surplus 3. Pte Lawley to CCS suffering fr. To hospit Pte Larner h.To. Unit left at 11 am for FIENVILLERS.	AYP
Fienvillers	19/9/18	noon	Sick ind. Hospit 11. Surplus 3. To hospit Pte Imy, Sick from Williams. Reynolds. Lahin Stevens v Potts. (due 15 England). Others hospital fr Brigade sick to beds.	AYP
Fienvillers	20/9/18	noon	Sick 1 Hosp 5 Surplus 3. To hop. Pte Hyphnon, Bott from Lahn Williams Lowle.	AYP/1.
Fienvillers	21/9/18	noon	Sick 4 Hosp 5 Surplus 3	? Cap Hugh. Pte Allen leave to England. To Hospital Pte Bentee ex Hospital " Reynolds.	AYP
Fienvillers	22/9/18	noon	Sick 4. Hosp 5 Surplus 3.	Jean to hospit In ex hospit-	AYP

Army Form C. 2118.

WAR DIARY
or
INTELLIGENCE SUMMARY
(Erase heading not required.)

Instructions regarding War Diaries and Intelligence Summaries are contained in F.S. Regs., Part II. and the Staff Manual respectively. Title Pages will be prepared in manuscript.

Place	Date	Hour	Summary of Events and Information	Remarks and references to Appendices
Feuilleres	23/9/16	noon	Sick 2 Hospl 8 Surplus 3. To hospl- Lacelly.	aayl.
Feuilleres	24/9/16	noon	Sick 2 Hospl 2 Surplus 3 Co hospl- Pte Goodyer, Brown W. Bird, Orchard, Such	aayl
Feuilleres	25/9/16	noon	Sick 6 Hospl 2 Surplus 2 Dr Whitaker to hospl-. Pte Stone to CCS off strength La Fuente, Lemacier returned from leave.	aayl.
Feuilleres	26/9/16	noon	Sick 3 Hospl 4 To hospl- Cpl Bird to hospl- Capt Audwin reports for duty. Pte Brodener returned from leave.	aayl.
Feuilleres	27/9/16	noon	Sick 2 Hospl 2 To hospl- Pte Petache, Dean. Capt Anthrom to no 11 CCS temp duty. Cpl Buck S to other ranks to no 9 CCS "	aayl.
Feuilleres	28/9/16	noon	Sick 4 Hospl 1 Surplus 2 Pte Dozaith ex hospl- "Littlewood rec'd as reinforcement. Capt Williams went on leave. & 3 other ranks to 1st Bn A Co. Provale dubr-	aayl.
Feuilleres	29/9/16	noon	Sick 4 Hospl 1 Surplus 1 Cpl Cole to Base for Munitions	aayl.
Feuilleres	30/9/16	noon	Sick 1 Surplus 1 Hospl 1 Ambulance En route march to VAUCHELLES.	aayl.

WAR DIARY
or
INTELLIGENCE SUMMARY

Army Form C. 2

1/2 2/ya Amb 48

Vol 19

Place	Date	Hour	Summary of Events and Information	Remarks and references to Appendices

Summary of admissions & discharges 1/2 South Mid. Field Amb. 16 – 30 Sept.

ADMITTED			DISCHARGED		
	Sick	I.B.	C.C.S.	Duty	Died
Officers	4	—	4	—	—
O.R.	207	—	98	99	1
Total	211	—	102	99	1

16 Oct 12.

Appendix i.

[Stamp: SOUTH MIDLAND FIELD AMBULANCE 0 SEP 1916]

a/ [signature] Major
O.C. 1/2 S.M.F.A.
Commanding 2nd Fd. Amb.
48 Div.

48th Dwight

112 J Maitland F Ambrose

40/1-188

Oct 1916

COMMITTEE FOR THE
MEDICAL HISTORY OF THE WAR
Date -2 DEC. 1916

From Officer Commanding
   1/2nd South Mid Field Amb.
To:
   ADMS
   48th Division

   Herewith please War Diary for the unit under my command, for the month of October 1916.

   A W Livingston
   Major R.A.M.C.T.
   COMMANDING 2ND FD. AMB.
   48 DIV.

1/2nd SOUTH MIDLAND FIELD AMBULANCE.
No. Fd. 366
Date 31.10.16.

Army Form C. 2118.

WAR DIARY
or
INTELLIGENCE SUMMARY

(Erase heading not required.)

Vol 20

Place	Date	Hour	Summary of Events and Information	Remarks and references to Appendices

Confidential

1/2 South Midland Fld Ambulance.
B.E.F.

1 Oct 1916 — 31 Oct 1916.

Oct. 13.

A J Murphy

Murphy R.A.M.C. T.
Commanding 2nd Fd. Amb.
48 Div.

Vol 13
Pages 6 —
Appendices

1/2nd
SOUTH MIDLAND
FIELD AMBULANCE.
No. Ja 366
Date 31 OCT 1916

Army Form C. 2118

WAR DIARY
or
INTELLIGENCE SUMMARY
(Erase heading not required.)

Instructions regarding War Diaries and Intelligence Summaries are contained in F.S. Regs., Part II. and the Staff Manual respectively. Title Pages will be prepared in manuscript.

Place	Date	Hour	Summary of Events and Information	Remarks and references to Appendices
Vauchelles	Oct 1 – 1/10/16	noon	Sick 0. Hosp 1. Suph[os] 1.	Left Vauchelles & route march to D 26 Central.	A/y 1.
D 26 Cent Hosp	2/10/16	noon	Sick 3. Hosp 4. Suphos 1.	Lt Richards Pte Logged W.C. Benn to hospital. 12 O.R. returned from detached duty at Warloy. Capt Murray & 26 O.R. went to A.D. Helsetenes Park.	A/y 1.
D 26.C.	3/10/16	noon	Sick 0. Hosp 5. Suphos 1.	Capt Anderson & Capt Lang returned from ho. 11 & 29 CCS. 27 O.R. returned from detached duty at 29 CCS. Pte Hands on leave. Lt Ridley to Hospital.	A/y 1.
D 26.C.	4/10/16	noon	Sick 3. Hosp 7. Suphos 1.	Pte Moorch Terry. Boucher J. Dr Howell to hospital.	A/y 1
D 26.C.	5/10/16	noon	Sick 1. Hosp 8. Suphos 1.	Dr Cullen to hospital. Dr Jackson have returned from duty with 1st Battn. Pte Jolle & Roberts to water duty = 241 R.F.A.	A/y 1.
D 26.C.	6/10/16	noon	Sick 2. Hosp 8. Deficient 1.	Pte Smith RC to hospital. Lt Benn to hospital. Cpl Morris on leave.	A/y 1.
D 26.C.	7/10/16	noon	Sick 2. Hosp 8. Deficient 1.	Pte Terry ex hospital. Cpl Davis to school of cooking for 14 days.	A/y 1.

WAR DIARY
or
INTELLIGENCE SUMMARY

(Erase heading not required.)

Army Form C. 2118.

Instructions regarding War Diaries and Intelligence Summaries are contained in F. S. Regs., Part II. and the Staff Manual respectively. Title Pages will be prepared in manuscript.

Place	Date	Hour	Summary of Events and Information	Remarks and references to Appendices
B.2.C.	8/10/16	noon	Sick 2. Pte Boucher to hospital Hosp 1 Deficient 1.	aayl.
Gaudiempré	9/10/16	am	Sick 3. Pte Team to hospital. Left by route march to Gau dieu pré. Hosp 3. Capt Richards & Capt Murray & 26 O.R. reporting Deficient 1. for Pte left & to hospital. rejoint from St Polincino.	aayl.
Gaudiempré	10/10/16	noon	Sick 1. L/C Cartright. Pte Ivy to Hospital. Hospital 6. Pte Shoreer to hospital. Deficient 1. Lieu Gen Irwin. Col Gray A.M.P. visits ambulance.	aayl.
Gaudiempré	11/10/16	noon	Sick 3. Hospital 6. Deficient —	aayl.
Gaudiempré	12/10/16	noon	Sick 1. 3 O.R. received as reinforcements. Hospital 6. 1 Hears do have off strength. Surplus 2	aayl.
Gaudiempré	13/10/16	noon	Sick 1. Pte Wood, Smith R.E. D' Crley to hospital. Hospital 9. Col Gray A.M.D. gave lecture to Officers. Surplus 2.	aayl.

WAR DIARY
or
INTELLIGENCE SUMMARY

(Erase heading not required.)

Army Form C. 2118.

Place	Date	Hour	Summary of Events and Information	Remarks and references to Appendices
Gaudiempre	14/10/16	noon	Sick 3 Capt Wilkinson returned from leave to England. Hospital 3. Pte Eastwood to 2H (Bar for wrist club) off strength. Surplus 1. Capt A.S. McConnell attached to strength. Capt Roch (Warwicks) have attached. 5 NCOs received from Reinforcements.	Appx 1.
Gaudiempre	15/10/16	noon	Sick 5. 1 Cpl Cashington Pte Jenny to hospital. Lewis & Rowland Roath. Hospital 1. Col Gray Adm. gave lecture to officers on highest wounds. Surplus 1.	Appx 1.
Gaudiempre	16/10/16	noon	Sick 1. Pte Ivy to hospital. Hospital 1. Pte Loomi O.E. to hospital. Surplus 1. Capt Bailey Butler Off strength leaving returns to England.	Appx 1.
Gaudiempre	17/10/16	noon	Sick 2. Pte Davis J. to hospital. Hospital 2. Capt Wilkinson to 38 C.C.S. a/off strength. Surplus 1.	Appx 1.
Gaudiempre	18/10/16	noon	Sick 0. Pte Inns H. to hospital. Corp Thomas returned from leave. Hospital 3. 3 O.R. reinforcements. Establishment of officers + tobacco Surplus 4. to 8. M.O & Q.M.	Appx 1.
Gaudiempre	19/10/16	noon	Sick 5. Capt Coo on leave. Hospital 3. Corp Davis returned from school of cooking. Surplus 4.	Appx 1.

WAR DIARY
or
INTELLIGENCE SUMMARY

(Erase heading not required.)

Army Form C. 2118.

Instructions regarding War Diaries and Intelligence Summaries are contained in F. S. Regs., Part II and the Staff Manual respectively. Title Pages will be prepared in manuscript.

Place	Date	Hour	Summary of Events and Information	Remarks and references to Appendices
Gaudiempré	20/10/15	noon	5 at Strpt 1st Suptn 3. B. Wheeler to hospital.	Appx
Gaudiempré	21/10/15	noon	Sick 1. Strpt 0. Suptn 3. B. Wheeler. Pte Wood. Davis to hospital. Pte Ind to CCS. Lt Ellis attached for duty. Unit moved to the other side of the village on being relieved by 3rd West Riding Division. Capt Maud Roch on leave to England.	Appx
Gaudiempré	22/10/15	noon	Sick 5. Strpt 0. Suptn 3. Unit moved by route march to Beauval via Luchuse o Bouteux arrived at 3 pm. (16 mile march)	Appx
Beauval	23/10/15	9 pm	Sick 16. Strpt 0. Suptn 3. Unit marched to Lahuss arriving at 5.30.	Appx
Lahuso	24/10/16	9 pm	Sick 7. Strpt 0. Suptn 3. Unit marched to Behencourt arriving at 12 pm.	Appx
Behencourt	25/10/15	9 pm	Sick 12. L/Cpl Rowe to hospital. Strpt 1. Unit marched to Franvillers. arrived at 11.30. Suptn 3. B.O. Tent Subdivision to no 16 Bottom Wood in 2nd half union 3rd Amb. front at Fricourt.	Appx

WAR DIARY
or
INTELLIGENCE SUMMARY

(Erase heading not required.)

Army Form C. 2118.

Place	Date	Hour	Summary of Events and Information	Remarks and references to Appendices
Granvillers	26/10/18	9 pm	Sick 3. Hospital 4. Surplus 4. Pte Bain J Crawford invalided home to hospital. Pte Stone returned from CCS on strength. Capt Anderson 472 OR to No 11 CCS to temp duty. Capt Longe Lt Edw. Skytime to Boulogne board to temp duty. Capt Buchanan & O Beaver scoton to 27 J Amb to take over at Boisieux.	asgd.
Granvillers	27/10/18	9 pm	Sick 0. Hospital 4. Surplus 4.	asgd.
Granvillers	28/10/18	9 pm	Sick 3. Hospital 1. Surplus 3. Pte Crawford invalided to Le Havre to hospital. Dr Wheeler to CCS off strength.	asgd.
Granvillers	29/10/18	9 pm	Sick 1. Hospital 1. Surplus 3.	asgd.
Granvillers	30/10/18	9 pm	Sick 4. Hospital 2. Surplus 4. Expected to hospital. Capt McConnell returned from sick leave on strength.	asgd.
Granvillers	31/10/18	9 pm	Sick 0. Hospital 3. Surplus 3. Pte Williams Geo. to hospital.	asgd.

Army Form C. 2118.

WAR DIARY
or
INTELLIGENCE SUMMARY
(Erase heading not required.)

Appendix 1

Summary of admissions & discharges 1/2 South Midland 16 Ambulance.
1 – 31 Oct. 16.

	ADMITTED			DISCHARGED			
	SICK	WDD	C.C.S	C.R.S & DRS	DUTY	DIED	TRANSFERRED
OFFICERS	23	2	10	2	9	–	4
O.RANKS	719	74	191	137	239	4	215
TOTAL	742	76	201	139	248	4	219

Watlington
Major
COMMANDING 2/1 F.A. AMB.
48 DIV.

WAR DIARY
or
INTELLIGENCE SUMMARY

Army Form C. 2118

Confidential

48 Div

1/2 South Midland Fd Ambulance
B.E.F.
1 hrs 1916 — 30 hrs 1916.
Vol II.

Vol II
pages 6.
Appendix 1.

1/2nd SOUTH MIDLAND FIELD AMBULANCE
No. Fd. Amb
Date 30 NOV 1916

COMMITTEE FOR THE
MEDICAL HISTORY OF THE WAR
Date 3 JAN 1917

Vol 2 1

R.A.M.C. 1
COMMANDING 2ND FD. AMB.
48 DIV

Place	Date	Hour	Summary of Events and Information	Remarks and references to Appendices

Army Form C.2...

WAR DIARY
or
INTELLIGENCE SUMMARY
(Erase heading not required.)

Instructions regarding War Diaries and Intelligence Summaries are contained in F.S. Regs., Part II and the Staff Manual respectively. Title Pages will be prepared in manuscript.

Place	Date	Hour	Summary of Events and Information	Remarks and references to Appendices
Franvillers	1/11/16	9 pm	I.C.R. 1, Hospital 4, Surplus 2. Corp bio to Base and off strength. Capt Buchanan - 32 of C Section returned from Barocourt. Capt Edw to 1/3 Fd Amb. off strength. Capt re-enlisted to No 2 h.S.	aayl.
Franvillers	2/11/16	9 pm	I.C.R. 0, Hospital 4, Surplus 3. Pte Goodeye + received as Reinfts from 9th Fd Amb.	aayl
Franvillers	3/11/16	9 am	Sick 3, Hospital 3, Surplus 3. Flat Nulis. to hospital. 86 O.R. went to Contalmaison for temp duty with 1/3 Fd Amb. Capt CoO o Capt Maude Roely. returned from leave.	aayl.
Franvillers	4/11/16	9 pm	I.C.R. 2, Hospital 4, Surplus 3.	anyl.
Franvillers	5/11/16	9 pm	I.e.h. 1, Hospital-2, Surplus 3. Pte Brick to hospital. Pte Davis to. Corps R.F.	aayl.
Franvillers	6/11/16	9 pm	Sick 1, Hospital-3, Surplus 3. Capt Coe to Martinpuich for duty. Pte Glendon to hospital. Capt Roch to 1/2 Fd Amb. off strength. Servant o 2 horses.	aayl.

2449 Wt. W14957/M90 750,000 1/16 J.B.C. & A. Forms/C.2118/12.

WAR DIARY
or
INTELLIGENCE SUMMARY

Army Form C. 2118.

Place	Date	Hour	Summary of Events and Information	Remarks and references to Appendices
Franvillers	7/11/16	9 pm	Sick 0 Hospit- 3. Surplus 3.	asgh.
Franvillers	8/11/16	9 am	Sick 1 Hospit 1 Surplus 2	Pte Gladwin sent to hospital. Pte Brown to 6 Stationary Hospital for duty off strength. Dr Cross on leave. Corporal Le Turier to base off Strength. 3 Ambulances 12 Horses 3 Surveys 3 troops whilst to 4" 9in Hospit.	asgh.
Franvillers	9/11/16	9 pm	Sick 2 Hospit 0 Surplus 2.	L/Cpl Cartwright to hospital.	asgh.
Franvillers	10/11/16	9 pm	Sick 2 Hospit 0 Surplus 1.	Pte Sharpe to CCS (wounded) off Strength. Pte Huin returned from CRE.	asgh.
Franvillers	11/11/16	9 am	Sick 1 Hospit 1 Surplus 1.	Dr Davis to hospital. 2 light draught horses received.	asgh.
Franvillers	12/11/16	9 pm	Sick 0 Hospit 1 Surplus 1.		asgh.

WAR DIARY
or
INTELLIGENCE SUMMARY

(Erase heading not required.)

Army Form C. 2118

Instructions regarding War Diaries and Intelligence Summaries are contained in F.S. Regs., Part II. and the Staff Manual respectively. Title Pages will be prepared in manuscript.

Place	Date	Hour	Summary of Events and Information	Remarks and references to Appendices
Louvilliers	13/11/18	9 pm	Sick O. Hopital Surplus O. Pte Witham H. to CCS. Sick off strength.	A.A.F.
Louvilliers	14/11/18	9 pm	Sick R.O. Hopital Surplus O. Dr Davis 1 to hospital	A.A.F.
Louvilliers	15/11/18	9 am	Sick O. Hopital O. Wastage 4 Rank. Surplus 1 A.S.C.	L Cpl Lewis H. died from wounds. L Cpl Beddoe & Pte Wounded to CCS. 11 strength.	A.A.F.
Louvilliers	16/11/18	9 pm	Sick 1. Hopital o. Wastage 4 Rank. Surplus 1 A.S.C.		A.A.F.
Louvilliers	17/11/18	9 pm	Sick 2. Hopital o. Wastage 3 Rank. Surplus 1 A.S.C.	Pte Matthews rejoined from detached duty and taken on strength.	A.A.F.
Louvilliers	18/11/18	1 pm	Sick 4. Hopital 2. Wastage 3 Rank. Surplus 1 A.S.C.		A.A.F.

WAR DIARY
or
INTELLIGENCE SUMMARY

Army Form C. 2118

(Erase heading not required.)

Instructions regarding War Diaries and Intelligence Summaries are contained in F. S. Regs., Part II. and the Staff Manual respectively. Title Pages will be prepared in manuscript.

Place	Date	Hour	Summary of Events and Information	Remarks and references to Appendices
Franvillers	19/1/16	6 pm	Sec R 2 Staph 0 Woolage 3 Rawe Septhus 1 ASC	Pte Shaw G. Staffers Cldr. Colley on leave	aayl.
Franvillers	20/1/16	9 am	Sec R 2 Staph 0 Capt Coe o 3 O R returned from attached duty at Martin pinch Capt Murran o 1 P O R returned from attached duty at No 2 man Woolage 3 Rawe during Dr Batesman leave Septhus 1 ASC 2 O R went to ADS Martin puich 1 O R went to Bri Schort at Istpalica	aayl.
Franvillers	21/1/16	9 am	Sec R 2. Dr Batesman to hospital. Staph 1 Woolage 3 Rawe Septhus 1. ASC.	aayl.
Franvillers	22/1/16	9 am	Sec R 3 Staph 1. Woolage 3 Rawe Septhus 1 ASC. Conference at Adm Sir Officer.	aayl
Franvillers	23/1/16	9 pm	Sec R 2. Staph 1. Woolage 4 Rawe Septhus 1 ASC. 1 P O R went to N 3 Hosp tr attached duty at Becourt Pte Whitelier to no 2 main dressing station Pte Ireson Iw. returned from ho 2 main dressing a ward 241 R R.A.O. with Rhumpta	aayl.

2449 Wt. W14957/M90 750,000 1/16 J.B.C. & A. Forms/C.2118/12.

WAR DIARY or INTELLIGENCE SUMMARY

Army Form C.2118

Place	Date	Hour	Summary of Events and Information	Remarks and references to Appendices
Rawville	20/11/16	9 p.m.	Sick 1. Sgt Clark K to hospital. Pte Hazelton to Base sick. Wastage 1. Rank 2 OR 2/2 9 m F Amb attacked to duty. A.S.C. took over Officers rest station. Sent hospital annexe to Surplus. Civil hospital at Warloy. Capt Munn evacuated to RWR. Capt Atkinson attacked.	a.a.f.
Warloy	20/11/16	9 a.m.	Sick 9. Hospital 1. Pte Taylor to base sick. Capt Newman to hospital Le Tourne. 73 Hospital 1 & 8 Officers Surplus 1. A.S.C. proceed at 15 for Travillers to Warloy	a.a.f.
Warloy	26/11/16	9 a.m.	Sick 1. Hospital 3. Pte Foley, Cartwright, R to Base sick. Wastage 8. Hughes 1 Agt. Pte Evans L Cpl Cope to hospital.	a.a.f.
Warloy	28/11/16	9 a.m.	Sick 1. Pte Epsom to Base sick. Hospital 3. 9 OR returned from detached duty. Wastage 8. 8 OR returned from detached duty at 1/1 9m FCS	a.a.f.
Warloy	28/11/16	9 p.m.	Sick O. JC Ince. Pte Valentine, Thomas. Clifton proceed Hosp. Hospital 9. Wastage 9. Rank. Surplus 1. A.C.C.	a.a.f.
Warloy	29/11/16	9 a.m.	Sick 2. Hospital 9. Wastage 9. R.A.M.C. Surplus 1. A.C.C.	a.a.f.

WAR DIARY
or
INTELLIGENCE SUMMARY

(Erase heading not required.)

Army Form C. 2118

Instructions regarding War Diaries and Intelligence Summaries are contained in F. S. Regs., Part II. and the Staff Manual respectively. Title Pages will be prepared in manuscript.

Place	Date	Hour	Summary of Events and Information	Remarks and references to Appendices
Varley	30/1/16	9 pm	1 CR 2 1 Cpl Cook sic hospital Strophic P. Boatage 9. Strength 1,800.	asyl.

WAR DIARY or INTELLIGENCE SUMMARY

Army Form C. 2118.

Summary of admissions & discharges 1/2 South Midland Field Amb.
Nov 1 – 30.

	ADMITTED			DISCHARGED		
	SICK	WOUNDED	CCS	DUTY	DIED	TRANSFERRED
OFFICERS	11	1	4	5	–	–
O. RANKS	190	–	32	127	–	19
TOTALS	201	1	36	132	–	19

Aylmer
Major R.A.M.C.T.
Commanding 2nd Fd. Amb.
48 Div

1/2nd SOUTH MIDLAND FIELD AMBULANCE.

140/1900.

1/2nd L.M. Field Ambulance

43rd Div.

Dec 1916

COMMITTEE FOR THE
MEDICAL HISTORY OF THE WAR
Date 31 JAN. 1917

Army Form C. 2118.

WAR DIARY
or
INTELLIGENCE SUMMARY

(Erase heading not required.)

Instructions regarding War Diaries and Intelligence Summaries are contained in F. S. Regs., Part II. and the Staff Manual respectively. Title Pages will be prepared in manuscript.

Vol 22

Confidential

1/2 South Midland Field Ambulance
B.E.F.

Vol 45.

1 Dec — 31st Dec
1916.

Vol 15
Pages 5
Appendix 1.

Place	Date	Hour	Summary of Events and Information	Remarks and references to Appendices

Army Form C. 2118.

WAR DIARY
or
INTELLIGENCE SUMMARY

(Erase heading not required.)

Instructions regarding War Diaries and Intelligence Summaries are contained in F. S. Regs., Part II. and the Staff Manual respectively. Title Pages will be prepared in manuscript.

Place	Date	Hour	Summary of Events and Information	Remarks and references to Appendices
Warloy	1/12/16	9 pm	Sick: Pte Gunter to hospt. Depot 4 left men. Pte Thomas Goddard from Clyphi to hospt. Wastage 11. Capt Anderson to base sick, off strength. Sick ASC 1 reinforcement on strength. 3 hCOs 20 OR. Pte Griffiths received on strength. 9o SM W Amb attached rejoined their unit.	a wyl
Warloy	2/12/16	9 pm	Sick 2. Hospt 3. Wastage 11. 2 Cpl Tolentive to hospt. Pte hom Conj retn. Call no. Smith RC. on leave.	h wyl
Warloy	3/12/16	9 pm	Sick 2. Hospt 3. Wastage 12. Pte Sullvn When sick off strength. G JC + 1	a wyl
Warloy	4/12/16	9 pm	Sick 2. Hospt 3. Wastage 12.	a wyl
Warloy	5/12/16	9 pm	Sick 1. Dr Gunter ex hospt. Hospt - 2. 1 Officer + 22 OR returned from detached duty at Wastage 12. B Wm hosp. 3 OR returned from leave	b wyl
Warloy	6/12/16	9 pm	Sick 2. Hospt - 2. Wastage 12. W.O. + 1	a wyl

WAR DIARY
INTELLIGENCE SUMMARY
(Erase heading not required.)

Army Form C.

Place	Date	Hour	Summary of Events and Information	Remarks and references to Appendices
Wanly	7/12/16	9pm	Sec 3. Sgt Clark R to hospital. Hospital 6. Pte Bell, Thicar, Hipkins returned from detaches duty admitted hospital. Wastage 12.	acyl.
Wanly	8/12/16	9pm	Sec R1. Pte Griffiths to W.O. Bates jun to W.D. C/M Shinglia hospital. Pte Carlong u-R returnes as reinforcement. Wastage 12. Q.S.C. +1.	acyl.
Wanly	9/12/16	9pm	Sec 1. Capt Buchanan on leave to Scotland = 40 R. Hospital 6. Pte Martin to leave. O.R. Wastage 13. Q.S.C. +1.	acyl.
Wanly	10/12/16	9pm	Sec R.2. Pte Mercer to hospital. Pte Gellyman to hospital. Hospital 6. Wastage 13.	acyl.
Wanly	11/12/16	9pm	Sec R1. Pte Hipkins to hospital. Pte Harpin & Scott to hospital. Hospital 8. Sgt Clark. Wastage 13.	acyl.
Wanly	12/12/16	9pm	Sec R 3. Pte Baker C.C. hospital. Hospital 8. Sgt Rutherford, Morris, Pte Rawlings to hospital. Wastage 13. Capt Lang to hospital.	acyl.
Wanly	13/12/16	9pm	Sec R 3. Dr Jacobs to hospital. Hospital 9. Cpl Rogers on leave. Wastage 13.	acyl.
Wanly	14/12/16	9pm	Sec R 3. Pte Brown A.B. received as new Piercement. Hospital 11. St George, Gibson to hospital. Wastage	acyl.

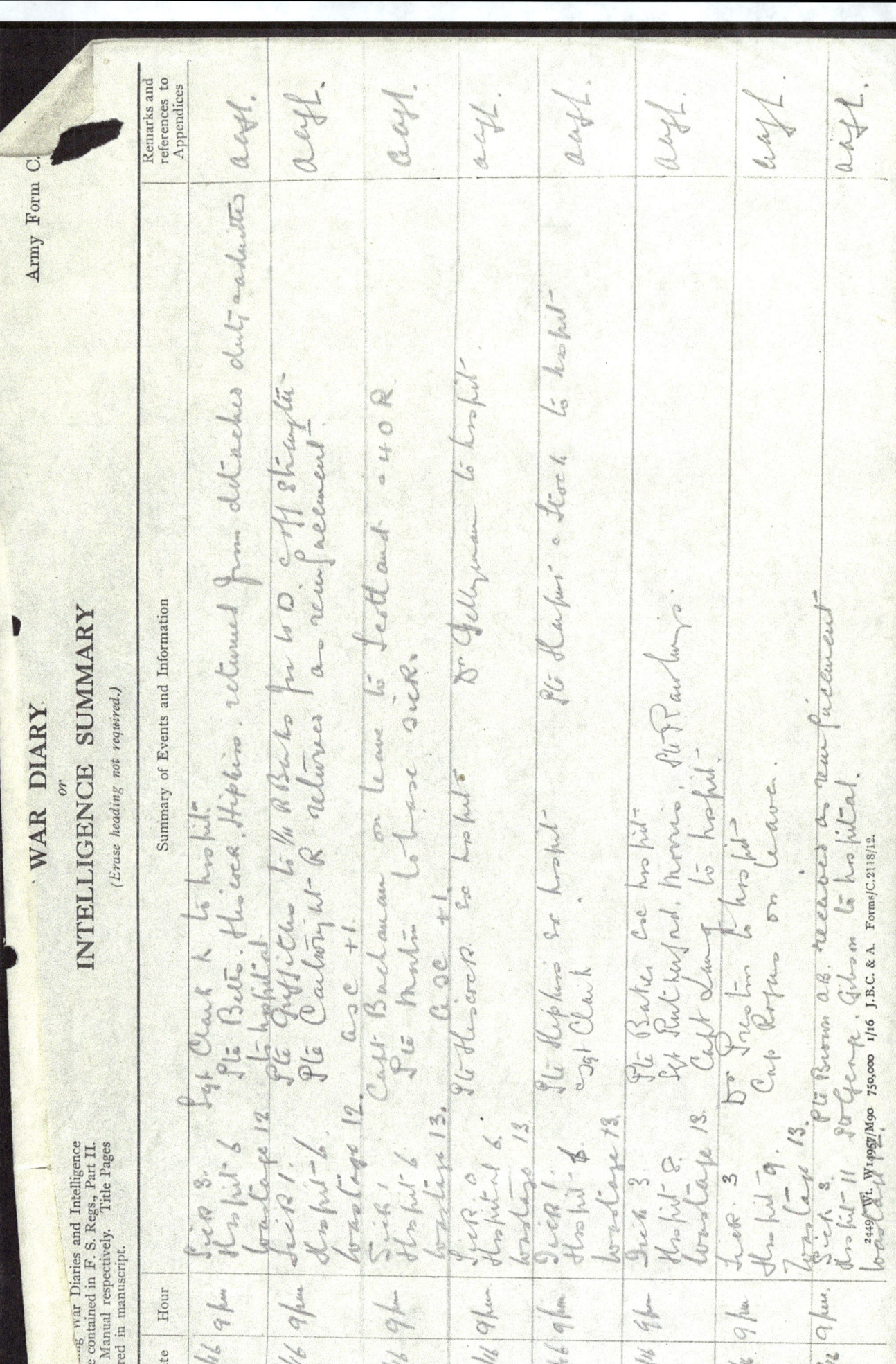

WAR DIARY or INTELLIGENCE SUMMARY

Army Form C. 2118

(Erase heading not required.)

Place	Date	Hour	Summary of Events and Information	Remarks and references to Appendices
Warley	15/12/15	9 pm	Sick. Pte Shirguison to hospital #12. Wastage 12.	acyl.
Warley	16/12/15	9 pm	Sick. Pte Tillyman to hospital. Capt Bortwick to hospital. Capt Bortwick McConnell & 8 G o R returned from detached duty at Harwich punch. Hospital 12. Pte Lord Donnelly, Edmondson to Base D.R. Lt Laing to hospital. Wastage 12.	acyl.
Warley	17/12/15	9 pm	Sick 2. Pte Edmondson to hospital. Cpl Kineon rejoins 8 G o R. Hospital 20. Lt Ashby attached on strength. Capt Trueman & Servant rejoined. Cap Bodman, Busby Balmore. Dr Curro to hospital. Capt M Gunnell. Wastage M. Corp Stevenson, Pte Stevenson B'n on leave.	acyl.
Warley	18/12/15	9 am	Sick 4. Pte George to hospital. Hospital 19. Pte Allen to W.O. to 2nd Bn. R.F.A. Wastage 12.	acyl.
Warley	19/12/15	9 am	Sick 4. Pte Ranking, Brook, Bracker to hospital. Hospital 16. Pte Church from 11 Sm Fd Amb on strength. Pte Bonnelly to base sick. Pte hitched to Sch School of Cookery. Took over Civil Hospital Wastage N. and billets temporarily.	acyl.
Warley	20/12/15	9 pm	Sick 6. Pte Betts, Pte Reid to hospital. Hospital #13. Wastage 12.	acyl.
Warley	21/12/15	9 pm	S.of S. Sgt Rutherford to hospital. Pte Cunning to hospital. Hospital 12.	acyl.

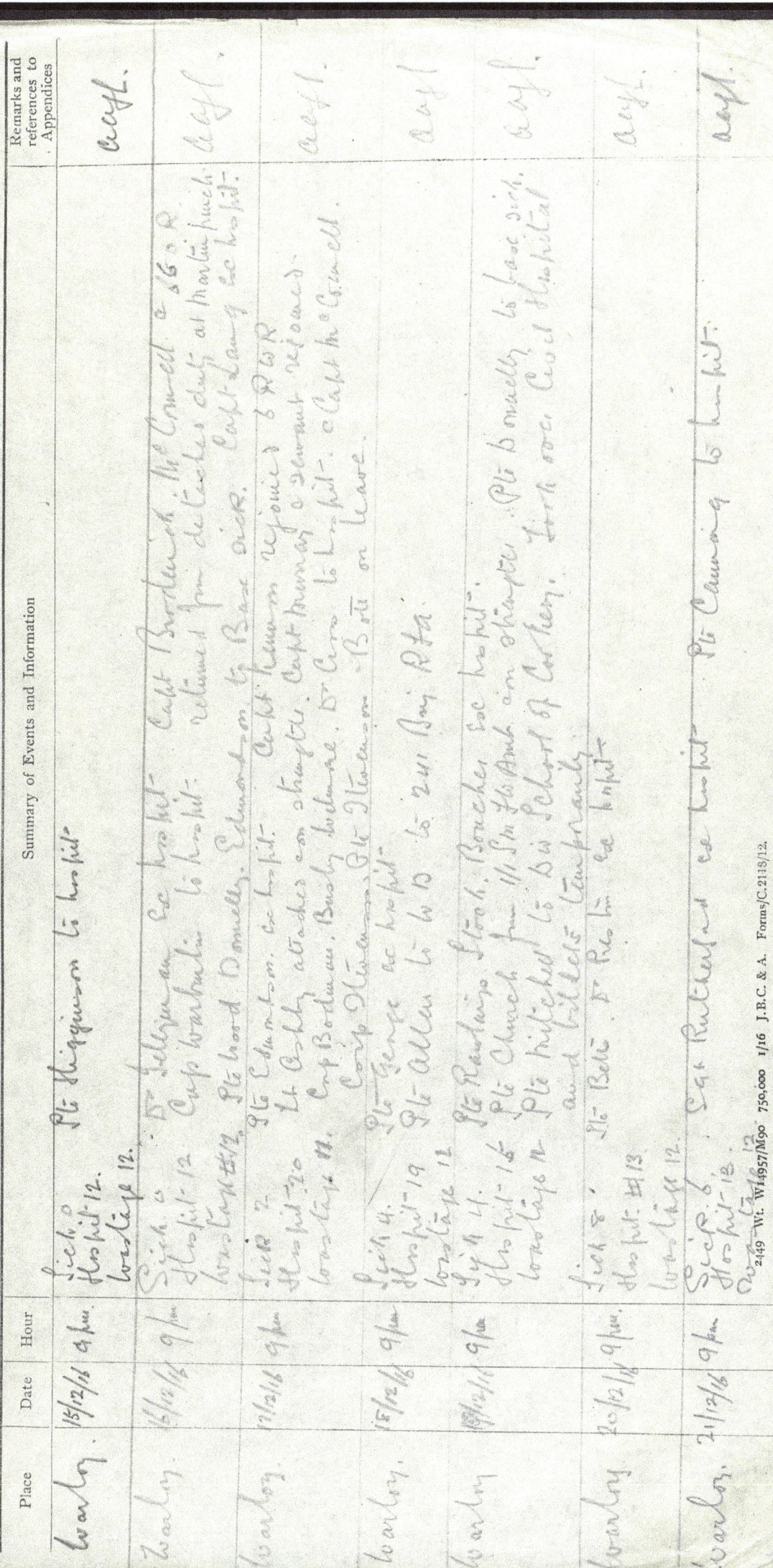

WAR DIARY or INTELLIGENCE SUMMARY

Army Form C. 2118

(Erase heading not required.)

Instructions regarding War Diaries and Intelligence Summaries are contained in F.S. Regs., Part II. and the Staff Manual respectively. Title Pages will be prepared in manuscript.

Place	Date	Hour	Summary of Events and Information	Remarks and references to Appendices
Warloy	22/12/16	9 pm	Sick 5. Pte Edmundson to hospital. Cpl Bowman, Capt Barker, Osborn exc hospital. Corpl Morrison to Bn Depot. Lt Pte Dawson on leave. Wastage 12.11. Pte Standly received as new recruit.	asf.
Warloy	23/12/16	9 am	Sick 3. Pte Hargan to lab & 24th Bn R.T.A. to replace Pte Jeans. Hospital 14. Sgt Aris exc hospital. Wastage 11. Pte Beardsley, Mayhew, Deakin, Osborn to hospital.	asf.
Warloy	24/12/16	9 pm	Sick 2. Capt McClary to 8 lines for duty. Sgt Stumpter. Hospital 14. Pte Jeans returned from lvs. Wastage # 11	asf.
Warloy Recreation	25/12/16	9 pm	Sick 0. GC Jones to hospital. Hospital 15. Wastage # 11	asf.
Warloy	26/12/16	9 am	Sick 1. 40 R returns from leave. Hospital 16. Pte Moon to hospital. Wastage # 11	asf.
Warloy	27/12/16	9 am	Sick 2. Pte Mayhew, Beardsley, OT Brew exc hospital. Hospital 13. Pte Gibson to Dn Qno Depot. Wastage # 11	asf.
Warloy	28/12/16	9 am	Sick 1. Pte Mitchell, Capt Buck to hospital. Hospital 13. Pte Wilson exc hospital. Pte Standly to Base (underage). Wastage 13. Wagaman to Base (sick)	ayf.

2449 Wt. W14957/M90 750,000 1/16 J.B.C. & A. Forms/C.2118/12.

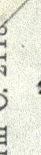

Army Form C. 2118.

WAR DIARY
or
INTELLIGENCE SUMMARY
(Erase heading not required.)

Instructions regarding War Diaries and Intelligence Summaries are contained in F. S. Regs., Part II. and the Staff Manual respectively. Title Pages will be prepared in manuscript.

Place	Date	Hour	Summary of Events and Information	Remarks and references to Appendices
Warloy	29/12/16	9 am	S/cR 4. " 7 Pte Beaken to hospital. Pte Brown, Hanbury, Harris, Collins, Lakin to hospital. Hospital 1st. 4 OR on leave. Corp Rogers returns from leave. Wastage 13. Cpl Harrison returns from Div Gas School.	Regt.
Warloy	30/12/16	9 am	S/cR 5. Cpl Hartabin, Pte Mitchell to hospital. Hospital 15/14. Pte Sutton returns from Base hospital on sthought. Wastage 13. Pte Sadly awarded 28 days Field punishment No 1.	Regt.
Warloy	31/12/16	9 am	S/cR 2. Pte Joy Boucher, Mitchell to hospital. Hospital 17. 4 On Bought. 3 OR on leave. Wastage 13.	Regt.

Army Form C. 2118.

WAR DIARY
or
INTELLIGENCE SUMMARY
(Erase heading not required.)

Summary of admissions & discharges
1/2 South Midland Fd Amb. R87
1 Dec — 31 Dec 1916.

	ADMITTED		DISCHARGED			
	SICK	WOUNDED	C.C.S	DUTY	DIED	TRANSFERRED
OFFICERS	38	1	11	24	—	—
O.RANKS	549	—	198	280	1	12
	587	1	209	304	1	12

Appendices:
Col 165.   31/12/16

Appendix:
R.A.M.C.
Commanding 2nd Fd Amb

46

'40/104-1

48th Div.

1/2nd S.M. Field Ambulance.

Ja. 1917

COMMITTEE FOR THE
MEDICAL HISTORY OF THE WAR
Date 13 MAR. 1917

Army Form C. 2118.

WAR DIARY
or
INTELLIGENCE SUMMARY

(Erase heading not required.)

Vol 23

Place	Date	Hour	Summary of Events and Information	Remarks and references to Appendices

Confidential.

1/2 South Midland Field Ambulance
B.E.F.

Vol 16.

1 Jan 1917 — 31 Jan 1917.

Waynforth
Lt. Col.
LIEUT. COL. R.A.M.C. T.
COMMANDING 2ND FD. AMB.
48 DIV.

Vol 16.
Pages 6.
Appendix 1.

Army Form C. 2118.

WAR DIARY
or
INTELLIGENCE SUMMARY

(Erase heading not required.)

Summary of Events and Information

Summary divisions discharges
1/2 bowels kidland Fils Ambulance
Jan 1917.

	ADMITTED		DISCHARGED.			
	SICK	WOUNDED	C.C.S.	DUTY	DIED	TRANSFERRED
OFFICERS.	18	—	8	12	—	5
O. RANKS.	420	—	250	203	—	56
	438	—	258	215	—	61

A J W go hn
LIEUT.COL. R.A.M.C. T.
COMMANDING 2ND FD. AMB.
48 DIV.

WAR DIARY
or
INTELLIGENCE SUMMARY

(Erase heading not required.)

Army Form C. 2118.

Place	Date	Hour	Summary of Events and Information	Remarks and references to Appendices
Warloy	1/1/17	9 pm	Sick 3. Pte Wilmore 144th Machine Co. to hospl. 1 O R on leave. Strength 17. Casualties 14.	a/eft.
Warloy	2/1/17	9 pm	Sick 2. B/Sgn'n to hospl. Walford to hospl. Hospl 17. Pte Boucher 1. to Base Sick. L/Cpl Rau to Dn Gas School for instruction. Casualties 13.	a/eft.
Warloy	3/1/17	9 pm	Sick 3. Pte Dale to hospl. Hospl 15. Casualties 15.	a/eft.
Warloy	4/1/17	9 pm	Sick 4. Pte La tur, Bush, Co to hospl. Hospl 17. Pte Gordge 1 to hospl. Casualties 15.	a/eft.
Warloy	5/1/17	9 pm	Sick 4. Pte Cumming, Collins Co hospl. Cpl Stevenson Pte B&T Pte Stevenson a Capt Buchanan returns from leave. Pte Moore to CCS. Died. Pte Hamlin to hospl.	a/eft.
Warloy	6/1/17	9 pm	Sick 4. Pte Cumming, Yapp, Beadslin to hospl. Hospl 15. Pte Evans, Edmonston, Cum Co. ho hpl. Casualties 16. Handed over Annex to 47 Bn Ply Pmt.	a/eft.

WAR DIARY
or
INTELLIGENCE SUMMARY
(Erase heading not required.)

Army Form

Instructions regarding War Diaries and Intelligence Summaries are contained in F.S. Regs., Part II. and the Staff Manual respectively. Title Pages will be prepared in manuscript.

Place	Date	Hour	Summary of Events and Information	Remarks and references to Appendices
Wardrop	7/1/17	9 pm	Strath. Sgr 4 Potratz, Sgr Inos. Goodyer J. Cpl Birch to hospital. Hospit. 12 Pte Brazia. Wda to hospital. Wastage 16. 1 Cpl Bell returned from Open School. Capt Buchanan "B" OR advance party to Mallen court. 4 OR on leave.	ayl
Wardrop	8/1/17	9 pm	Sick 4. Pte hurn returned from CCS taken on strength Hospit. 11 C Section Transport with Lord RAMC moved with 145 Bgd Transport Wastage 16. to Western Training Area	RMcB
Wardrop	9/1/17	9 pm	Sick 4 C Section depart by train for Western Training Area Hosp. 9 Lt. Col. Hingston on leave Wastage 15. Ptes Morris J. S. + Mitchell E. ex Hospital.	RMcB
Wardrop	10/1/17	9 pm	Sick 6 Staff Sgt. Mercer returned from leave Hosp. 9 Wastage 15.	RMcB
Wardrop	11/1/17	9 pm	Sick 3. 1 Reinforcement received. Hosp. 12. Wastage 15.	RMcB

Army Form C. 2118.

WAR DIARY
or
INTELLIGENCE SUMMARY

(Erase heading not required.)

Instructions regarding War Diaries and Intelligence Summaries are contained in F. S. Regs., Part II. and the Staff Manual respectively. Title Pages will be prepared in manuscript.

Place	Date	Hour	Summary of Events and Information	Remarks and references to Appendices
Wanley	12/1/17	9pm	Sick 2 Hosp. 7 Wastage 14. Pte Hawley to C.C.S. S/Sgt Dames, Sgt Mathy to C.C.S. Pte Cannigo Wastage Dublin et habit.	RWB
Wanley	13/1/17	9pm	Sick 3 Hosp. 2 Wastage 17. All patients evacuated to C.C.S. N&B, by order of D.D.M.S. Pte Hamlin Pneumonia to hosp. Pte's Mayberry, Yapp, Beardsley, Baker, Sgt Rutterford. No 3 Ambulance sta. Amb. arrived to take over S.A. site I Section stationery equipment. Pte Butler, Allen S.M. detached from C. Section to Cpl Washington. Dis' Baths at Hallencourt	RWB
Wanley	14/1/17	9pm	Sick 4 Hosp 3 Wastage 17. Pte Elliott admitted Hosp. M. Transport mounted personnel depart by road for Area 5. Dismounted personnel entrained at Hallencourt for Area 5.	RWB
Fricourt	15/1/17	9pm	Sick 2 Hosp 5 Wastage 17. Pte's Moon & Yapp admitted hosp. Dr Brown, Dr David, Sto. Gondai, Church, Chatterton Stamfra on leave Sections A&B with Transport arrived at Area 5	RWB
Fricourt	16/1/17	9pm	Sick 6 Hosp 5 Wastage 19. Capt Kiell to England by order of D.D.M.S. Cpl Tryanski Div' School for Instruction. Lt. Bright returned from leave	RWB

Army Form C. 2118.

WAR DIARY
or
INTELLIGENCE SUMMARY
(Erase heading not required.)

Instructions regarding War Diaries and Intelligence Summaries are contained in F. S. Regs., Part II. and the Staff Manual respectively. Title Pages will be prepared in manuscript.

Place	Date	Hour	Summary of Events and Information	Remarks and references to Appendices
Fricourt	17/1/17	9pm	Sect 10 Hop 6 boxtage 18	Dr Joker (MCC M.7.) Dr Jackson (RMC H7) returned from leave	RMB
Fricourt	18/1/17	9pm	Sect 7 boxtage 19 Hop 2	Pte Mitchell to C.C.S. Capt Tonnall Pte Saxelby to CRS for instruction in treatment of trench feet. Pte Bowater + CRS Ptes Moon + Tapp ex hop. Pte Heawin returned from leave	RMB
Fricourt	19/1/17	9pm	Sect 6 boxtage 19 Hop 2	Sgt Humpherson admit Etaples	RMB
Fricourt	20/1/17	9pm	Sect 4 boxtage 19 Hop 3	Sgt Humpherson to C.C.S Pte Hamblin to CCS Capt Murray on leave, Sgt Clark R. Pte Spavins on leave for 1 month, Cpl Pembrton ↔ Pte Handley for leave Pte Elliot ex hop.	RMB
Fricourt	21/1/17	9pm	Sect 1 boxtage 21 Hop 1		RMB

Army Form C. 2118.

WAR DIARY
or
INTELLIGENCE SUMMARY

(Erase heading not required.)

Instructions regarding War Diaries and Intelligence Summaries are contained in F. S. Regs., Part II. and the Staff Manual respectively. Title Pages will be prepared in manuscript.

Place	Date	Hour	Summary of Events and Information	Remarks and references to Appendices
Frévent	22/1/17	9pm	Lieut Ince to England to take up Com. Mon. Lt Lieut Sewell & Pte Saxelby returned from instruction at C.R.S. Pte Elliot to Hosp. Wastage 2.	RAH
Frévent	23/1/17	9pm	Sgt Johnson att. to No 34 Squad RFC. Cpl Rogers returned from Div. School. Wastage 2. Hosp 1	RAH
Frévent	24/1/17	9pm	Pte Slim Arthur sent to Base for rheumatism. Pte Kilcot to Base Hosp. Pte Griffin returned from leave. Sept 4 Hosp - 1 Wastage 24	RAH
Frévent	25/1/17	9pm	96 Coyston to Base, N.Y.D. Pte Gregory to hospital. Lt Col Humpston returned from leave. 1 to I hosp 02 OR returned from leave. Hosp - 10 Wastage 25.	NH
Frévent	26/1/17	9pm	Lieut Abrahams to CCS. Hosp 2 Pte Davis to hospital. Wastage 25.	RAH

2449 Wt. W14957/M90 750,000 1/16 J.B.C. & A. Forms/C.2118/12.

Army Form C. 2118.

WAR DIARY
or
INTELLIGENCE SUMMARY
(Erase heading not required.)

Instructions regarding War Diaries and Intelligence Summaries are contained in F. S. Regs., Part II. and the Staff Manual respectively. Title Pages will be prepared in manuscript.

Place	Date	Hour	Summary of Events and Information	Remarks and references to Appendices
Lucecourt	27/1/17	2pm	Sick R 3. Transport what 8.30 to Argorures. Evacts for Maud area.	aatl.
Lucecourt	28/1/17	9/am	Sick 5 - 1 Reinforcement received evacuates to Maud Hospt. Pte George Davis to hospt. Evacd - 2 On large 2t.	aatl.
Lucecourt	29/1/17	9/am	Sick 9. 1st Increment at 8 am en-trained at Onicourt for Cering in Maud area arrived to him. Hospt - 0 On large 2t.	aatl.
Maud	30/1/17	9/am	Sick 6 - C section threw Maud 150 beds. Dr Matthew to hospit. Hospt - 1 On large 2t.	aatl.
Maud	31/1/17	9/am	Sick - 7 Pte George Davis, Pte Jackson to hospital. Hospt - 1 On large 2t.	aatl.

140/1994.

1/1st S.M. Fields Ambulance

COMMITTEE FOR THE
MEDICAL HISTORY OF THE WAR
Date 4— APR. 1917

A.D.M.S.
48th Division

Herewith please -
War Diary for the Unit
under my command
for the month of
February 1917

Ralph Rodwick
Capt.
28/2/17. Commanding

1/2nd
SOUTH MIDLAND
FIELD AMBULANCE

Army Form C. 2118.

WAR DIARY
or
INTELLIGENCE SUMMARY

(Erase heading not required.)

Vol 24

Confidential 1/2 South Midland Field Ambulance
B.E.F
Vol 17.
1 Feb. 1917 – 28 Feb. 1917

Ralph Broderick
Capt. Commanding

1/2nd SOUTH MIDLAND FIELD AMBULANCE.
No..........
Date..........

Vol 17b.
Page 6.
Appendix 1.

Place	Date	Hour	Summary of Events and Information	Remarks and references to Appendices

Army Form C. 2118

WAR DIARY
or
INTELLIGENCE SUMMARY

(Erase heading not required.)

Instructions regarding War Diaries and Intelligence Summaries are contained in F.S. Regs., Part II. and the Staff Manual respectively. Title Pages will be prepared in manuscript.

Place	Date	Hour	Summary of Events and Information	Remarks and references to Appendices
Hamel	1/2/17	9 pm	Sick 7. Pte Latham to hospital. Hospital 5. Wastage 26.	aapl.
Hamel	2/2/17	9 pm	Sick 8. St Sgt Isaacs. Sgt Watts returned from C.C.S. Hospital 8. Wastage 28.	aapl.
Echzicon	3/2/17	4 pm	Sick 12. Davis. Sutton. George. Hartpree. Jackson & Co. Corpt Stead returned as reinforcement. Hospital 1. Dr Lewis to C.R.S. Wastage 22. Unit left at 11 by route march for Echzicon area, arrived at Echuries at 6 pm.	aapl.
Echzicon	4/2/17	9 pm	Sick 8. B" Stephens. Hartpree to hospital. Hospital 3. Wastage 22.	aapl.
Echzicon	5/2/17	4 pm	Sick 2. Cpl Thomson. Harrison, Rodgers, Hadley returned from 3rd Fd Amb. Lt Col. Kingston on special leave. Hospital 3. Wastage 22. Route march via Lucenne.	aapl.

Army Form C. 2118.

WAR DIARY
or
INTELLIGENCE SUMMARY

(Erase heading not required.)

Instructions regarding War Diaries and Intelligence Summaries are contained in F. S. Regs., Part II. and the Staff Manual respectively. Title Pages will be prepared in manuscript.

Place	Date	Hour	Summary of Events and Information	Remarks and references to Appendices
Eclusier	6/2/17	9pm	Sick 20 Hosp 3 wastage 22	Ptes Bhiring, Goddard, Stanford, Chatterton, Bro Brown & Brown returned from leave.	RWB
Eclusier	7/2/17	9pm	Sick 21 Hosp 0 wastage 22	Capt Murray returned from leave. Route march 10 - 12.30	RWB
Eclusier	8/2/17	9pm	Sick 11 Hosp 10 wastage 25	Dr Hepburn attached per to C.O.S. for water duty. C Section tent subdivision made Capt. Buchanan depart to take over Isola Amb. site from 10/1 Amb. 24 Div French Army. Dr Lewis ex hosp. Capt Stell & 37 O.R. att. to 3rd Harpe Pte Deakin to 241 R.F.A. for duty.	RWB
Cappy	9/2/17	9pm	Sick 0 Hosp 0 wastage 26	Move to Cappy of remaining 2 sections into Isola Amb. site here. Pte Bradley, Church, Cann, Then & Mann's returned from leave. Pte Wood to England sick.	RWB
Cappy	10/2/17	9pm	Sick 5 Hosp 0 wastage 26	Capt Stell relieved by Capt. McConnell at 3rd Hussars	RWB

2449 Wt. W14957/M90 750,000 1/16 J.B.C. & A. Forms/C.2118/12.

Army Form C. 2118.

WAR DIARY
or
INTELLIGENCE SUMMARY
(Erase heading not required.)

Instructions regarding War Diaries and Intelligence Summaries are contained in F.S. Regs., Part II. and the Staff Manual respectively. Title Pages will be prepared in manuscript.

Place	Date	Hour	Summary of Events and Information	Remarks and references to Appendices
Cappy	11/2/17	9pm	Sick 9 Hosp 0 Wastage 27	Staff Sgt. Dancer to 1/ SMO, CCS on A/CM. Corps. letter No P 800 of 9/2/17) Capt Stott on special leave to England
Cappy	12/2/17	9pm	Sick 10 Hosp 0 Wastage 27	Cpl Warburton returned from leave.
Cappy	13/2/17	9pm	Sick 6 Hosp 1 Wastage 27	Pte Blake to Hosp.
Cappy	14/2/17	9pm	Sick 9 Hosp 1 Wastage 14	1 RAMC reinforcements received 1 ASC reinforcement received.
Cappy	15/2/17	9pm	Sick 4 Hosp 1 Wastage 14	

Army Form C. 2118.

WAR DIARY
or
INTELLIGENCE SUMMARY
(Erase heading not required.)

Instructions regarding War Diaries and Intelligence Summaries are contained in F. S. Regs., Part II. and the Staff Manual respectively. Title Pages will be prepared in manuscript.

Place	Date	Hour	Summary of Events and Information	Remarks and references to Appendices
Cappy	16/2/17	9pm	Sick 3 Hosp 1 Wastage 14	RMB
Cappy	17/2/17	9pm	Sick 7 Hosp 1 Wastage 14	Pte Cook H.S. returned from Div. School	RMB
Cappy	18/2/17	9pm	Sick 5 Hosp 1 Wastage 14		RMB
Cappy	19/2/17	9pm	Sick 4 Hosp 1 Wastage 14 or 10+	Lt. Col. Stimpson placed on Home Establishment for 2 months vis accompany. Struck off strength W.O. letter No 118/17(A.M.D.) d/- 12/2/17 from 16/2/17	RMB
Cappy	20/2/17	9pm	Sick 5 Hosp 1 Wastage 14 or 10+	Working Party sent to Herbécourt to prepare Divisional Collecting Station	RMB

Army Form C. 2118.

WAR DIARY
or
INTELLIGENCE SUMMARY
(Erase heading not required.)

Instructions regarding War Diaries and Intelligence Summaries are contained in F. S. Regs., Part II and the Staff Manual respectively. Title Pages will be prepared in manuscript.

Place	Date	Hour	Summary of Events and Information	Remarks and references to Appendices
Cappy	21/2/17	9pm	Sick 7 Hosp 1 Wastage 14 OR + 1 OH	RMB
Cappy	22/2/17	9pm	Sick 9 Hosp 1 Wastage 14 OR + 1 OH	RMB
Cappy	23/2/17	9pm	Sick 7 Hosp 0 Wastage 16 OR + 1 OH. Pte Blake to C.C.S. A/S/t Johnson transferred on probation to R.F.C. R.O. No 9/1149 a/f 14/2/17 35a	RMB
Cappy	24/2/17	9pm	Sick 5 Hosp 0 Wastage 17. 2 NCOs + 23 OR attached to C.R.S. at Cerisy. Capt D.A. Mackay reported for duty	RMB
Cappy	25/2/17	9pm	Sick 4 Hosp 0 Wastage 16 OR + 1 OH. Sgt Payton on special leave to England. Lt Ashley seconded to England R.O. No 259 b a/f 25/2/17 132.63	RMB
Cappy	26/2/17	9pm	Sick 4 Hosp 0 Wastage 16 OR + 1 OH. Capt Steele returned from leave. Capt Buchanan attached 1/4 R. Berks	RMB

Army Form C. 2118.

WAR DIARY
or
INTELLIGENCE SUMMARY

(Erase heading not required.)

Instructions regarding War Diaries and Intelligence Summaries are contained in F. S. Regs., Part II. and the Staff Manual respectively. Title Pages will be prepared in manuscript.

Place	Date	Hour	Summary of Events and Information	Remarks and references to Appendices
Capby	27/1/17	9pm	Sick 3 Capt Skall to No 4 Stationary Hosp. S. Omer, DGMS letter No B/1483 Hosp. O. Pte Thomas C & Dunn J.G. to transport depot, 63 dtd 25/1/17 Wastage 22 CEB No. 18745-2.17- 13 - A. a/2/1/17 Pte Allen GM, Busby, Edmondson to water duty. Pte Day returned from water duty Pte Whitwick, Bennett, Moon return from 4th R- 5th rate Corpls Pay Pte Beech from 4th R - 5th rate, Pte Smith to 5th rate	RMJ
Capby	28/1/17	9pm	Sick 3 36 O.R. returned from 13 Hosp Rest. Hosp. O Pte Hawthorn to water duty Wastage 23 Good Conduct Badges awarded to 79 O.R.	RMJ

WAR DIARY
or
INTELLIGENCE SUMMARY

Army Form C. 2118.

Appendix

Summary of Admissions & Discharges

February 1917.

	ADMITTED		DISCHARGED			
	SICK	WOUNDED	CCS	DUTY	DIED	TRANSFERRED
OFFICERS.	-	-	-	-	-	-
O RANKS.	536	5	99	164	-	127
	536	5	99	164	-	127

Ralph R. Broderick
Capt. Commanding

1/3rd SOUTH MIDLAND FIELD AMBULANCE

140/2042

48th Div.

1/1st S.M. Field Ambulance.

Mar 1917

COMMITTEE FOR THE
MEDICAL HISTORY OF THE WAR
Date   11 MAY 1917

WAR DIARY
or
INTELLIGENCE SUMMARY

Army Form C. 2118.

Confidential

1/2 South Midland Field Ambulance

B.E.F.

Vol 18.

1 March 1917 — 31 March 1917.

T. Munro
Cpt. ⟨?⟩
LIEUT. COL. R.A.M.C.T.
COMMANDING 2ND Fd. AMB.
48 DIV.

Vol 18
Pages 6
Appendix 1

1/2nd
SOUTH MIDLAND
FIELD AMBULANCE.
No.
Date 31 MAR 1917

Army Form C. 2118.

WAR DIARY
or
INTELLIGENCE SUMMARY

(*Erase heading not required.*)

Instructions regarding War Diaries and Intelligence Summaries are contained in F. S. Regs., Part II. and the Staff Manual respectively. Title Pages will be prepared in manuscript.

Place	Date	Hour	Summary of Events and Information	Remarks and references to Appendices
Cappy	1/3/17	9pm	Sick 3 Hop 0 Wastage 23. 36 O.R. attached to 1st Hampshires for duty.	RMcB
Cappy	2/3/17	9pm	Sick 2 Hop 0 Wastage 23. Capt McConnell returned to unit for duty from 1/3rd the Hants.	RMcB
Cappy	3/3/17	9pm	Sick 0 Hop 0 Wastage 23.	RMcB
Cappy	4/3/17	9pm	Sick 2 Hop 0 Wastage 23.	RMcB
Cappy	5/3/17	9pm	Sick 1 Hop 0 Wastage 23.	RMcB

Army Form C. 2118.

WAR DIARY
or
INTELLIGENCE SUMMARY

(Erase heading not required.)

Instructions regarding War Diaries and Intelligence Summaries are contained in F. S. Regs., Part II. and the Staff Manual respectively. Title Pages will be prepared in manuscript.

Place	Date	Hour	Summary of Events and Information	Remarks and references to Appendices
Cappy	6/3/17	9 pm	Sick 2 Hosp 0 Wastage 23	RWB
Cappy	7/3/17	9 pm	Sick 5 Hosp 0 Wastage 22	1 Reinforcement received	RWB
Cappy	8/3/17	9 pm	Sick 2 Hosp 1 Wastage 21	Ptes Mattocks to Hospital 1 reinforcement received	RWB
Cappy	9/3/17	9 pm	Sick 3 Hosp 1 Wastage 22	Pte Black sent to C.C.S. from 7/S HantRub.	RWB
Cappy	10/3/17	9 pm	Sick 3 Hosp 1 Wastage 24	Capt Lang reported for duty	RWB
Cappy	11/3/17	9 pm	Sick 3 Hosp 1 Wastage 21		RWB

Army Form C. 2118.

WAR DIARY
or
INTELLIGENCE SUMMARY

(Erase heading not required.)

Instructions regarding War Diaries and Intelligence Summaries are contained in F. S. Regs., Part II. and the Staff Manual respectively. Title Pages will be prepared in manuscript.

Place	Date	Hour	Summary of Events and Information	Remarks and references to Appendices
Cappy	12/3/17	9pm	Lt. Maule (T.C.) reported for duty to 1/5 O.B. Pte Watkins returned from D.H.Q. Sick 3 Hosp 1 Wastage 5	P.M.B
Cappy	13/3/17	9pm	Capt. Buchanan to D.H.Q. Capt. MacKay to 1/4 Royal Berks - both struck off strength - Pte Bisson attached to D.H.Q. Sgt Ponden returned from leave. Sick 3 Hosp 1 Wastage 7	P.M.B
Cappy	14/3/17	9pm	Capt Meek reported for duty taken on strength Sick 7 Hosp 1 Wastage 6	P.M.B
Cappy	15/3/17	9pm	Pte Gadane attached 474 to R.E. to supervise Clothing Store at Batho. Sick 7 Hosp 1 Wastage 6	P.M.B
Cappy	16/3/17	9pm	Pte Blackwell returned from C.C.S. Pte Griffiths to hospital Pte Brown to C.C.S. Capt. Meek to 1/4 O.B. + Buabos Sick 5 Hosp 2 Wastage 7	P.M.B

Army Form C. 2118.

WAR DIARY
or
INTELLIGENCE SUMMARY

(Erase heading not required.)

Instructions regarding War Diaries and Intelligence Summaries are contained in F.S. Regs., Part II. and the Staff Manual respectively. Title Pages will be prepared in manuscript.

Place	Date	Hour	Summary of Events and Information	Remarks and references to Appendices
Cappy	17/3/17	9pm	Ptes Blackwell, Riddle to Hosp. Capt Ferguson reported for temporary duty — not taken on strength. Sick 2 Hosp 4 Wastage 7	RMG
Cappy	18/3/17	9pm	Sick 4 Hosp 4 Wastage 7	RMG
Cappy	19/3/17	9pm	Pte Moon & Pte Brown S. to Corps Rest Station. Pte Beadle to C.C.S. Sick and off strength. Capt Ferguson proceeded to England. Sick 5 Hosp 6 Wastage 8	RM
(Wken?)	20/3/17	9pm	Capt Rev'd AE Broderick on leave to England (10 days). Sick 5 Hosp 6 Wastage 8	RM
Cappy	21/3/17	9pm	Pte Pritchard to CCS and off strength. Pte Griffiths & Pte Matlock discharged from hospital. 22 other ranks returned from detached duty at Arras. Sick 5 Hosp 4 Wastage 9	RM

2449 Wt. W14957/M90 750,000 1/16 J.B.C. & A. Forms/C.2118/12.

Army Form C. 2118.

WAR DIARY
or
INTELLIGENCE SUMMARY

(Erase heading not required.)

Instructions regarding War Diaries and Intelligence Summaries are contained in F. S. Regs., Part II. and the Staff Manual respectively. Title Pages will be prepared in manuscript.

Place	Date	Hour	Summary of Events and Information	Remarks and references to Appendices
Cappy	22/3/17	9pm	Pte Poole discharged from Hospital Sick 6 Stop 3 Wastage 9	KM
Cappy	23/3/17	9pm	Pte Pritchard died at C.C.S Sick 6 Stop 3 Wastage 9	KM
Cappy	24/3/17	9am	Sick 3 Stop 3 Wastage 9	KM
Cappy	25/3/17	9am	2 M.S. Ingham to leave on Commission of Service 9 Off Strength Sick 3 Stop 3 Wastage 10	KM
Cappy	26/3/17	9am	7 Reinforcements Received Sick 3 Stop 3 Wastage 3	KM

Army Form C. 2118.

WAR DIARY
or
INTELLIGENCE SUMMARY

(Erase heading not required.)

Instructions regarding War Diaries and Intelligence
Summaries are contained in F. S. Regs., Part II.
and the Staff Manual respectively. Title Pages
will be prepared in manuscript.

Place	Date	Hour	Summary of Events and Information	Remarks and references to Appendices
Capph	27/3/17	9pm	Sick 6 Hosp 3 Wastage 3	K.M.
Capph	28/3/17	9pm	Sick 5 Hosp 3 Wastage 3	K.M.
Capph	29/3/17	9pm	Sick 3 Hosp 2 Wastage 4	Pte Blackwell to C.C.S. & off Strength	K.M.
Capph	30/3/17	9pm	Sick 3 Hosp 2 Wastage 4		K.M.
Capph	31/3/17	9pm	Sick 3 Hosp 1 Wastage 5	Pte Brunner to C.C.S. & off Strength	K.M.

Army Form C. 2118.

WAR DIARY
or
INTELLIGENCE SUMMARY

(Erase heading not required.)

Instructions regarding War Diaries and Intelligence Summaries are contained in F. S. Regs., Part II and the Staff Manual respectively. Title Pages will be prepared in manuscript.

Place	Date	Hour	Summary of Events and Information	Remarks and references to Appendices
			Appendix Summary of Admissions & Discharges March 1917.	

	ADMITTED			DISCHARGED		
	SICK	WOUNDED	C.C.S.	C.R.S.	DUTY	REMAINING
OFFICERS	–	–	–	–	–	–
O. RANKS	521	5	260	33	322	86
	521	5	260	33	322	86.

Appendix 1
Volume 18

1/2nd SOUTH MIDLAND FIELD AMBULANCE
No. Fa.366
Date 31 MAR 1917

K Ahmad
Capt. for
LIEUT. COL. R. A. M. C. T.
COMMANDING 2ND FD. AMB.
48 DIV.

2449 Wt. W14957/M90 750,000 1/16 J.B.C. & A. Forms/C.2118/12.

140/2026

48 K Div

1/2nd South Midland F.A.

April 1917

COMMITTEE FOR THE
MEDICAL HISTORY OF THE WAR
Date -6 JUN.1917

WAR DIARY
or
INTELLIGENCE SUMMARY

Army Form C. 2118.

Vol 26

Confidential

1/2 South Midland Field Ambulance
B.E.F.

Vol 19

1 Ap. 1917 – 30 Ap. 1917

Vol 19
Pages 7.
Appendix 1

1/2nd
SOUTH MIDLAND
FIELD AMBULANCE
No. ......JA/306.......
Rec'd 30 APR 1917

Ralph J Brookwith
Lt Col
LIEUT COL. R.A.M.C.T.
COMMANDING 2ND FD AMB
48 DIV.

Army Form C. 2118.

WAR DIARY
or
INTELLIGENCE SUMMARY

(Erase heading not required.)

Instructions regarding War Diaries and Intelligence Summaries are contained in F.S. Regs., Part II. and the Staff Manual respectively. Title Pages will be prepared in manuscript.

Place	Date	Hour	Summary of Events and Information	Remarks and references to Appendices
Capps	Apl 1	9pm	Lt Thomas (TC) reported for duty. taken on strength. Lt Col R.H Brocklehurst return from leave. Sick 4 Hosp 2 back 4	R.H.B
Capps	Apl 2	9pm	Capt McConnell 7 3 O.R. 1 Motor Amb. 1 Horse Amb. } att. to 1/1 Sh. Hadnts for duty. 5 Reinforcements received. Sick 3 Hosp 2 wastage 1 officers 2 O.R. Surplus 2. O.R.	R.H.B
Capps	Apl 3	9pm	Sick 2 Hosp 2 wastage 1 OR Surplus 2 OR	R.H.B
Capps	Apl 4	9pm	Pte Moon to C.B. Sick 6 Hosp. 1 wastage 1 OR Surplus 1 OR	R.H.B

Army Form C. 2118.

WAR DIARY
or
INTELLIGENCE SUMMARY

(Erase heading not required.)

Instructions regarding War Diaries and Intelligence Summaries are contained in F. S. Regs., Part II. and the Staff Manual respectively. Title Pages will be prepared in manuscript.

Place	Date	Hour	Summary of Events and Information	Remarks and references to Appendices
Cappy	Apr 5	9pm	Sick 6. Hosp. 0. Wastage 6 off. Surplus 10 off. Pte Brown or Hosp. Lt Hards rejoined sent out car to Tire court to report to Capt the Coroner	RAB
Cappy	Apr 6	9pm	Sick 4. Hosp. 0. Wastage 10 off. Surplus 10 R.	RAB
Cappy	Apr 7	9pm	Sick 2. Hosp. 0. Wastage 10 off. Surplus 10 R.	RAB
Cappy	Apr 8	9pm	Sick 2. Hosp. 0. Want 10 off. Surplus 10 R.	Capt Kent Newsome detached to D.H.Q. RAB

Army Form C. 2118.

WAR DIARY
or
INTELLIGENCE SUMMARY

(Erase heading not required.)

Instructions regarding War Diaries and Intelligence Summaries are contained in F.S. Regs., Part II. and the Staff Manual respectively. Title Pages will be prepared in manuscript.

Place	Date	Hour	Summary of Events and Information	Remarks and references to Appendices
Cappy	8/4/17	9pm	Sick 4 Hosp. 0 wastage 10ft Surplus 1 OR.	R/R/B
Cappy	10/4/17	9pm	Sick 5 Hosp 0 wastage 10ft Surplus 1 OR	R/R/B
Cappy	11/4/17	9pm	Sick 3 Hosp. 0 wastage 10ft	Pte Parker evac. to C.C.S. struck off Strength. R/R/B
Cappy	12/4/17	9pm	Sick 2 Hosp 0 wastage 10ft	R/R/B

2449 Wt. W14957/M90 750,000 1/16 J.B.C. & A. Forms/C.2118/12.

Army Form C. 2118.

WAR DIARY
or
INTELLIGENCE SUMMARY
(Erase heading not required.)

Instructions regarding War Diaries and Intelligence Summaries are contained in F. S. Regs., Part II. and the Staff Manual respectively. Title Pages will be prepared in manuscript.

Place	Date	Hour	Summary of Events and Information	Remarks and references to Appendices
Cappy	13/4/17	9pm	Sick 4. Hosp. 0. Wastage 10% 10R. Pte Hutchinson on leave to England	R/L
Cappy	14/4/17	9pm	Sick 5. Hosp. 0. Wastage 10ft 10R.	Pte Wright & L.A.C. attached I.L.D. sent to M.T.S.	R/L
Cappy	15/4/17	9pm	Sick 5. Hosp. 0. Wastage 10ft 10R/ASC Surplus 10R/RAMC	Pte Tolson reported at 11.p.m. returned for reinforcement of 1/2 on S.B. returned at 11pm at M.S.	R/L
Cappy	16/4/17	9pm	Sick 3. Hosp. 0. Wastage 10ft 10R/ASC	Pte Attwell transferred to 1/3 Lon Platoon	R/L
Cappy	17/4/17	9pm	Sick 3. Hosp. 0. Wastage 10ft 10R/ASC 1 Surplus R/Amc	Staff Sgt Baker ceased as reinforcement	R/L

2449 Wt. W14957/M90 750,000 1/16 J.B.C. & A. Forms/C.2118/12.

Army Form C. 2118.

WAR DIARY
or
INTELLIGENCE SUMMARY

(Erase heading not required.)

Instructions regarding War Diaries and Intelligence Summaries are contained in F.S. Regs., Part II. and the Staff Manual respectively. Title Pages will be prepared in manuscript.

Place	Date	Hour	Summary of Events and Information	Remarks and references to Appendices
Coppey	18/4/17	9 pm	Sick 3 H.P.O. Wastage 10ft 10RAHSC Surplus 10RAHMC	RMB
Doignt	19/4/17	9 pm	Sick 4 H.P.O. Wastage 10ft 10RAHSC Surplus 10RAHMC	H.Qrs moved to DOIGNT to build RE Corps Clearing Station remain to administer DRS	RMB
Doignt	20/4/17	9 pm	Sick 7 H.P.O. Wastage 10ft 10RAHSC Surplus 10RAHMC	Pte Butler on leave	RMB
Doignt	21/4/17	9 pm	Sick 6 H.P.O. Wastage 10ft 10RAHSC Surplus 10RAHMC		RMB

Army Form C. 2118.

WAR DIARY
or
INTELLIGENCE SUMMARY
(Erase heading not required.)

Instructions regarding War Diaries and Intelligence Summaries are contained in F. S. Regs., Part II. and the Staff Manual respectively. Title Pages will be prepared in manuscript.

Place	Date	Hour	Summary of Events and Information	Remarks and references to Appendices
Doiran	22/4/17	9pm	Lt 3 Hosp 0 Wastage 10ff 10RMFC Surplus 10R RBMC	Lt Made Lieutenant to 241 Bde RFA for temp duty.	Kits
Doiran	23/4/17	9pm	Sick 1 Hosp 1 Wastage 10ff 10RMF 0	Pte Jellyman to Hosb. Pte Faithnow transferred to 1/1 Can. Fld Amb.	12823
Doiran	24/4/17	9pm	Sick 2 Hosp 1 Wastage 10ff 10RMF 30		Kits
Doiran	25/4/17	9pm	Sick 1 Hosp 0 Wastage 1 oft 10RMFoc	Pte Jellyman ex Hosp. Pte Mitton to CCS S/Sgt Stevenson received as reinforcement	12823
Doiran	26/4/17	9pm	Sick 0 Hosp 1 Wastage 10ff	Pte Perons to Hosp. Dvr Smith TR. rec'd as reinforcement.	12823

Army Form C. 2118.

WAR DIARY
or
INTELLIGENCE SUMMARY

(Erase heading not required.)

Instructions regarding War Diaries and Intelligence Summaries are contained in F. S. Regs., Part II. and the Staff Manual respectively. Title Pages will be prepared in manuscript.

Place	Date	Hour	Summary of Events and Information	Remarks and references to Appendices
Doriful	27/4/17	9pm	Sick 1. Hosp 1. Wastage 1 off.	Lt Smith opleave to England	Ref 5
Doriful	28/4/17	9pm	Sick 1. Hosp 1. Wastage 1 off.	Dr Jenkinson returned from leave. Opened to received patients as Corps section Station	Ref 5
Doriful	29/4/17	9pm	Sick 1. Hosp 1. Wastage 1 off.	Interpreter reported for duty. Dr Jenkins reported from ADMS for duty	Ref 5
Doriful	30/4/17	9pm	Sick 3. Hosp 1. Wastage 1 off.		Ref 5

Army Form C. 2118.

WAR DIARY
or
INTELLIGENCE SUMMARY

(Erase heading not required.)

Instructions regarding War Diaries and Intelligence Summaries are contained in F. S. Regs., Part II. and the Staff Manual respectively. Title Pages will be prepared in manuscript.

Place	Date	Hour	Summary of Events and Information	Remarks and references to Appendices
			Appendix. Summary of Admissions & Discharges April 1917	

	ADMITTED			DISCHARGED		
	S.	W.	C.C.S.	D.R.S.	DUTY.
OFFICERS	-	-	-	-	-
O. RANKS.	212	1	84	2	132.
	212	1	84	2	132

REMAINING :- O. Ranks. 82.

1/2nd
SOUTH MIDLAND
FIELD AMBULANCE.

No.......
Dated 30 APR 1917

Rupert L Rookwick
LIEUT COL R. A. M. C. T.
COMMANDING 2ND FD. AMB.
48 DIV.

Lt Col

48th Div.

1/2nd South Midland F.A.

COMMITTEE FOR THE
MEDICAL HISTORY OF THE WAR
Date   10 JUL. 1917

Army Form C. 2118.

WAR DIARY
or
INTELLIGENCE SUMMARY
(Erase heading not required.)

Vol 27

Place	Date	Hour	Summary of Events and Information	Remarks and references to Appendices

Confidential

1/2 South Midland Field Ambulance.
B.E.F.
—
Vol. 20.

1 May 1917 — 31 May 1917.

Vol. 20.
Pages 8.
Appendix. 1.

Maplewright
Lt Col

1/2nd
SOUTH MIDLAND
FIELD AMBULANCE
No. M366
3 1 MAY 1917

WAR DIARY
or
INTELLIGENCE SUMMARY

(Erase heading not required.)

Instructions regarding War Diaries and Intelligence Summaries are contained in F. S. Regs., Part II. and the Staff Manual respectively. Title Pages will be prepared in manuscript.

Place	Date	Hour	Summary of Events and Information	Remarks and references to Appendices
Dorjot	1/5/17	9pm	Sick 3 Hosp 1 Wastage 10ff. Lt hu home on 3 days special leave to Flower.	RHB
Dorjot	2/5/17	9pm	Sick 1 Hosp 1 Wastage 10ff. B. Section returns to head quarters from Tincowali. Capt McConnan & servant detached to 2nd Bgd. RFA for duty.	RHB
Dorjot	3/5/17	9pm	Sick 1 Hosp 1 Wastage 14ff.	RHB
Dorjot	4/5/17	9pm	Sick 4 Hosp 0 Wastage 10ff. 10R Adbne	Stevens evac. to CCS RHB

Army Form C. 2118.

WAR DIARY
or
INTELLIGENCE SUMMARY
(Erase heading not required.)

Instructions regarding War Diaries and Intelligence Summaries are contained in F. S. Regs., Part II. and the Staff Manual respectively. Title Pages will be prepared in manuscript.

Place	Date	Hour	Summary of Events and Information	Remarks and references to Appendices
Doignt	5/5/17	9 pm	Sect 4 Hq 0 Front 10ft 10R. Lt Thurlow returned from leave to Rouen	Ptff
Doignt	6/5/17	9 pm	Sect 2 Hq 0 Front 10ft 10R. 3 RE's Tanks attached for instr.	Ptff
Doignt	7/5/17	9 pm	Sect 3 Hq 0 Frontage 10ft 10R.	Ptff
Doignt	8/5/17	9 pm	Sect 6 Hq 0 Frontage 10ft 10R. Lt Monds Tennant reported at H.Q. from 241 Bgn RFA	Ptff
Doignt	9/5/17	9 pm	Sect 1 Hq 1 Frontage 10ft Platoon returned to Front from Base Pte Vireo to Hosp.	Ptff

WAR DIARY
or
INTELLIGENCE SUMMARY

(Erase heading not required.)

Instructions regarding War Diaries and Intelligence Summaries are contained in F. S. Regs., Part II. and the Staff Manual respectively. Title Pages will be prepared in manuscript.

Place	Date	Hour	Summary of Events and Information	Remarks and references to Appendices
Doingt	10/5/17	9 pm	Sick 2 Hosp 1 To Base 1 oR 1 oR/RAMC Sgt Lacey transferred to 1st Hussars.	RAMB
Dorigt	11/5/17	9 pm	Sick 3 Hosp 0 Lost 1 oR 1 oR RAMC Capt Cox & 2 OR orders to England Pte Vivian ex Hosp.	RAMB
Le Transloy	12/5/17	9 pm	Sick 0 Hosp 0 Lost 1 oR 2 RAMC Capt McDonnell Lieut van t returned from detached duty with 240 Bde RFA	Corps Bearer Station at Doingt handed over to 1/3 E Lancs Fd Amb. but 1 car C Section, moved at 6.15 A.M. with 143 B'd'e to Le Transloy arriving at 12 Noon. Bivouaced for Night at O 31.B.4.2 Sheet 57c. All surplus stores at Doingt handed over to 1/3 E. Lancs also all books of Patients complete. C. Section at Cappy ordered to clean patients to CRS + e.g. to hand over Stores to Learmoneet with 9 men standing to moving. Surplus stores sent to Divn Dump at Cappy. Water clothing & to blankets of Unit sent to Divn Dump at Peronne. Pte Cohot 15 29 C.C.S. ? Dysentery	RAMB

WAR DIARY
or
INTELLIGENCE SUMMARY

Army Form C. 2118.

Place	Date	Hour	Summary of Events and Information	Remarks and references to Appendices
Lebucquière	13/5/17	9pm	Sick 5 H to O Eval. 10 H. 30R Ritrue. Pte Jennell to 29 C.C.S. Unit moved to Lebucquière to take over advanced area from 34 Fd. Amb. and in 12 Noon. C. Seaton crossed to move to Corbléo Pavronne for night. 3 Advance Posts taken over. Capt McConnell party to Hermies Capt Kent Marle party to Doignies S/Sr Matty party to Beaumetz Capt Stork party to takeover Battn at Velu	RAB
Lebucquière	14/5/17	9pm	Sick 4 H to O Eval. 10H 30R Ritrue. Creation under Capt Murray. Lieut Thomas reported Hospence. Lieut Thomas to take over post at Beaumetz. Capt Longh report headquarters for duties. J. Rices evacuated.	RMH

Army Form C. 2118.

WAR DIARY
or
INTELLIGENCE SUMMARY

(Erase heading not required.)

Instructions regarding War Diaries and Intelligence Summaries are contained in F. S. Regs., Part II. and the Staff Manual respectively. Title Pages will be prepared in manuscript.

Place	Date	Hour	Summary of Events and Information	Remarks and references to Appendices
Lebruguire	15/5/17	9pm	Sick 9 Hosp 0 Wounds 10ff 30R	MB
Lebruguire	16/5/17	9pm	Sick 4 Hosp 0 Wounds 10ff 30R	Heavens Posts at Heumes Dorjee "Beaumais" to be moved as they are unsuitable & unsafe positions Heumes 10ff 30R for newones chosen work commenced at Heumes	M.B
Lebruguire	17/5/17	9pm	Sick 2 Hosp 0 Wounds 10ff 30R	Report to ADMS on situation at Heumes 27 Evacuation	M.B
Lebruguire	18/5/17	9pm	Sick 3 Hosp 0 Wounds 10ff 30R		M.B.
Lebruguire	19/5/17	9pm	Sick 1 Hosp 0 Wounds 10ff 2oR	Pte Jenell returned from Hospital	M.B

Army Form C. 2118.

WAR DIARY
or
INTELLIGENCE SUMMARY

(Erase heading not required.)

Instructions regarding War Diaries and Intelligence Summaries are contained in F. S. Regs., Part II. and the Staff Manual respectively. Title Pages will be prepared in manuscript.

Place	Date	Hour	Summary of Events and Information	Remarks and references to Appendices
Lebucquiere	20/5/17	9pm	Sick 1 Hosp 0 Strt 10ft 2OR. 3 OR. detached to 3 Kents for duty. An officer from II Royal Sussex reported for duty with 30 pioneers for purpose of burying men advanced dressing stations at HERMIES, DOIGNIES & BEAUMETZ. L.Cpl. Bradnock, No. 708 & Pte. Hughes to Hd. on leave	MHS
Lebucquiere	21/5/17	9pm	Sick 1 Hosp 0 Strt 10ft 3OR. Sgt. Smith returned from leave. Cpl. Warburton to Base, authority DAG. Base telegram No H.R. 2377 of 19/5/17	R.B.
Lebucquiere	22/5/17	9pm	Sick 2 Hosp 0 Strt 10ft 4OR. Pte. Day on water duty to 1 Bucks Bn.	MHS
Lebucquiere	23/5/17	9pm	Sick 1 Hosp 0 Strt 10ft 4OR. Pte. Phillips returned from III Corps Rest Station	appd

Army Form C. 2118.

WAR DIARY
or
INTELLIGENCE SUMMARY

(Erase heading not required.)

Instructions regarding War Diaries and Intelligence
Summaries are contained in F. S. Regs., Part II.
and the Staff Manual respectively. Title Pages
will be prepared in manuscript.

Place	Date	Hour	Summary of Events and Information	Remarks and references to Appendices
Lebucquiere	24/5/17	9pm	Sick 1 to Hosp. Hosp 1 Capt McConnell on leave West 1 Off 4 O.R. Capt Murray to HERMIES as relief	R.H.S
Lebucquiere	25/5/17	9pm	Sick 4 Dr Newell JC to Hosp. Hosp 2 West 1 Off 4 O.R.	R.H.S
Lebucquiere	26/5/17	9pm	Sick 3 S/S Hatty to Hosp Hosp 3 Capt Cox MO Supern returned from leave West 1 Off 4 O.R	R.H.S
Lebucquiere	27/5/17	9pm	Sick 2. Pte Hickman to CCS Hosp. 2 Lt Col Murgah: reported unit from Home Establishment West 5 O.R. took over command.	Rept.
Letrucquiere	28/5/17	9pm	Sick 2. Water advanced Patrol Stewner Capt Murray in Hosp. 2 to Glendon to C.C.S. charge. West 5 O.R.	Rept.

Army Form C. 2118.

WAR DIARY
or
INTELLIGENCE SUMMARY
(Erase heading not required.)

Instructions regarding War Diaries and Intelligence Summaries are contained in F. S. Regs., Part II. and the Staff Manual respectively. Title Pages will be prepared in manuscript.

Place	Date	Hour	Summary of Events and Information	Remarks and references to Appendices
Retrospective	29/5/17	9/am	Lieut R¹ Lt Watty, Dr Newell F.C. to O.C.P. Major's Lt Price returned from leave. L.C. Valentine - 2 O.R. returned from detached duty at Cathy. Leaf 8 O.R. visited advanced posts at Bahveio (Lt Marle) and Beaumetz (Lt Thomas).	nil
Retrospective	29/5/17	9/am	Lieut R² P.C. Littlewood to O. Bath for walk duty. Major's Hospital Lost 9 O.R.	nil
Retrospective	30/5/17	9/am	Lieut R¹ Medical Board held at Aust H⁰ on men taken sick. Major's Regimental Employed. Lost 9 O.R.	nil

Army Form C. 2118.

WAR DIARY
or
INTELLIGENCE SUMMARY

(Erase heading not required.)

Instructions regarding War Diaries and Intelligence Summaries are contained in F.S. Regs., Part II. and the Staff Manual respectively. Title Pages will be prepared in manuscript.

Place	Date	Hour	Summary of Events and Information	Remarks and references to Appendices
			Appendix.	
			Summary of Admissions and Discharges. MAY 1917	

	ADMISSIONS				DISCHARGES						
	OFFICERS		O.R.		C.C.S.		CYRS or DRS		TRANSFERS		DUTY
	S	W	S	W	OPRS	OR	OPRS	OR	OPRS	OR	OPRS	OR
48th Div. D.R. Stn.	2	.	113	2	1	22	1	46	.	.	.	118
III Corps Schools Sn.	.	.	176	.	.	6	.	.	.	138	.	32
A.D.S. Ledeghere	.	.	87	23	.	54	.	46	.	9	.	1
TOTALS	2	.	376	25	1	82	1	92	.	147	.	151

REMAINING - NIL -

[signature]

1/2nd
SOUTH MIDLAND
FIELD AMBULANCE
No. ____
Date 31 MAY 1917

14/220

Ward South Mid. T.A.

June 1917

COMMITTEE FOR THE
MEDICAL HISTORY OF THE WAR
Date -7 AUG.1917

Army Form C. 2118.

WAR DIARY
or
INTELLIGENCE SUMMARY

(Erase heading not required.)

Place	Date	Hour	Summary of Events and Information	Remarks and references to Appendices

JA 28

Confidential

1/2 South Midland Field Ambulance.

B.E.F.

Vol. 21.

1 June 1917 — 30 June 1917.

Vol 21.
Pages 4.
Appendices 1.

Washington
Lt Col.

WAR DIARY or INTELLIGENCE SUMMARY

Army Form C. 2118.

Place	Date	Hour	Summary of Events and Information	Remarks and references to Appendices
Hougumont	1/8/17	9 pm	Lieut. O. Stopford O. Wastage 8. Large Bug out of C.O.S. Bourges finished. It will accommodate 10 lying & 50 sitting cases. Sent up splints just head covering and timber to Capt Hurworth Hermes for construction of improved accommodation. Pte. Fletchman returned from C.C.S.	acyl.
Hougumont	2/8/17	9 am	Lieut. O. Stopford O. Wastage 8. Col Meek A.D.M.S. 4th Corps visited. Went to Beaumetz A.D.S. which can now accommodate 20 lying cases in dug-out. This place has been regularly shelled lately as there are some artillery posts near. At 11 pm 3 Bombs were dropped in the Hospital from an aeroplane. Capt Cox was wounded (slight) and much damage was done to tents and their contents (officers mess). Very fortunately the other officers had not gone to bed at the time it happened.	acyl.

WAR DIARY
or
INTELLIGENCE SUMMARY

(Erase heading not required.)

Army Form C. 2118.

Instructions regarding War Diaries and Intelligence Summaries are contained in F.S. Regs., Part II. and the Staff Manual respectively. Title Pages will be prepared in manuscript.

Place	Date	Hour	Summary of Events and Information	Remarks and references to Appendices
Letraquire	3/6/17	9 pm	Sick 2. Capt Cox to O/P. wounded. Shot at 0. Church service at 11. by Capt Shields. Wastage 1 Officer & O.R.	Weather
Letraquire	4/6/17	9 pm	Sick 3. Shot at 0. Water tank R destroyed by shell fire at Plemnes. New dug out there now complete. Trenches have also been dug with splinter proof head cover along which wounded can be taken to that dressing station. Wastage 1 Officer & O.R.	Weather
Letraquire	5/6/17	9 pm	Sick 3. Shot at 0. Capt King, L.Q.M. tonight went on leave to England. Pte Heymont received an reinforcement. Wastage 1 Officer & two returned from leave. 1 O.R.	Weather
Letraquire	6/6/17	9 pm	Sick 2. Shot at 0. Pte Hutchen to C.C.S. Pte Butler A returns from leave. Cpl Brown to Cookery School at Bovee. Wastage 1 Officer. Prising have M Strength. & O.R. Capt Broderick awarded M.C.	Weather

2449 Wt. W14957/Mgo 750,000 1/16 J.B.C. & A. Forms/C.2118/12.

WAR DIARY
or
INTELLIGENCE SUMMARY

Army Form C. 2118.

Place	Date	Hour	Summary of Events and Information	Remarks and references to Appendices
Le Hesquin	7/8/19	9 pm	Sick 3 Pte Daniels returned to 1/2 hours. Strength O. Wastage 1 Officer E.O.R.	aoyl.
Le Hesquin	8/6/19	9 pm	Sick 1. Strength O. Wastage 1. O.	aal.
Le Hesquin	9/6/19	9 pm	Sick 1 Capt Shelton & 6 O.R. went on leave. Strength O. Wastage 1. O. 8. O.R.	aal.
Le Hesquin	10/6/19	9 pm	Sick 2 4 O.R. went to Rest Camp at Valerie Strength O 3 O.R. returned from Rest Camp. Wastage 1. O Pte Bissett returned from detached duty. 8. O.R. Lt Cap howell returned from leave. Court Martial held on Capt Mackay at D.H.Q. Lt Col Humphris detailed to be on the Court.	aoyl.

WAR DIARY
or
INTELLIGENCE SUMMARY

(Erase heading not required.)

Army Form C. 2118.

Instructions regarding War Diaries and Intelligence Summaries are contained in F. S. Regs., Part II and the Staff Manual respectively. Title Pages will be prepared in manuscript.

Place	Date	Hour	Summary of Events and Information	Remarks and references to Appendices
Lahaquin	11/6/17	9 pm	Sick 1. 2 O R recvd as reinforcements. Capt McConnell returned from leave. Wastage 1.O. 6 O.R.	all.
Lahaquin	12/6/17	9 pm	Sick 2. Pte Mitchell returned from C.C.S. Stopd 0. bodies A.O.S. Beaumetz into A.O.M.S. Wastage 1.O. 5.OR.	nil.
Lahaquin	13/6/17	9 pm	Sick 2. RC Phipps to A.C.S. Stopd 0. Wastage 1.O. 6.O.R.	nil.
Lahaquin	14/6/17	9 pm	Sick 2. bodies A.D.S. at Boisjeux. Stopd 0. bodies 1.O. 6.O.R.	nil.
Lahaquin	15/6/17	9 pm	Sick 3. Pte Stone H Shingli new bring out Heavy shelling — Brigmont Station at Boisjeux. Stopd 0. heavy shelling for 2 hours and much damaged. Wastage 6.O.R. Removed to the old place in the trenches road	nil.

WAR DIARY or INTELLIGENCE SUMMARY

Army Form C. 2118.

(Erase heading not required.)

Instructions regarding War Diaries and Intelligence Summaries are contained in F.S. Regs., Part II. and the Staff Manual respectively. Title Pages will be prepared in manuscript.

Place	Date	Hour	Summary of Events and Information	Remarks and references to Appendices
Refrognière	16/6/17	9 p.m.	Sick 5:- 2 OR on leave. Hospital O. visits ADS. Hennies, hers dug out has complete accommodation for 12 stretcher cases. And all the wastage 6. OR personnel	Appx.
Etrequière	17/6/17	9 p.m.	Sick 4. Capt. Bowman reports to duty. Hospital O. Lts Phillips Rawnell & Kent returned from leave. Wastage 6.	Appx.
Etrequière	18/6/17	9 p.m.	Sick 5:- Hospital O. Lts Flemming returned from duty with ADMS. GOC. (Lt. Rout. Fawshaw) visits the Ambulance. Wastage 6.	Appx.
Etrequière	19/6/17	9 p.m.	Sick 3. Hospital O. 2 Cars sent up to Boisieux during night operations as casualties. Capt Bowman to Bucks Bn for temp. duty. Wastage 6.	Appx.
Etrequière	20/6/17	9 p.m.	Sick 3. Hospital O. Lt. Col. DDMS (3rd Army) (Lt. Capp) visits Ambulance. Wastage 6.	Appx.
Refrognière	21/6/17	9 p.m.	Sick 5:- Hospital O. Wastage 6.	Appx.

Army Form C. 2118.

WAR DIARY
or
INTELLIGENCE SUMMARY
(Erase heading not required.)

Instructions regarding War Diaries and Intelligence Summaries are contained in F. S. Regs., Part II. and the Staff Manual respectively. Title Pages will be prepared in manuscript.

Place	Date	Hour	Summary of Events and Information	Remarks and references to Appendices
Letacquise	22/6/17	9 pm	Sick 1. Lt Thomas 29 O.R. detailed for Camp duty at 29 C.C.S. Hospl. o. Grevillers. Capt McConnell returned Lt Thomas at A.O.S. Wastage 6. Beauval.	nil.
Letacquise	23/6/17	9 pm	Sick 1. Lt hy Soffer o P.O. Murphy returned from leave. Hospl. o. 2.O.R. on leave. Capt Evans returned from School of Wastage 6.O.R. Cookery. Capt Davis went to Cookery school. I.O.	nil.
Letacquise	24/6/17	9 pm	Sick 1. Capt Lang transferred to home Establishment of Shingles Hospl. o. Capt Helm his service to the unit. Wastage 10. 6.O.R. Pte Jackson to St Vallerie.	nil.
Letacquise	25/6/17	9 pm	Sick 1. H.O.R. returned from out camp at St Vallerie Hospl. o. 3 O.R. to Amiens for a days leave. Wastage 1. Off. 6.O.R.	nil.
Letacquise	26/6/17	9 pm	Sick 2. Hospl. o. Wastage 1. Off. 10 O.R.	nil.

Army Form C. 2118.

WAR DIARY
or
INTELLIGENCE SUMMARY
(Erase heading not required.)

Place	Date	Hour	Summary of Events and Information	Remarks and references to Appendices
Lebucquire	27/6/17	9 am	Sick 1. Shofit~0. Wastage 1 off. 6 O.R.	all.
Lebucquire	28/6/17	9 am	Sick 1. Shofit~0. Wastage 1 off. 6 O.R. 5.bn. L (Chuck). Motor Ambulance.	aeph.
Lebucquire	29/6/17	9 am	Sick 1. Shofit~0. Wastage 1 off. 6 O.R. Cap Harrison & Cap Rowe returned from leave.	aell.
Lebucquire	30/6/17	9 am	Sick 4. Shofit~0. Wastage 1 off. 6 O.R. 3 O.R. went on leave to England.	aeph.

Army Form C. 2118.

WAR DIARY
or
INTELLIGENCE SUMMARY
(Erase heading not required.)

Place	Date	Hour	Summary of Events and Information	Remarks and references to Appendices
			— Appendix —	

Summary of Admissions & Discharges. June 1917.

	Admissions.			Discharges.				
	Officers	O.R.		C.C.S.		Transfers	Duty	Died
	S W	S W		Offrs OR	Offrs OR	Offrs OR	Offrs OR	Offrs OR
Advanced Dressing Station Lebucquière	- 1	123 71		- 105	- 62	- 24	- 1	- 1

Remaining 30 June 1917
O Ranks (sick) 1.

Appendix. Pages 1.

A. W. Musgrove
LIEUT. COL. R.A.M.C. T.
COMMANDING 2ND FD. AMB.
48 DIV

140/2354.

1 1st South Midwx F.A.

COMMITTEE FOR THE
MEDICAL HISTORY OF THE WAR
Date -1 OCT.1917

Army Form C. 2118.

WAR DIARY
or
INTELLIGENCE SUMMARY
(Erase heading not required.)

Vol 29

Confidential.

1/2 South Midland Field Ambulance.

For B.E.F.

Feb 22 -

1 Feb 1917 — 31st Feb 1917.

Vol 22
page. 1
Appendix 1.

1/2nd
SOUTH MIDLAND
FIELD AMBULANCE.
No. 70 376
Date 1 JUL 1917

Wyburgh
Lt Col.

LIEUT. COL. R.A.M.C.
COMMANDING 2nd S.M. FD. AMB.
48 DIV.

Place	Date	Hour	Summary of Events and Information	Remarks and references to Appendices

WAR DIARY
or
INTELLIGENCE SUMMARY

Army Form C. 2118.

Place	Date	Hour	Summary of Events and Information	Remarks and references to Appendices
Rebecquit	1/7/17	9 pm	Strength 4 officers 100. 2 O.R. Col. heek took Major Stong U.S.A. visited Ambulance & inspected advanced post at Hennen. 2 O.R. received as reinforcement. Lieut. Clark returned from leave.	asph.
Rebecquit	2/7/17	9 pm	Strength 2 officers 100. Wastage 1 off. 4 O.R. Pte Gibson returned from detached duty. Capt Bowman returned from temp duty with 1 Ranks Highland Inf.	asph.
Rebecquit	3/7/17	9 pm	Strength 1 officer 100. Wastage 1 off. 3 O.R. Handed over advanced dressing station at Hennen. Bearers Reserves at 10 pm to parties of 142 Fld Amb. Handed over H.Q. at Retraquie to 142 Fld Amb at 12 am. 1 O.R. a/c received as reinforcement. Departed enroute march at 12.15 with 145 Inf. Brigade to Bihucourt. G.17.d.7.9. (map 51 C.). Arrived at 4.30 pm.	map.
Bihucourt	4/7/17	9 pm	Strength 3 O.R. A & C Sect. departed enroute march at 6.15 for Bihucourt with 112 & 145 Inf Brigade. B Sect. remaining. R.31.b.2.3 map 51 C.	asph.

Army Form C. 2118.

WAR DIARY
or
INTELLIGENCE SUMMARY

(Erase heading not required.)

Instructions regarding War Diaries and Intelligence Summaries are contained in F. S. Regs, Part II. and the Staff Manual respectively. Title Pages will be prepared in manuscript.

Place	Date	Hour	Summary of Events and Information	Remarks and references to Appendices
Bellacourt	5/7/17	9 pm	Sick 0. Ambulance closed. Conference with O.C. Brigade commanders. Hospital: Pte Bennett: leave. L/Cpl Cork: went on leave. Wastage 1 off. 3 O.R. Bar't arrived with new draft of 1st & 2nd Brigade at 10 pm.	appx
Bellacourt	6/7/17	9 pm	Sick 2. Hospital 0. Wastage 1 off. 2 O.R. Ambulance training commenced.	appx
Bellacourt	7/7/17	9 pm	Sick 8. Hospital 0. Wastage 1 off. 3 O.R. Pte Heiron returned from leave. Route march.	appx
Bellacourt	8/7/17	9 pm	Sick 4. Hospital 0. Wastage 1 off. 2 O.R. Pte Heiron received as reinforcement. Capt Kemmy & 2 O.R. went on leave to England. Pte Ritchie A. L. to 5th Army Rest Camp.	appx
Bellacourt	9/7/17	9 pm	Sick 1. Hospital 0. Wastage 1 off. 1 O.R. Brigade Field Day. The whole ambulance with transport engaged. Capt Towstino, C.F. (hon CyS) attached to the ambulance. 1 8 O.R. returned from detached duty at 2/g CCS.	appx

2449 Wt. W14957/M90 750,000 1/16 J.B.C. & A. Forms/C.2118/12.

WAR DIARY
or
INTELLIGENCE SUMMARY

(Erase heading not required.)

Army Form C. 2118.

Place	Date	Hour	Summary of Events and Information	Remarks and references to Appendices
Bellacourt	10/7/17	9/am	Sick 5. Hospital 0. Wastage 1 off. 2 O.R. Dr Jackson returned from 3rd Army rest Camp. Pte Parker, his Employment Co. attached as servant to Rev Winter. Conference with G.O.C. Pte Whyton, Parlg., 2nd Section on leave to England.	Appx.
Bellacourt	11/7/17	9/am	Sick 2. Hospital 0. Wastage 1 off. 2 O.R. L/C Jephcott, Pte Fewell, George Slade on leave to England. Training continued. Conferences, sketches, drill.	Appx.
Bellacourt	12/7/17	9/am	Sick 3. Hospital 0. Wastage 1 OR. Pte Rowland Stammers received as reinforcement. Route march, passed on the march the Major of the Kings.	Appx.
Bellacourt	13/7/17	9/am	Sick 1. Hospital 1. Wastage 1 off. In Tripoli Barbe to Hospital Sick. 3 O.R. returned from leave.	Appx.
Bellacourt	14/7/17	9/am	Sick 8. Hospital 1. Wastage 1 off. Influenza 1 O.R. 1 O.R. received as reinforcement. Pte C.C.S. McDowell detached to Coy H.Qrs. Corpl Davis returned from Army Cookery School.	Appx.

WAR DIARY or INTELLIGENCE SUMMARY

Army Form C. 2118.

(Erase heading not required.)

Instructions regarding War Diaries and Intelligence Summaries are contained in F. S. Regs., Part II. and the Staff Manual respectively. Title Pages will be prepared in manuscript.

Place	Date	Hour	Summary of Events and Information	Remarks and references to Appendices
Bellacourt	15/7/17	9 am	Sick 1. Stopt 1. 4 OR went on leave to England. Athletic Sports held for 1st Ambulance. Postings 1 Off. Joined 1 OR.	a & l.
Bellacourt	16/7/17	a/pm	Sick 5. Stopt 1. 1 OR transferred to 1/2 Fld Amb. BdMS 1st Corps visited ambulance. Wastage 1 Off. 2 OR went on leave to England.	a & f.
Bellacourt	17/7/17	9 pm	Sick 4. Interpreter Boule to CCS. Stopt 0. Field day under 145 Bde orders. Wastage 1 Off. 3 officers a bearer subdivisions of B & C 2nd: entrained march at 2pm at Beaumetz for XVIII Corps area.	a & l.
Bellacourt	18/7/17	9 pm	Sick 2. Pte Kerr & Yelp. Cpl returned from leave. Stopt 0. 1 motor Ambulance to XVIII Corps workshop. Wastage 1 Off.	a & l.
Bellacourt	19/7/17	9 pm	Sick 3. Sit Major trepand to England on appointment as Lt & Qm. Stopt 0. 10 R to the advance party to XVIII Corps area. Wastage 1 Off. (aoc) 1 OR.	a & f.

2449 Wt. W14957/M90 750,000 1/16 J.B.C. & A. Forms/C.2118/12.

Army Form C. 2118.

WAR DIARY
or
INTELLIGENCE SUMMARY
(Erase heading not required.)

Instructions regarding War Diaries and Intelligence Summaries are contained in F. S. Regs., Part II and the Staff Manual respectively. Title Pages will be prepared in manuscript.

Place	Date	Hour	Summary of Events and Information	Remarks and references to Appendices
Bellacourt	20/7/17	9/pm	Sick 2. Hospital- 0. Casualties 1 Off. 1 O.R. Route march.	R.M.
Bellacourt	21/7/17	9/pm	Sick 2. Hospital- 0. Casualties 1 Off. 1 O.R. 3 O.R. Bomd. Cartwright, Davis W.J. on leave to England. ADMS G.I. Young Li. L. Bom S. 1st Cdn. Cent Murray 2 O.R. returned from leave.	R&L.
Bellacourt	22/7/17	9/pm	Sick 0. Hospital- 0. Casualties 1 Off. 1 O.R. Unit moved to Mondicourt arriving 4.10 and entrained complete with transport.	R&L.
Marcaut Farm	23/7/17	9/pm	Sick 2. Hospital- 0. Casualties 1 Off. 1 O.R. Arrived at Godeweersvelde at 4 am. detrained and marched to Mouthurspe and on to Marcaut Farm. remained closed. collected sick of 145 Bde. 1 O.R. on leave to England.	R&L.
Marcaut Farm	24/7/17	9/pm	Sick 3. Hospital- 0. Casualties 1 Off. 1 O.R. Deports by 1st march to L'Elsie Farm. to bivouac where Lt. ambulance remained parked. Capt. Marle + their subdivision remained at Marcaut Farm to collect sick of 145 Bde. Capt Murray + 1 Lieut- first division to No. 3 Canadian C.C.S. Remy siding for temp duty.	R&L.

Army Form C. 2118.

WAR DIARY
or
INTELLIGENCE SUMMARY

(Erase heading not required.)

Instructions regarding War Diaries and Intelligence Summaries are contained in F. S. Regs., Part II and the Staff Manual respectively. Title Pages will be prepared in manuscript.

Place	Date	Hour	Summary of Events and Information	Remarks and references to Appendices
R'Elbo Farm	25/7/17	9/am	Sick 2. Major J.O Summerhays B.S.C. Capt McArthur taken to Shingle Hospital. Capt Bowman to 1/6 Glos. off Shingle. Casualties 10R. L/Cpl Clayton returned from leave. Major Summerhays to No 3 Canadian C.C.S. in relief of Capt Murray. Capt McConnell & Lt Munro returned from detached duty at Corps main Dressing Station. Lt Qm Wright Shuck M Shingles from 20th inst. Col Richard Chg. to med Lt W Division ADMS	Appx.
R'Elbo Farm	26/7/17	9/am	Sick 2. Hospital O. Pte Batin returned from V Corps Rest Camp. Casualties 10R. Lt Qm Wright leave Batentes to aug 6th and hit as above.	Appx.
R'Elbo Farm	27/7/17	9/am	Sick 1. Hospital O. 2 OR. returned from leave. Casualties 10R. Conference at L O M S office Capt McConnell & Capt Munro — 2 OR. detached to Bde Div. for temporary duty.	Appx.

Army Form C. 2118.

WAR DIARY
or
INTELLIGENCE SUMMARY
(Erase heading not required.)

Instructions regarding War Diaries and Intelligence Summaries are contained in F. S. Regs., Part II. and the Staff Manual respectively. Title Pages will be prepared in manuscript.

Place	Date	Hour	Summary of Events and Information	Remarks and references to Appendices
P. Eske Farm	28/7/17	9 pm	Sick 1. O.R. Sick. 6 O.R. returned from leave. Capt Bodem & Pte Silvers on leave to England. Wastage 2.	aaft
P. Eske Farm	29/7/17	9 pm	Sick 1. 6 O.R. returned from attached duty with 133 Fd Amb. 3 O.R. on leave to England. 6 Pack battles received as additional equipment. Wastage 2.	aaft.
P. Eske Farm	30/7/17	9 pm	Sick. 2. Pte Brenner Harley to CCS Mshingtoi. Pte Roberts Jnr. to 31 Labour Group. Pte Maher to 6 Oxford Bucks. Pte Barrett to 2/1 Devons Rtn. private duty off Shingtoi. Lt Wade - 25 O.R. returned from Marcant Farm. Montebroth to No 145 Fd Bce. Wastage 7.	aaft.
P. Eske Farm	31/7/17	9 pm	Sick 5 Motor Ambulance. +14 O.R. attached to M.A.C. Hosp 3. 2 O.R. arrived from leave. Wastage 7.	aaft.

Army Form C. 2118.

WAR DIARY
or
INTELLIGENCE SUMMARY
(Erase heading not required.)

Place	Date	Hour	Summary of Events and Information	Remarks and references to Appendices
			July 1917	
			Appendix	
			SUMMARY OF ADMISSIONS & DISCHARGES.	
			OFFICERS — NIL.	
			ORANKS:—	
			ADMITTED (SICK) 9	
			TO. C.C.S. " 4	
			TRANSFERS " 5	
			WOUNDED — NIL.	
			Appendix 1.	W.J. Wingate Lt Col.
			Volume 22.	1/2 I.M. Fld Amb.
2/2nd SOUTH MIDLAND FIELD AMBULANCE 31 JUL 1917				

14/2264

1/3rd South Midland F.A.

COMMITTEE FOR THE
MEDICAL HISTORY OF THE WAR
Date -1 OCT. 1917

Aug. 15. 17

Army Form C. 2118.

WAR DIARY
or
INTELLIGENCE SUMMARY.
(Erase heading not required.)

1/2 South Midland Field Ambulance

Volume 23

1 Aug 1917 – 31 Aug 1917

CONFIDENTIAL

Pages to.

Rupert Brotherwick
Capt RAMC T.F.
RO C/2 S.M. Field Amb.

Army Form C. 2118.

WAR DIARY
or
INTELLIGENCE SUMMARY

(Erase heading not required.)

Instructions regarding War Diaries and Intelligence Summaries are contained in F. S. Regs., Part II. and the Staff Manual respectively. Title Pages will be prepared in manuscript.

Place	Date	Hour	Summary of Events and Information	Remarks and references to Appendices
P'Esse Farm	1/8/17	6pm	Sich 12. Conference with AOMS. Hospital 2. on leave 7.	Appx.
P'Esse Farm	2/8/17	6pm	Sich 14. Pte Oetrie to CCS off through. Hospital 2. on leave 8.	Appx.
P'Esse Farm	3/8/17	6pm	Sich 17. Pte Jackson (M.T) to CCS, wounded. Hospital 2. 2 OR returned from leave. on leave 9.	Appx.
P'Esse Farm	4/8/17	6pm	Sick 14. 4 OR on leave to England. Hospital 2. Pte Beach, Owen, Whittaker returned from leave. on leave 9.	Appx.
Goudol Farm A.28.a.2.4.	5/8/17	6pm	Sick 9. HQ Ok. Transport moved to Goudal Farm A.28.a.2.4. Hospital 2. 3 Officers and 3 Bearer Sub-divisions of 1st Sub-division on leave 9. moved to Div Collecting Post. C.21.c.4.3. map 28. 1 Sect Sub-division to walking wounded Collecting Post. Pte Thompson, Goodyer to 5th Army rest camp. H. B. d. Pte Matthews, Hickman dropall off a leave to England. 1 Cpl Conkanti returned from leave.	Appx.

WAR DIARY
or
INTELLIGENCE SUMMARY

(Erase heading not required.)

Army Form C. 2118.

Place	Date	Hour	Summary of Events and Information	Remarks and references to Appendices
Quetta Cann.	6/6/17	9 pm	Sick 3. Pte Hughes E.M. Welsh. Hall. marked to CCS wounded. Habit 2. Visits by P. & the ADMS. the C.V.S & Lt Birch. Indian 13. Convoys at intervals by 4 teams of elephant rotary. Established two relay posts. Detached & leave to act as runners to line at Batt. of 145 Bgs in his line. 2 Officers & 3 Bearer Subdivisions of 1/3 F.S.Amb. attached for Bearer work. Pte Cartwright R. returned from leave.	acpl.
Quetta Cann.	7/8/17	9 am	Sick R. 3. Cpl Knight on leave to England. Habit 1. Pte Hatton & Whitaker, Pt Gardner to CCS wounded. Indian 16. Cpt Bruce returned from detached duty with 3 Bos.	chapl.
Quetta Cann.	8/8/17	9 am	Sick R. 3. Pte Griffiths to CCS sick. Pte Croyats to CCS wounded. Habit 1. 2 Heavy draughts & light draughts have killed 2 " wounded & Invalids Indianape 18. Pte Bond to hosp. wounded. Pte Dunsmore leave to England.	acpl

2449 Wt. W14957/Mg0 750,000 1/16 J.B.C. & A. Forms/C.2118/12.

WAR DIARY
or
INTELLIGENCE SUMMARY
(Erase heading not required.)

Army Form C. 2118.

Place	Date	Hour	Summary of Events and Information	Remarks and references to Appendices
Gustot Farm 9/6/17	9/6/17	9 pm	SiR 3. Pte Bahn A. Killed in action. Pte Beardsley to CCS wounded. Pte B most disch hospt. Hospt 6. to cut up to DCP this place has been much bombed also work proceeding at the new DCP informed. C.22 C.1.E. Lt Thomas and 65 Bearers relieves to Walwortage 20. Wd Oc Fr 4 & hrs rest. Pte Walter Pritchard sent to hospt. Pte to eight to hospt.	aayh
Guest Farm	10/6/17	9 pm	SiR 19. Pte Warrington to CCS sickness. Hospt 6. 3.O.R. returned from leave. Wortage 21.	aayh
Gust Farm	11/6/17	9 pm	SiR 21. Lg. Pritchard on leave to England. Hospt 3. Bearers all returned to DCP under Capt McConnell. Wortage 20. Lt Hanly returned to the OC for 24 hours rest. Capt Murray Lt Thomas Lt Capt to W CP. with remainder of 6 Sect. Tent sub division in Pte Pritchard, Gough, Clithoe returned from Corps rest station	aayh

WAR DIARY
or
INTELLIGENCE SUMMARY

Army Form C. 2118.

(Erase heading not required.)

Place	Date	Hour	Summary of Events and Information	Remarks and references to Appendices
Godwit Farm	12/5/17	9am	Sick 1. 15 OR. Rand recvd as reinforcement. Hospl 3. 1 OR. ASC (HT) recvd as reinforcement. Pt Martin returned to W.W.O.Q. Casltic 4. Pt. Mullin, Walsh, Manuel on leave to England.	aaU.
Godwit Farm	13/5/17	9am	Sick 4. Pt Pickles to CCS wounded. Hospl 3. Dr Nealin Mostly returned from leave. Wastings 5. Pte Corben on leave to England. 29. OR reports to duty from 23 Dvn. (6a Festubert). 2 mules sent to 145 Bde. Lys Shingle 1846 somewhere sick.	aaU.
Godwit Farm	14/5/17	9am	Sick 2. Sgt Majr Pickles reports from ADMS office for duty. Hospl 4. Lt Capt Greenaway, D.r Greenwood to OCS wounded. Wastings 1. Belgian interpreter D. Important attached to us 3. Our Ambulance for duty. Pte Tolloff to hospital, sick	aaU.

WAR DIARY
or
INTELLIGENCE SUMMARY

Army Form C. 2118.

Place	Date	Hour	Summary of Events and Information	Remarks and references to Appendices
Canal Farm.	15/6/17	9 pm	Sch 2 Lt-Col Hungerton proceeded to D.C.P. August 5 Below disposition of R.A.M.C. bearers on Y day. meeting 8.	

Alberta Fm.
1 Platoon, 12 R.A.M.C.
Capt McConnell.

St Julien.
1 Platoon,
12 R.A.M.C.

RP 3.
1 off + sjt,
1 Platoon.

RP 2.
1 off + sjt,
1 Platoon.

RP 1.
1 off + sjt,
1 Platoon.

RP. (Vanheule St)
Capt Newman
40 R.A.M.C.

RP. (California)
Lt Poole
40 R.A.M.C.
2 bert orderlies.

RP. 40 R.A.M.C.

D.C.P.
C. 21. C.4.2.
Map 28.

½ test bat division
Reserve Bearers.
Lt-Col Hungerton
Capt Broderick M.C.
Capt Hodges.
Canal Bank.

Army Form C. 2118.

WAR DIARY
or
INTELLIGENCE SUMMARY

(Erase heading not required.)

Instructions regarding War Diaries and Intelligence Summaries are contained in F. S. Regs., Part II. and the Staff Manual respectively. Title Pages will be prepared in manuscript.

Place	Date	Hour	Summary of Events and Information	Remarks and references to Appendices
Goudberg Farm.	16/8/17	9 p.m.	Sick 2. 3 Rank & File. 3 O/C Buch admitted to Hospital while on leave in England — Strength Pte Jenn on leave. During the day 264 lying wounded (officers) were cleared. Casualties this D.C.P.	nil.
Goudberg Farm	17/8/17	9 p.m.	Sick 3. Hospital 5. Casualties 6. The front was practically cleared of wounded during the night and the numbers coming thro' fell considerably during the afternoon. 2. O.R. returned from leave. Pte Foley, Brazier, Weston leave to England.	nil.
Goudberg Farm.	18/8/17	9 p.m.	Sick 5. Hospital 4. Casualties 10. Sgt Thomas, Butler A, Delaney to C.C.S. wounded. Pte Waite to C.C.S. sick. Pte Worrall A.H. returned from leave. Pte Goodzys G. Thurston returned from 5th Army. Lieut Sewart returned to H.Q. Sh. Pte Wade wounded. D.C.P. at Hamond's Corner reported by La Belle Alliance on account of the former place being destroyed by shell fire!	nil.

Army Form C. 2118.

WAR DIARY
or
INTELLIGENCE SUMMARY
(Erase heading not required.)

Instructions regarding War Diaries and Intelligence Summaries are contained in F. S. Regs, Part II. and the Staff Manual respectively. Title Pages will be prepared in manuscript.

Place	Date	Hour	Summary of Events and Information	Remarks and references to Appendices
Gwent Farm	19/8/17	9 pm	List 4. Hospit 4. Pte Cottingham to CCS wounded. Wastage 11.	all
Gwent Farm	20/8/17	9 pm	List 4. Hospit-4. 1 male returned to S.C.P. La Belle Alliance Wastage 11. Corpl bought returned from leave.	all
Gwent Farm	20/8/17	9 pm	Sick 4. Hospit-4. Wastage 11. Pte Bryan, Goff. L/Cpl Pratt. L/Cpl Valentine wounded. Sgt Gill wounded remaining on duty. 1 tin hair received. 2 males handed over. 1 male to Mot Tpt Sect. Sgt Lewis, Yapp, Birs on leave to England.	acpt.
Gwent Farm	20/8/17	9 pm	Sick. 10. Hospit-8. Wastage 11. Pte Shaler returned from CCS on strength. Pte Duncan returned from leave. Pte Bryan to CCS wounded. Lt made SoRnd returned from S.C.P.	acpt.

2449 Wt. W14957/M90 750,000 1/16 J.B.C. & A. Forms/C.2118/12.

Army Form C. 2118.

WAR DIARY
or
INTELLIGENCE SUMMARY

(Erase heading not required.)

Instructions regarding War Diaries and Intelligence Summaries are contained in F.S. Regs., Part II and the Staff Manual respectively. Title Pages will be prepared in manuscript.

Place	Date	Hour	Summary of Events and Information	Remarks and references to Appendices
Gwalt Farm	23/8/17	9am	Sick 4. 6 OR on leave to England. Strtht-8. Returns to no 3 Canadian CCS for duty. Contag. 9. 2.OR. ASC (MT) unpleaded returns.	AAyL
Gwalt Farm	24/8/17	9am	Sick 4. 1 OR on leave to England. Strtht-5. Lieut Ruthven returned from leave. Contag.12. Pte Hitchcock. Gott. L.Cpl Prett to CCS wounded.	AAyL
Gwalt Farm	25/8/17	9am	Sick R. 2. 4 OR returned from leave. Strtht-5. Pte Orchard on leave to England. Contag 12.	AAyL
Gwalt Farm	26/8/17	9am	Sick 3. Lt Marle to 46 Warw.Regt and AA Strngth. Strtht-5. Capt Mc Arthur proceeded to England at his Return of his Contract- off strngth. hosptal 1/5. 5 Troops on to CCS wounded.	AAyL

2449 Wt. W14957/M90 750,000 1/16 J.B.C. & A. Forms/C.2118/12.

WAR DIARY
or
INTELLIGENCE SUMMARY

(Erase heading not required.)

Army Form C. 2118.

Place	Date	Hour	Summary of Events and Information	Remarks and references to Appendices
Gwalt Farm	27/8/17	9am	Sick 1. Pte Crozier returned from leave. Hospl → 3 Pte Bennett W. & Hines H. to CCS Wounded Wastage 17 *	RWB
Gwalt Farm	28/8/17	9pm	Sick 1 Hosp. 3. Wastage 17	2 Officers & 20 O.R. returned from C.W.W.C.S.	PAB
Gwalt Farm	29/8/17	9pm	Sick 1 Hosp 3 Wastage 16	Forward area handed over to 5-8th Div. Hamoyses hts Ronnel to France. Capt McDonnell detached to Buckleston for duty. Capt Forderick & OR returned to HQ. Cpl Martin & 5 OR detached to 5-8 Div for duty. 3rd Can. att. to 58 Div. for our ty. Pte Wright retd from CCS stamp 1/8	RAB

Army Form C. 2118.

WAR DIARY
or
INTELLIGENCE SUMMARY

(Erase heading not required.)

Instructions regarding War Diaries and Intelligence Summaries are contained in F. S. Regs., Part II. and the Staff Manual respectively. Title Pages will be prepared in manuscript.

Place	Date	Hour	Summary of Events and Information	Remarks and references to Appendices
L'Eppe Farm	30/8/17	9 am	Unit moved to L'Eppel Farm's closed. Stop. 4 OR 1 Off. Cpl Davis from leave. Wantage 16 Lt-Col Kingston to hosp. Pte Cannings to hosp. Pte Thomas to Band Bn for duty (vice Capt McDonnell returned) reporting strength home Establishment Lt + Un bought reported for duty from	RMB
L'Eppel Farm	31/8/17	9 pm	L/Cpl Stott reformed from CCS. von strength Stop. 4 OR 1 Off. Dr Attfield returned to No 4 Co hosp appt through Wantage 16 Dr Williams (rcd) on new appointment Pte Frazier retd from leave Lt Tickell, Shutcross Left Baker B, Preston Dr Dowell + Dr Chilton on leave to England	RMB

2449 Wt. W14957/M90 750,000 1/16 J.B.C. & A. Forms/C.2118/12.

1/2nd South Midland F.A.

40/499.

COMMITTEE FOR THE
MEDICAL HISTORY OF THE WAR
Date -8 DEC. 1917

Army Form C. 2118.

WAR DIARY
or
INTELLIGENCE SUMMARY.
(Erase heading not required.)

Vol 31

CONFIDENTIAL.

1/2nd SOUTH MIDLAND FIELD AMBULANCE.

1st September 1917 to 30th September 1917.

VOLUME 24.

Ralph R Roderick

LIEUT COL R.A.M.C.
COMMANDING FIELD AMB.
48 DIV.

Pages 10
Appendix 1. and 2.

Army Form C. 2118.

WAR DIARY
or
INTELLIGENCE SUMMARY.
(Erase heading not required.)

Place	Date	Hour	Summary of Events and Information	Remarks and references to Appendices
L'EBBE FARM	1/9/17	9pm	Sick 4. Hosp. 5 +10H wastage 17. Cpl Martin (attacked 5th Dr) killed in action. Lt. Col. things to C.C.S. 4 O.R. ret'd from leave 5 O.R. proceeded on leave 7 O.R. to 5th D.R. to duty 3 O.R. returned from 5th D.R. Incl Ca. ranker ret'd from 5th Dr.	Rifles
L'EBBE Farm	2/9/17	9am	Sick 3 Hosp 5 all ranks 10 R. on leave wastage 17	Pte Donnelly ret'd from hospital Pte Phillips ret'd from C.M.D.S.	RAB.
L'EBBE Farm	3/9/17	9pm	Sick 6 Hosp 3 wastage 18	Ptes Powney Hoeft to hosp. Pte Moon to C.C.S. sick Sgt Morris ret'd from leave C. Sect. Tent Subdivision returned from No.3 Canadian C.C.S. Inspection by A.D.M.S.	Rifles

WAR DIARY
or
INTELLIGENCE SUMMARY.
(Erase heading not required.)

Army Form C. 2118.

Instructions regarding War Diaries and Intelligence Summaries are contained in F. S. Regs., Part II. and the Staff Manual respectively. Title pages will be prepared in manuscript.

Place	Date	Hour	Summary of Events and Information	Remarks and references to Appendices
L'EBBE FARM	4/9/17	9 am	Pte Brunner retd. from C.C.S. Lt Maule rejoined for duty Capt Murray & servant detached to 91 H.A.G. Physical duties - Company Stretcher Drill Sick 8 Hosp. 3 Wastage 16	RMB
L'EBBE Farm	5/9/17	9 am	Capt MacDermott T.E. reported for duty. 3 O.R. on leave. Baths for unit Sick 6 Hosp. 3 Wastage 15.	RMB
L'EBBE Farm	6/9/17	9 am	Pte Cannings to hosp. 3 O.R. from leave. 5 O.R. off on leave, leave to England. Physical Company & Stretcher Drill Sick 2 Hosp. 2 Wastage 15.	RMB
L'EBBE Farm	7/9/17	9 am	Ptes Latch & Krant S.J. admitted to hosp. 2 O.R. on return from leave roft. strength. Capt Read reported for duty 3 O.R. returned from leave. 6 O.R. on leave. Pte Carruthers on leave to Cookery School. Training continued Sick 3. Hosp. 2 Wastage 16	RMB

Army Form C. 2118.

WAR DIARY
or
INTELLIGENCE SUMMARY.
(Erase heading not required.)

Instructions regarding War Diaries and Intelligence Summaries are contained in F.S. Regs., Part II. and the Staff Manual respectively. Title pages will be prepared in manuscript.

Place	Date	Hour	Summary of Events and Information	Remarks and references to Appendices
L'EBRE FARM	8/9/17	9 p.m.	Sick 3. Capt Read T.F, Capt Merkle T.F, Capt Samuel T.F. reported for duty. Taken on Strength. Capt Merkle on leave to England - reporting at to Division on Return. Major Penman-Hayes T.F. to 1st Can Field Amb off Strength. Wastage 5.O.R. 1 O.R. Bruce O.R.A. as reinforcement. Surplus 1 O.R. 1 O.R. on leave to England. 2 O.R. on leave. 3 O.R. returned from leave. Route march. Training continued.	RW&B
L'EBRE Farm	9/9/17	9 a.m.	Sick 1. 7 O.R. sent to 58 D.R. to relieve leaves in the line. Hosp 2. Lt Piper ACR MS reported for duty taken on strength. Wastage 5 O.R. Surplus 20 O.R.	RW&B
L'EBRE Farm	10/9/17	9 p.m.	Sick 5. Pte O'Hara R/5131 driver returned to Strength. Hosp 2. the Farrier returned to unit from s/Sussex. On Strength. Wastage 5 O.R. Lt Price, Lt Giles & 125 dgd for instruction in SbL Parie Surplus 2 O.H. Athletic club. Authority an thorise to Mintleny Cross by Capt McDonnell & Company Ostellackowitz. Training continued. Physical in	RW&B

Army Form C. 2118.

WAR DIARY
or
INTELLIGENCE SUMMARY.
(Erase heading not required.)

Place	Date	Hour	Summary of Events and Information	Remarks and references to Appendices
L'EBRE Farm	11/9/17	9am	Sick 3 Hosp 2 boat. 5 OR Surplus 2 OR	Capt McDonnell on 3 days leave to Paris. Dr Hartspe arrived on reinforcement. Dr Litiquano returned to No 2 by train. Route March.	RKB
L'EBRE Farm	12/9/17	9am	Sick 3 Hosp 2 boat. 2 ASC Surplus 2 OR 10 R Rhine	Cpl Pratt & Pte Foaye & ree'd as reinforcements 2 Ace Drivers rec'd as reinforcements. 2 OR on leave. 2 OR returned from leave. Training continued.	RKB
L'EBRE Farm	13/9/17	9am	Sick 3 Hosp 1 boat. 2 ASC Surplus 10 R 10 R Rhine	Lt Col Hampton to Boy land sick 4 OR Hosp & Pte Fraye & Ace & ree'd as reinforcements. 7 OR on leave 5 OR returned from leave Training continued	RKB
L'EBRE Farm	14/9/17	9am	Sick 4 Hosp 0 boat 2 ASC Surplus Nott	Pte Colliott to England sick & off strength 2 OR deture on leave. 2 OR on leave. Capt Muirhead returned from leave to Paris Capt Read to 1/8 wore. for duty 10 off strength	RKB

Army Form C. 2118.

WAR DIARY
or
INTELLIGENCE SUMMARY.
(Erase heading not required.)

Place	Date	Hour	Summary of Events and Information	Remarks and references to Appendices
L'ROBBE Town	15/9/17	9pm	Sec T4 Hosp 2 wast 2 Offs	Pte Phillips J Harold C to Hosp. 10/R on leave. 10/R returned from leave. 10/R movement to 145 Bde transport to Zeggers Cappell.	RMB
LIEQUES	16/9/17	9pm	Sick 2 Hosp 3 wast 2 Offs	Motor lorry transport moved by train to XIX Corps Area, detraining at AUDRUCQ. Proceeded by route march to LIEQUES, taking over from 1/6 Lancs Stat Amb. the rest of XIX Corps Road Transport. Strength of 2/48 I Div. Transport Station reporting for sick 6pm. Interpreter to Stat. reports or at 6pm.	RMB
LIEQUES	17/9/17	9pm	Sick 2 Hosp 3 wast 2 Offs	30/R on leave. Arrangements for collecting sick & healing them completed.	RMB

WAR DIARY
or
INTELLIGENCE SUMMARY.
(Erase heading not required.)

Army Form C. 2118.

Place	Date	Hour	Summary of Events and Information	Remarks and references to Appendices
LIEQUES	18/9/17	9pm	Sick 2. Both on leave. 1 offr returned. 1 offr returned from leave. Hosp 2. 8 P.B. men arrived to replace 8 Batmen. Creat - Surplus 60R.	PHR
LICQUES	19/9/17	9pm	Sick 4. Pte Phillips & Arnold returned from hosp. Hosp. — 20R. on leave. Creat — 30R. MSO to 19 T.S. after Hosp. Surplus 30R RSO. Pte La Barbara transferred to become x1x C.P.S. Hospital.	PHR
LIEQUES	20/9/17	9pm	Sick 3. Hosp — Lost — Surplus 30R RSO	Nothing to report. PHR
LICQUES	21/9/17	9pm	Sick 2. Hosp — Creat — Surplus 30R RSO	3 ORs returned from leave. 1 Cpl to men to 58 I.B.D. to relieve leave absent. attached there. hill from Staff Instructor in Physical Drill from 14S — R9H	PHR

WAR DIARY
or
INTELLIGENCE SUMMARY.

(Erase heading not required.)

Army Form C. 2118.

Instructions regarding War Diaries and Intelligence Summaries are contained in F.S. Regs., Part II. and the Staff Manual respectively. Title pages will be prepared in manuscript.

Place	Date	Hour	Summary of Events and Information	Remarks and references to Appendices
Licques	22/9/17	9 pm	Sick 3 Adm — boat. 1 O.R. 2 officers Surplus 3 O.R. A.F.C.	Interpreter to C.C.S. Sick — Off Strength 10 men returned from leave Capt Samuel to 33 C.C.S. off strength Capt MacDermott to 1/5 R.W. Regt on Strength. Bearers returned from leave on being relieved.	MHB
Licques	23/9/17	9 pm	Sick 4 Adm — Wastage 2 off. Surplus 3 O.R. A.F.C.	Pte Tapp reported from Base on Strength L.Cpl Sellars returned from leave 1 O.R. proceeded on leave.	MHB
Licques	24/9/17	9 pm	Sick 3 Adm — Wast.k. 1 off. Surplus 1 O.R. A.F.C. 3 O.R. A.F.C.	Interpreter reported for duty Capt Lang joined for duty, taken on strength Orders received to re-evacuate patients to duty or C.C.S.	MHB
Licques	25/9/17	9 pm	Sick 2 Adm — Wast. 1 off. R.A.M.C. Surplus 1 O.R. A.F.C. 3 O.R. A.F.C.	Evacuation of patients completed – Hospital clean by Noon. Capt Kemp R servant for temporary duty to 1/5 R. Regs.	MHB

WAR DIARY
or
INTELLIGENCE SUMMARY.

Army Form C. 2118.

Place	Date	Hour	Summary of Events and Information	Remarks and references to Appendices
Loc Q.4.25	26/9/17	9 P.m.	Sect 4. Transport moved at 6 P.M. under Lt Moule to Kopsel bec. Sect 1. Personnel moved at 12 N. to ZUTKERQUE (pronounced) from Pas 10A. Supplies 20R Ptme for the night. 30R HRC Prs to Burgham (returned from 24 S return on strength to Army Rest Camps. 20R 30R returned from 5 Army Rest Camp. 70R returned from leave.	
ZUDOVES ZUTKERQUE	27/9/17	9 P.m.	Sub 3. Transport moved under LT MAPLE to XVIII Corps main transport station arrived at 4 P.M. Sub 1. Personnel moved to AUDRICQ UE rendezvous for Brataye 70ff 30RABe BRIELEN r ten touched to XVIII Corps Main Qmps Divs 30R.Ptme 20R Ptme Dressing Station	

Army Form C. 2118.

WAR DIARY
or
INTELLIGENCE SUMMARY.
(Erase heading not required.)

Instructions regarding War Diaries and Intelligence Summaries are contained in F. S. Regs, Part II. and the Staff Manual respectively. Title pages will be prepared in manuscript.

Place	Date	Hour	Summary of Events and Information	Remarks and references to Appendices
GwAllA 22RM A28 2.3 Sheet 28	28/9/17	9pm	Sick 4 Hosp. 0 Took 10h Duty 30 Offic Lt Marks RB Tent Subdivision with Chams Bgt moved to XVth Corps walking wounded post. 19 Reserves under Cpl Roadman moved to HRS Du Sullows for duty, man OC 13 Lu SB. A.Y.C. Sent subdivisions took over Hospital Antus from 2/Ho SB at 12 noon. 30A returned from leave AgRD 1963. Pte Barner to Res sick Pte Goodall	RHJ RHJ
GwAllA James	29/9/17	9pm	Sick 2 Hosp. 1 Took 1 Duty 6 OR Capt Dobson T.C. attached temporarily for duty 8 OR returned from 58 Div. 6 OR returned from leave Surplus 30R ASC Pte Cawkitter returned from Cookery School	RHJ

Army Form C. 2118.

WAR DIARY
or
INTELLIGENCE SUMMARY.

(Erase heading not required.)

Instructions regarding War Diaries and Intelligence Summaries are contained in F. S. Regs., Part II. and the Staff Manual respectively. Title pages will be prepared in manuscript.

Place	Date	Hour	Summary of Events and Information	Remarks and references to Appendices
GWALIA FARM	30/9/17	9pm	Sent to Hosp. Corpl. 1 Off. Surplus 30R Bde. 50R relieved from Leave. Pte Hay to and to Office of D.A.D.M.S. for temporary duty.	RAMC

WAR DIARY or INTELLIGENCE SUMMARY

Army Form C. 2118.

XIXth CORPS REST STATION. (LICQUES, PAS DE CALAIS)

Date	Hour	ADMISSIONS				DISCHARGES.							REMAINING.		Remarks
		Officers		o.ranks		To C.C.S.		Duty		Transfer		Died		Offrs	o.ranks	
		S	W	S	W	Offrs	O.R.	Offrs	O.R.	Offrs	O.R.	Offrs	O.R.			
Hospital OPENED 10/9/17 CLOSED 26/9/17																
Sept. 17		-	-	2	-	-	-	-	-	-	-	-	-	-	2	
18		-	-	6	-	-	-	-	-	-	-	-	-	-	6	
19		-	-	8	-	-	-	-	2	-	-	-	-	-	11	
20		-	-	16	-	2	-	-	-	-	-	-	-	-	26	
21		-	-	23	-	1	-	-	1	-	-	-	-	-	40	
22		-	-	19	-	8	-	-	1	-	-	-	-	-	53	
23		-	-	14	-	6	-	-	1	-	-	-	-	-	61	
24		-	-	21	-	5	-	-	1	-	-	-	-	-	75	
25		1	-	22	-	2	1	-	28	-	-	1	-	-	1	
						69										
		1	-	131	-	1	96	-	34	-	1	-	1	-	-	

Appendix 1.
Volume 24.

Ralph R...
LIEUT. COL. R.A.M.C.T.
COMMANDING 2ND FD. AMB.

WAR DIARY
or
INTELLIGENCE SUMMARY.
(Erase heading not required.)

Army Form C. 2118.

Place	Date	Hour	Summary of Events and Information	Remarks and references to Appendices
			XVIII Corps Main Dressing Station (Sheet 28. 1/40,000. A.23 c.29)	
			Total cases passed through Ambulance & Discharge points of this S.M.Ambulance from 12 noon 28/9/17 to 9 p.m. 30/9/1917 } Officers. 19 O.Ranks. 350.	
			Of the above, 9 Officers and 157 O.Ranks were "Gassed" cases	
			XVIII Corps Walking Wounded Collecting Post (Sheet 28 1/40,000 H 3 d 5.8)	
			The numbers passed through are not to hand, but they will be included in next month's diary.	

Appendix I.
30/9/17.

R.R. Rolleuck
Lt Col.
Commanding 1/2 S.M.a. Ma. Amb.

COMMITTEE FOR THE
MEDICAL HISTORY OF THE WAR
Date -8 DEC. 1917

Army Form C. 2118.

WAR DIARY
or
INTELLIGENCE SUMMARY.
(Erase heading not required.)

Y/132

CONFIDENTIAL

1/2nd SOUTH MIDLAND FIELD AMBULANCE.

1st October 1917 to 31st October 1917.

VOLUME 25.

Pages 14.
Appendix 1.

H.P. Welwell
Captain R.A.M.C. T.
a/for O.C. 2nd S.M. Field Amb.
48th Division.

Army Form C. 2118.

WAR DIARY
or
INTELLIGENCE SUMMARY.
(Erase heading not required.)

Instructions regarding War Diaries and Intelligence Summaries are contained in F. S. Regs., Part II. and the Staff Manual respectively. Title pages will be prepared in manuscript.

Place	Date	Hour	Summary of Events and Information	Remarks and references to Appendices
Goolia Farm	29/10/17	9pm	Sick 1 1st 1 r.t. r.58 Beaumes to ADS Ambulance for duty in back 1st the front area. 30th ordered from leave. Hosp 1 Pte Purtell to Hosp. Surplus 30R.R.88.	R.R.8
Goolia Farm	30/10/17	9pm	Sick 4 Pte Rimmer to CCS. Pte Jacob to Hosp. Hosp 2 30th Pte leave to Base — MT r 3 Depot. Back 19A/10B. 30th. on leave 40th returned. Cpl Washbrook attached from 1st 3rd R.Ant Pte Kent awarded Military Medal	R.R.6
Goolia Farm	31/10/17	9pm	Sick 3 Dr Hall to CLS. Hosp 3 20th of 58 Div attached for duty at CMSS. Back 19A/10B. 30th returned from leave. T of R to CM. Ant attached for duty at CMSS.	R.R.6

Army Form C. 2118.

WAR DIARY
or
INTELLIGENCE SUMMARY.
(Erase heading not required.)

Instructions regarding War Diaries and Intelligence Summaries are contained in F. S. Regs., Part II. and the Staff Manual respectively. Title pages will be prepared in manuscript.

Place	Date	Hour	Summary of Events and Information	Remarks and references to Appendices
Gwaha Farm	4/10/17	9pm	Sick 2 Hosp 3 Total 10ft - 10R.	Capt Kay reinforcement returned to duty from K.R. Berks. 60 Sketch camps parade the "crypt" 24 hrs.	Riff
Gwaha Farm	5/10/17	9pm	Sick 2 Hosp 3 Total 10ft 10R.	Work as usual.	Riff
Gwaha Farm	6/10/17	9pm	Sick 1 Hosp 3 Total 10ft 10Off.	1 OR recd as reinforcement. 18 men sent to C.S.R. rept strength. Sgt Etta & 40 bearers returned from tse for rest	Riff
Gwaha Farm	7/10/17	9pm	Sick 2 Hosp 3 Total 10ft 10Off.	Sgt Giles & bearers returned to Du Talon Cpl Bott & 30 bearers returned for rest.	Riff

Army Form C. 2118.

WAR DIARY
or
INTELLIGENCE SUMMARY.
(Erase heading not required.)

Instructions regarding War Diaries and Intelligence Summaries are contained in F. S. Regs., Part II. and the Staff Manual respectively. Title pages will be prepared in manuscript.

Place	Date	Hour	Summary of Events and Information	Remarks and references to Appendices
Gwekin Farm	8/10/17	9am	Sick – Pte Lamb ex Hosp. Dr Hall to FCO. Pte Crowley to Hosp 1 FCS wounded – Pte Parker (P.B) to R.O. 2 O.R. returned from Rest Camp. 11 available bearers sent to detentions.	Field
Gwekin Farm	9/10/17	9pm	Sick 3 Pte Hodman & Wilson to Hosp Hosp 3 Pte travel by Sels from leave. Lost left 3 Pte Taylor killed in action 6 O.R. Pte Stair returned to CCS. bearers to Ashreight	R.H.B.
Gwekin Farm	10/10/17	9pm	Sick 1 Orders rec'd to hand over Pte D.S.T. to 6.6. C.P. Hosp 2 to 28th 2nd Aust. This was completed by 5 PM. Lost 108 t detachments moved to Turnells CRS Camp 6 O.R. Bearers reported from line. Pte Hardinn ex Hosp.	R.H.B.

Army Form C. 2118.

WAR DIARY
or
INTELLIGENCE SUMMARY.
(Erase heading not required.)

Instructions regarding War Diaries and Intelligence Summaries are contained in F. S. Regs., Part II. and the Staff Manual respectively. Title pages will be prepared in manuscript.

Place	Date	Hour	Summary of Events and Information	Remarks and references to Appendices
Tunnellers Camp	11/10/17	9pm	Sick – Lce Cpl returned for duty. Sgt. Sgt Baker & Sgt Gates to Hospital. Hosp 4 Evac. 1st C.C.S.	RWS
Tunnellers Camp	12/10/17	9pm	Sick 4 Hosp 6 Pte Hemir stood off. Pte W Piper returned to 1/6 barracks & off strength Evac. 2 off & B.o.R.	RWS
Tunnellers Camp	13/10/17	9pm	Sick 7 Hosp 6 Evac. 2 off & B.o.R. Dr Boydone on leave	RWS
In the Snow	14/10/17	9pm	Sick 2 Hosp 6 Evac. 2 off & B.o.R. Unit moved to HOPOUTRE station. Unit transport & Motor Ambulances moved more permanently to CAMBLIGNEUL	RWS

Place	Date	Hour	Summary of Events and Information	Remarks and references to Appendices
LES QUATRE VENTS	15/10/17	9pm	Sits. Hosp: 6 Wast: 204 BOR. Unit detrained at LIGNY ST FLOCHEL & proceeded by march route to LES QUATRE VENTS, N. of CAMBLIGNEUL & billeted in field Ambulance Ste here. Orders received to take over evacuation of front line from 3rd & 6th Canadian Field Ambulances by 17th inst. Visited part of the 3 posts. Pte Morris D.A. out from leave	Pfs
LES QUATRE VENTS	16/10/17	9pm	Sick 22 Hosp: 7 Wast 20h 5 BOR Pte Dorrington to Hosp. BOR. on leave. Capt Laws & 16 OR. 5 to LACHAUSSEE to take over huts there. Lieut Moule & BOR. to VANCOUVRE to take over huts at that point	Pfs

WAR DIARY or INTELLIGENCE SUMMARY

Army Form C. 2118.

Place	Date	Hour	Summary of Events and Information	Remarks and references to Appendices
Mont St Eloi	17/10/17	9am	Sect 3 units reinforce recd	
		9pm	Hos 7. Unit moved Headquarters Mont St Eloi took over from 5 K.C. Gun Posn.	Rpt
		10 A.M.	Capt McDowell & two men moved to 3 OR Neuville St Vaast to take over Bessey Station trie, pontoon to 90 to RMT J	
			Capt Potter 70. Rts R.E. 72. started for pontoon	
			Lt Burges left Reinforcements sent to Capt Laing & Lieut attaches from H.S.M. 2nd Bn made at these posts	
Mont St Eloi	18/10/17	9pm	Sect 3 Prestations to these	
			Hos 7, 6 Foremation from front line as follows Ref. MAP. 36.C & 1/40,000	
		10AM	Left Sector Station at La Haraucourt Remorny Harmed Arras Lens Rd. at SIO c 9.6. Rene Chaudière on Arras Lens Rd. 300B behind the Sector Cross are one Officer & 300B working the Sector Caves are collected from 2 Regimental Aid Posts at	Rpt

H AYTER T.8.c 9.6 & HURTON T.15.c 9.9. from

WAR DIARY
or
INTELLIGENCE SUMMARY.
(Erase heading not required.)

Army Form C. 2118.

Place	Date	Hour	Summary of Events and Information	Remarks and references to Appendices
MONT ST. ELOI	18/4/17	9 pm	Hayte Cases are brought by trench to the embankment at T.7.d.8.2. Thence by mule track to La Chaudière. from run to Cases are carried either by road into Vimy or to the top into La Chaudière or by trench to the Thence are entombment. Thence to La Chaudière. entombment Cases evacuate at dawn & sent from La Chaudière to Neuville St Vaast. Special cars can be used to Neuville if there is much urgent evacuation and so a day light if there is much urgent evacuation needs. Severe cases only are sent by railway to the head about there is a light railway to PÉGGY which could be midway between HAYTER & PÉGGY which could be Cases sent near La Chaudière. used in heavy fighting. Apps Pts 1.2 c.88 There is the commencement of a large wood A.A.P.S. L.d. be have occupied from it runs a light	Pth

A7093. Wt. W12539/M1295. 750,000. 1/17. D. D & L., Ltd. Forms/C2118/14.

WAR DIARY or INTELLIGENCE SUMMARY

Army Form C. 2118.

Place	Date	Hour	Summary of Events and Information	Remarks and references to Appendices
HON 7 9. E.10.1	14/10/17	9 pm	railway down to near Kalhandrie thence to Souchez. The work of completion is being proceeded with. A note as to light railways will be entered as soon as they have been thoroughly examined. **Right Sector.** The H.Q.s is at VAN COUVRE at T.22.c.7.2. Here are 1 M.O. & 2 R.M.Os. & 2 R.M.Ps. in the line at T.22.a.9.2 & T.16.a.5.3. Cases are brought overland by handcarriages. Clearance from the H.Q.S. is effected by car at dawn & such light as precedent soon on the left of railways are not so necedent. Up to VILLERS AUX BOIS which sector but there are routes to be made later when they have been explored.	[signature]

WAR DIARY
or
INTELLIGENCE SUMMARY.
(Erase heading not required.)

Army Form C. 2118.

Place	Date	Hour	Summary of Events and Information	Remarks and references to Appendices
Mont St Eloi	10/11/17	9pm	Affort has also been established at H.M.4 for the collection of local casualties. here are 1 off & 7 men this post is situated at T.25.a.9.3. they are cleared by car at dawn & dusk. NEUVILLE ST VAAST. This is the main Dressing Station. Cases are brought here from Lamance, Vimy & Vancouver. The accommodation is slight. Endeavour to try & establish an M.D.S. the occupants It is hoped to establish at RUE RIETZ about ½ of the present com[bi]ned A.D.S. now to-day which is route away W.H. to main [?] front. There are food deposits connected to the front. There are food deposits located for the occupation of huts accommodation &c for the Rifle regt food.	MY

Army Form C. 2118.

WAR DIARY
or
INTELLIGENCE SUMMARY.
(Erase heading not required.)

Place	Date	Hour	Summary of Events and Information	Remarks and references to Appendices
Mont St Eloi.	1/10/17	9 am	PLAN OF EVACUATION New ADS ⊗ — RAP — RAP Light Railway — Big Railway — RAP × — × VANCOUVRE Light Railway — × × LACHAUDIÈRE — × VIMY THÉLUS CORNER NEUVILLE ST VAAST × AUX RIETZ ×	PLAN

Army Form C. 2118.

WAR DIARY
or
INTELLIGENCE SUMMARY.
(Erase heading not required.)

Instructions regarding War Diaries and Intelligence Summaries are contained in F. S. Regs., Part II. and the Staff Manual respectively. Title pages will be prepared in manuscript.

Place	Date	Hour	Summary of Events and Information	Remarks and references to Appendices
Mont St Eloi	19/10/17	9h	Sick 2 Hosp 3 evac. 1 of SoR.	Sgt Giles ex hosp. Sgt Stephenson moved to CCS not at strength. Vancouver Bros 7 hrs visited. visit from DDMS 1st Army	AAH
Mont St Eloi	20/10/17	9hm	Sick 2 Hosp 2 evac 1 of SoR.	Sgt Sgt Baker ex hosp. Sgt Hall ex CCS now at strength	AAH
Mont St Eloi	21/10/17	9hm	Sick 2 Hosp 1 evac 1 of SoR.	Pte Barnden ex hosp.	AAH

Army Form C. 2118.

WAR DIARY
or
INTELLIGENCE SUMMARY.
(Erase heading not required.)

Instructions regarding War Diaries and Intelligence Summaries are contained in F. S. Regs., Part II. and the Staff Manual respectively. Title pages will be prepared in manuscript.

Place	Date	Hour	Summary of Events and Information	Remarks and references to Appendices
Mont St Eloi	22/10/17	9pm	Sect 4. Hop 1. Wout 1 off 7 OR.	took command
	23/10/17	9pm	Sect 3. Hop 1. Wout 1 Officer 4 OR.	Lt Col Bayard on leave for one month. Wout 1 officer — march forward gap.
	24/10/17	9pm	Sect 2. Hospital 1 OR. Wounded 1 Off. 7 OR.	Pte Goshman adm from Hospital. Visits with the R.War Regt. Staff Batt Pte Feron St + Church W.I. wounded & missing Lt & R.A.M.C. Medical to Offr XIII Bde, 1 OR returned from leave. Visited rail site at War Park.
Mont St Eloi to War Park	25/10/17	9pm	Sect 2. Hop 1. Wound 1 off 7 OR.	Removal Pte to Marine into train (Mil. H Zdn & Zdn cut) (continued). Pte Richardson [?] from Zdn to Hospital. Plc. Arrival 1 priest from school of Cookery, 1 OR (sgt) attached for supply duty on evac. Gas. March forward one hour distance.

A7092 Wt. w28397/M197 750,000. 1/17. D. D. & L. Ltd. Forms/C2118/14

Army Form C. 2118.

WAR DIARY
or
INTELLIGENCE SUMMARY.

(Erase heading not required.)

Instructions regarding War Diaries and Intelligence Summaries are contained in F.S. Regs., Part II. and the Staff Manual respectively. Title pages will be prepared in manuscript.

Place	Date	Hour	Summary of Events and Information	Remarks and references to Appendices
Mont St Eloi	26/10/17	4pm	Sect 1. Coy 1. Wadrop 1/A 7 AR	Conts moved from Mont Neck and commenced construction small at Gun Pits. 1 OR on leave. 1 OR (for soup kitchen) attached from 1/A CMFA	Appdx
Mont St Eloi	27/10/17	4pm	Sect 2. Sect 1. Tigsisque 1/A 7 OR	Work as usual. 1 OR returned from leave. 1 OR (for soup kitchen) attached from 1/3 CMFA	Appdx
Mont St Eloi	28/10/17	4pm	Sect 2. Coy 1. Wadrop 1/A 7 AR	1 OR returned from leave. 5th Coto commenced building Horse Watering Troughs on F.A. site at Gun Pits.	Appdx
Mont St Eloi	29/10/17	4pm	Sect 3. Coy 1. Wadrop 1/A 7 AR	6 OR attached from Band. 5th Coto Grand building Horse Watering Troughs on F.A. site at Gun Pits. Received 7 Nissen Huts supplied.	Appdx

WAR DIARY or INTELLIGENCE SUMMARY

Army Form C. 2118.

Place	Date	Hour	Summary of Events and Information	Remarks and references to Appendices
Mue Petz	30/9/17	4pm	Sect. O. Unit 2 Medical 3 Off 9 OR. H.20am. Headquarters and personnel moved to Aux Rietz. Visited Vancouver ADS tonight. Roads running about impassable to cars. Relieved 8th F.A. by two ambulances to Thury 9 La Chaudiere. Pte Cant W.S. to ORS. 6 OR sick on leave.	[appx]
Aux Rietz	31/9/17	4pm	Sect O. Unit 2 Medical 1 Off 7 OR. Visited Chaudiere & Dartmouth tunnel this morning. ADMS sent Dir. & DDMS 3rd Corps wanted Aux Rietz Maj. Roswell occupied in completion of road to stretcher bearing dugouts. etc.	[appx]

Army Form C. 2118.

WAR DIARY
or
INTELLIGENCE SUMMARY.
(Erase heading not required.)

Place	Date	Hour	Summary of Events and Information	Remarks and references to Appendices
			SUMMARY OF ADMISSIONS AND DISCHARGES during MONTH ENDING 31st October 1917	

	ADMISSIONS						DISCHARGES						
	Officers		O.R.		C.C.S.		C.R.S.		D.R.S.		DUTY		DIED.
	S	W	S	W	Offrs	O.R.	Offrs	O.R.	Offrs	O.R.	Offrs	O.R.	Offrs	O.R.
XVIII Corps M.D.S. *arrived 1st Oct to 7th Oct*	15	99	280	1253	111	1500	-	-	-	-	-	6	3	27
V Corps M.D.S. *arrived 18th Oct. 31st Oct.*	2	1	295	24	3	74	-	214	-	10	-	-	-	-
TOTALS.	17	100	575	1277	114	1574	-	214	-	10	-	6	3	27

Appendix page 1.

[signature] Captain
Officer Cmdg 2nd South Midland Field Ambulance

www.ingramcontent.com/pod-product-compliance
Lightning Source LLC
Chambersburg PA
CBHW080838010526
44114CB00017B/2331